Civic Youth Work

Civic Youth Work
Cocreating Democratic Youth Spaces

Editors

Ross VeLure Roholt
University of Minnesota, School of Social Work, Youth Studies

Michael Baizerman
University of Minnesota, School of Social Work, Youth Studies

R. W. Hildreth
Southern Illinois University, Political Science

LYCEUM
BOOKS, INC.

Chicago, Illinois

Published by
LYCEUM BOOKS, INC.
5758 S. Blackstone Ave.
Chicago, Illinois 60637
773 + 643-1903 fax
773 + 643-1902 phone
lyceum@lyceumbooks.com
www.lyceumbooks.com

6   5   4   3   2   1   13   14   15   16   17

ISBN 978-1-933478-84-5

Printed in the United States of America.

Library of Congress Cataloging-in-Publication Data

Civic youth work : cocreating democratic youth spaces / editors, Roholt, Ross VeLure,
Michael Baizerman, R.W. Hildreth.
      p.   cm.
   Includes bibliographical references and index.
   ISBN 978-1-933478-84-5 (pbk. : alk. paper)
   1. Youth—Political activity.   2. Political participation.
3. Civics. I. Roholt, Ross VeLure, 1970–   II. Baizerman, Michael.
III. Hildreth, R. W.
HQ799.2.P6C59   2013
320.40835—dc23
                                          2012014095

To the young people around the world who taught us civic youth work by doing and reflecting on it with us—thanks!

Contents

Preface ix

Acknowledgments xi

1. Introduction: A Big Surprise? 1
   Ross VeLure Roholt, Michael Baizerman,
   and R. W. Hildreth

Part 1: Civic Youth Workers

2. Critical Media Literacy in Action: Engaged Space in
   Urban Public Schools 21
   Katie Johnston-Goodstar and Joanne Krebs

3. Northern Ireland Museums as Sites of Youth Engagement 32
   Lisa Rea

4. Creating Spaces for the Next Generation of Civil Rights
   in Mississippi: Youth Participation in the Mississippi
   Safe Schools Coalition 43
   Sarah Young, Katie Richards-Schuster, Anna Davis,
   and Izzy Pellegrine

5. Engaging Youth in the Evaluation Process 55
   Rob Shumer

Part 2: Civic Youth Work Programs and Programming

6. School as a Site for Civic Youth Work Practices 67
   Terrance Kwame Ross

7. Manchester Craftsmen's Guild: Art, Mentorship,
    and Environment Shape a Culture of Learning
    and Engagement   81
      Mary Ann Steiner, Tracy Galvin, and Joshua Green

8. Leading the Way: Young People Cocreating a Safe
    Driving Culture   103
      Ofir Germanic

**Part 3: Policies Supporting and Challenging Civic
Youth Work**

9. Youth Civic Engagement in Korea: Past, Present,
    and Future   115
      Yun Jin Choi

10. Engaging Youth to Transform Conflict: A Study of Youth
    and the Reduction of War in Africa   126
      Jennifer De Maio

11. Croatian Youth Corner: Youth Participation and Civic
    Education from Practitioners' Eyes   139
      Emina Bužinkić

Part 4: Developing Civic Youth Work

12. Teaching and Training Civic Youth Workers: Creating
    Spaces for Reciprocal Civic and Youth Development   151
      R. W. Hildreth and Ross VeLure Roholt

13. Understanding Civic Youth Work: Touchstones
    for Practice   160
      *Ross VeLure Roholt, Michael Baizerman,
      and R. W. Hildreth*

References   187

Contributors   197

Index   201

Preface

This is one of two texts we have written on civic youth work; the other is *Becoming Citizens: Deepening the Craft of Youth Civic Engagement* (VeLure Roholt, Hildreth, & Baizerman, 2009), which introduced the term *civic youth work*. Here we aim to deepen an understanding of the civic youth work ethos, craft orientation, practices, policy, and programs to enhance young people's civic participation and to prepare workers who can develop, implement, and evaluate that work.

To accomplish this, we use practitioner-written stories to get at the flavor, style, and details—the practices—of civic youth work, and we introduce and explicate this in bookend chapters.

Among the topics we introduce here are the following: What is work with youth? What is youth work? What is civic youth work, and how is it similar to or different from normative, typical youth work? We note the rise of the positive youth development frame, an example of Eaton's (1962) scientific social movement of professionals, with its attention to positive youth development programming and youth work as applied developmental science. A later ideological movement began in response to sociopolitical moral panic (Thompson, 1998) and problems among youth (Cohen, 1997) with respect to what appeared to be the disinterest and noninvolvement of young Americans in electoral voting and in joining established political parties, as well as a seeming lack of interest in politics at all levels. This was called apathy, and the adult panic was that youth, by not actively living their sociopolitical rights and responsibilities when young, would inevitably not become involved in civic affairs as adults. The survival of democracy would then be at risk.

This read on young people came approximately thirty to forty years after the exuberant involvement of youth in the 1960s (e.g., Baizerman, 1974). However, scholars and civic actors were missing the realities of actual youth activism, which was substantial but accomplished outside normative political forms in schools, communities, places of worship, sport, and employment. It was shown that contrary to individual-level analysis that showed noninvolvement, group-level data revealed the existence of a variety of activist forms and documented how adults, intentionally or not, kept young people from participating in normative structures. Youth were being marginalized by the system, as some of them, and some adults, had suspected and claimed.

One response to these insights and findings was a renewed and invigorated effort to understand, invite, and support ongoing, authentic, meaningful, compelling, inclusive, just, and fun youth engagement on issues that matter to actual young people. Herein lies the origin of the recently named praxis civic youth work.

This new emphasis on substantive, not symbolic, youth involvement is a move from young person as citizen in the narrow sense of voting, rights, and civic duties to a richer, deeper conception of youth as living citizen(ship). In this book, this change is discussed theoretically and in relation to civic youth work practice.

This is the broad narrative that we sketch and at places fill in with shape, color, and texture. This text is our introduction to some of our civic youth work colleagues worldwide, to their work, and to the emergent practice called civic youth work.

Reading the Text

The text is designed to be read in at least three ways. Readers can follow along from start to finish; readers can begin with the introduction, then read the last chapter, and then the stories; or readers can begin with the stories and then read the remaining chapters. We suspect that practitioners will want to focus more on the stories and examine how we understand the practice as civic youth work. In any event, the more conceptual analysis is in the final chapter.

Michael Baizerman

Acknowledgments

This book has been a cocreative endeavor. The idea of the book first emerged in conversations with a group of youth workers, young people, and youth work scholars involved in the Youth Work in Contested Spaces project, which sponsored annual meetings in Northern Ireland between 2003 and 2007. We begin by thanking Paul Smyth, director of Public Achievement Northern Ireland, who supported the idea of civic youth work early on and helped secured funding to support ongoing conversations with youth workers from across the globe in order to refine, develop, and deepen our understanding of civic youth work. Public Achievement Northern Ireland continues to be an innovative hub for the refinement and development of civic youth work.

We also want to thank all of the very talented youth workers we have had the pleasure to meet and talk with, including but not limited to Lara Arjan, Tareq Bakri, Ofir Germanic, Suzanne Hammad, Kevin Hughes, Zane Ibrahim, Laura McFall, Thuqan Qishawi, Lisa Rey, and Nashira De Jongh, whose words we use to introduce the first chapter.

We also thank our academic colleagues from around the globe who have supported our work in a variety of ways, including Dr. Anthony Gallagher, Dr. Ken Harland, Dr. Choi, Dr. Rhissassi, and Dr. Anthony Morgan.

And to all the young people from Northern Ireland, Finland, the Netherlands, Ireland, Turkey, Israel, Palestine, Jordan, Morocco, Korea, Laos, Croatia, Serbia, the United States, South Africa, Canada, Libya, Yemen, Qatar, Lebanon, Egypt, and Syria who we have had the pleasure to meet, talk with, and learn from, and who have shown us again and again what young people can do to make a difference in the world.

CHAPTER ONE

Introduction

A Big Surprise?

Ross VeLure Roholt,
Michael Baizerman,
and R. W. Hildreth

They can do it, so we let them.
We let them and they do it.
—*South African youth worker*

There is a common conception that young people are apathetic, self-absorbed, and apolitical (Males, 1999). Yet youth workers have known for decades that young people can and do make important and significant contributions to their communities. Why is it that these young people's actual civic interests, capacities, and accomplishments are largely overlooked? Surely, part of the answer lies in how young people are portrayed in media and, related, the composition of the social roles of youth (e.g., age-, sex-, and place-specific social roles), such as student, teen, adolescent, student athlete, nerd, dropout, druggie, and the rest. Indeed, adults (and other youths) understand and respond to youth in general, as specific individuals, and as groups of individuals in terms of the images society has of youth. In the dominant public discourses on youth, there is not a social expectation for youth to be actively involved in public life, and there are limited formal social roles for youth as citizens. Recent events in Egypt, and elsewhere in the Middle East, where youth-led political demonstrations have led to powerful calls for and changes in political structure and citizen participation, disclose what is absent in most countries—active, organized, formal and informal political youth groups. In the United States, more quietly and possibly harder to notice, more and more young people are involved, engaged, and participants in efforts "to make the world a better place" and "to make a difference," most often as volunteers in social service–type efforts, such as tutoring, school cleanups, and neighborhood safety. Recent scholarship has shown that there is more going on— more young people and a wider variety of youth involved in a wide array of social issues—than was recognized or expected, much of it over the long term (Lopez et al., 2006). Despite these trends, the larger fact still holds: in the United States, at least, being an active citizen and doing "citizen work" is not typically expected of youth by themselves or expected of them by adults. Here we have a tension: youth can do that work and be citizens—some clearly want to be involved as citizens—but youth in general are not expected to do citizen work (VeLure Roholt, Hildreth, & Baizerman, 2009). They are rarely invited into established structures of engagement, and they are rarely coached and trained to participate in citizen work in small and larger groups.

This reader aims to address this tension by showing how adults who work with youth can conceive of and implement small, specific, practical, and often effective practices to invite and support viable, authentic, meaningful, and consequential youth engagement on issues of compelling interest and importance to them. This work we call civic youth work.

Civic Youth Work

As we described in our earlier work, *Becoming Citizens: Deepening the Craft of Youth Civic Engagement* (2009), civic youth workers support a particular ethos: an "invitation to young people to become and to stay involved in civic issues important to them" (VeLure Roholt et al., 2009, p. 165). Civic youth workers may appear very much like many other adults who work with youth (e.g., teachers, coaches, parents). They often use similar activities to engage and facilitate learning with young people. However, they bring a unique meaning to their work, to how they understand what they do and what young people can accomplish individually and in groups.

Civic youth workers want young people to experience democratic citizenship and not simply learn about it. We emphasize how civic youth workers often use experiential, informal, and dialogical pedagogies to support the "on-going cocreation with young people of [the] democratic citizen" (VeLure Roholt et al., 2009, p. 169). This work often begins by inviting young people to talk about public issues or problems they care about. In the process, civic youth workers invite young people to be responsible for addressing a public issue they find personally meaningful. To address the issue, young people often work with others, many of whom they have not met before; with several age peers (and across school grades); and with youth who are not friends. The civic youth worker reflects with the youth group about how they might best respond to the chosen issue and how everyone can contribute to what the group could do. As the group continues to work on addressing this issue, the civic youth worker seeks to build common understanding and collective decision making in the group. The group decides together, as a group, what it will do. Throughout this process, the civic youth worker embodies both care and the interrogatory.

How they work and what they do is refracted through a philosophy of care—for these young people and for others, and about issues and problems. Care guides their work from the initial meeting to civic action and beyond (Mayerhoff, 1971; Noddings, 1984). These workers also embody the interrogatory. They go to youth as questions, not as answers. This craft orientation (Bensman & Lilienfeld, 1973)—questioning, reflection, analysis—inquiry, is basic to a civic youth work ethos and practice, as is seen in the examples that make up this book.

Civic youth workers wrote this book with their stories. These describe how they facilitate, coordinate, support, and manage programs, initiatives, and efforts with young people. But these stories are not program descriptions, with an emphasis on design, strategy, curriculum, and outcomes. Rather, these stories illuminate civic youth work practice. Much has already been written about youth civic engagement approaches (Kirlin, 2003; Westheimer & Kahne, 2004), pathways (Walker, 2002), and programs (Gibson, 2001). But for us, this scholarship tends to miss the critical point that every program or initiative is carried out by someone. How this person does his or her work matters profoundly, because this shapes how young people experience and come to make sense of what they are doing. It is not civic work if it is not named and understood as such. This is why civic youth workers and their practice are crucial to understand.

Stories are a good way to get at practice in teaching (Coles, 1989), learning (Mezirow & Associates, 1990), and research (Polkinghorne, 1988; Wortham, 2001), and we believe they are a good way to get at civic youth work, also. We wanted a range of civic youth worker stories from practitioners in the United States and internationally. In the end, we have a majority of the stories about work in the United States. The relative absence of international stories has to do with time constraints and the limited support we, as editors, could provide to our international colleagues. But it should not be taken to mean that this work is more common in the United States than in other places in the world or that it is easier to do here or better supported. Indeed, good examples exist throughout the world and typically with more support than we see in the United States. Intentionally, these stories cross youth work domains and extend into what Delgado (2002) calls "new frontiers in youth work" (p. 11). The stories are in four domains of youth work—media, museums, community, and schools—and we have organized them into three groups: the civic youth worker, civic youth work programs, and civic youth work policy making and program development. At the end, we include a chapter on how we have taught civic youth work to others. The final chapter looks within and across the examples and illuminates what we can learn from the stories. As a beginning reader in the field of civic youth work, we wanted to emphasize how civic youth work is found in the typical categories of youth work and human services. We believe that we show with these cases, and by extension, the possibility of civic youth work throughout the youth work field. That is, civic youth work does not have to take place in a civic engagement program. Rather, it can take place in any work with young people. What matters is youth workers' craft orientation (Bensman & Lilienfeld, 1973)—ethos, knowledge, skill, and praxis—that is, what they do with whom, why, and how. Civic youth workers cocreate with young people spaces of democratic possibility and self-crafting. They cocreate spaces for living citizenship. Questions end each chapter to facilitate their use for workers reflection and for teaching.

Cocreating Spaces: From Engagement to Engaging Young People in Civic Work

In the late 1990s the moral panic in the United States about youth civic engagement was grounded in the example of voting. Young people were voting in small numbers (Bennett, 2000), and they were not active in established political parties. The 1960s, with its young people's antiwar and social reform involvements, were forgotten. The future of American democracy was considered at risk because of young people's apathy and nonparticipation in normative and explicit political structures. Scholars set about trying to measure and explain this youth nonengagement. Here we move from examining youth engagement to expanding on the notion of engaging in civic work.

The youth civic engagement moral crisis appeared in the 1990s. Several studies directed public attention toward seemingly alarming trends among young people: they were not voting in elections, joining political parties, or supporting formal political organizations—unlike generations before them (Bennett, 2000; Delli Carpini & Keeter, 1996). If this wasn't enough to worry about, Putnam (2000) described an American society that appeared to be moving away from supporting a democratic way of life, in part through the deterioration of community civic groups.

In general, civic organizations, what Alexis de Tocqueville (1835/2006) described as a unique hallmark of American democracy, struggled to find new members and to retain current members. Overall, scholarship indicated a social problem and a youth problem (Cohen, 1997), even a crisis. This was read as a call to intervene so as to prevent political apathy among young people and to motivate and activate the young in their civic duties, lest our democracy wither for lack of citizen involvement.

As evidence about what seemed to be youth disengagement mounted, a growing chorus of educators, researchers, youth organizations, and foundations sounded the alarm: "Something" must be done to counter these trends (Barber, 1992; Battistoni, 2000; Mann & Patrick, 2000; see also Murphy, 2004). High-level national and local task forces and commissions were appointed to assess these trends and to propose reactions, curative and preventative. One famously declared that "in a time that cries out for civic action, we are in danger of becoming a nation of spectators" (National Commission on Civic Renewal, 1998, p. 6; see also American Political Science Associations Task Force on Civic Education, in Mann & Patrick, 2000; Civic Mission of Schools, 2003). To address this alarming youth problem and to bring about youth civic activism, new initiatives received funding, new public and school policies required youth community service, and school civics curricula were refashioned and reinvigorated (by adult educators).

Those efforts gave attention to this youth problem (Cohen, 1997), to a variety of responses, and they also legitimated as a moral panic young people's disengagement from civic society and responsible citizenship. Over the past decade, the theme and tone of this concern about youth civic engagement has changed. Some scholars began looking at the seeming "problem" of youth disengagement in new ways and challenged the conclusion that youth apathy explains the low levels of civic engagement (VeLure Roholt et al., 2009; Yates & Youniss, 1999). Instead, these scholars found that young people are structurally, socially, and psychologically disenfranchised and disconnected from dominant structures of political life, but at the same time they care deeply about a wide range of issues in their communities and in the larger world (Biesta, Lawy, & Kelly, 2009; Llewellyn & Westheimer, 2009). These scholars witnessed young people working to address global epidemics (e.g., AIDS), raising awareness and advocating for policy changes in low-performing schools (Cammarota & Fine, 2008), volunteering at homeless shelters (Wuthnow, 1995), and tutoring children. Thus, what to adults was apathy was instead, and in general, uninvolvement, often resulting from blocked access to institutionalized participation structures (Watts & Flanagan, 2007), a lack of knowledge about and skills in doing "public work," and in turn an absence of helpful and knowledge-able adults, such as civic youth workers, to guide young people in this. Out of these policy and program responses to youth's seeming disengagement and actual nonparticipation, the very idea of youth civic engagement changed, and a new civic educator role was defined.

Engagement

Youth engagement became the new primary focus for much scholarship and practice. Why do some young people get involved while many do not? What are the benefits and consequences of civic involvement (and its absence) for young people? The focus was primarily on whether young people vote or volunteer, and on the outcomes of efforts to foster these forms of engagement. Much work has been done detailing how programs and initiatives can increase the level of civic and political knowledge, skills, and attitudes in young people (Sherrod, Torney-Purta, & Flanagan, 2010). Attention has been directed at developing youth civic engagement indicators that predict a young person's future political and civic engagement. The goal here is to increase the likelihood of young people becoming active citizens as adults. In all of this, adult conceived political and civic outcomes are given priority over young people's actual, lived civic and political experiences.

Not everyone agrees with this prioritization. Indeed, most youth workers care more about supporting young people's engagement in their communities than in preparing them for future engagement during their adulthood. These civic educators and other adults argue that the best way to foster civic participation later in life is to focus on supporting youth civic participation now. This book supports this shift away from preparation for engagement and toward engaging now. This we describe next.

Engaging

This idea of engaging connects to historical and contemporary community organizing approaches. Readers may recognize here older perspectives, strategies, and practices, what in the 1960s and 1970s were called the process orientation in several fields, including social work, and within it community work (Ross, 1955). Emphasis was on the how of the work, the doing of the work, and knowledge, attitudes, and skills were focused on these too. In the United States, the early work of Mike Schwartz at the School of Social Work at the University of Pittsburgh, who wrote the first National Association of Social Work monograph on community organizing; Jim Hackshaw and Sy Slavin at Columbia University School of Social Work; Dan Dodson at the School of Education, New York University; Preston Wilcox in East Harlem, New York City; Danny Kronenfeld and Ezra Birnbaun, also in New York City; and the Columbia University School of Social Work joined emergent social work notions of labor organizing approaches and practices and, for some, various (socialist and other) political strategies (e.g., C. W. Mills, Marxism) to fashion civic organizations. These came together in the pre–poverty program community-organizing efforts to reduce poverty and empower citizens in New York City's Mobilization for Youth and Harlem Youth Opportunities Unlimited, and in Newark's, New Haven's, and Boston's early demonstrations. Earlier, the ground had been laid by federal housing and community redevelopment legislation requiring citizen involvement in urban renewal planning. These are few of the perspectives, efforts, and sites for the larger process-oriented practice movement in social work in general and in community organizing in social work in particular, for what Ross (1955) called the process objective approach.

In this practice orientation emphasis is on the doing of the work, on collaboration and cooperative work with others. The outcome is a "development of community integration and capacity to function as a unit in respect to common problems" (Ross, 1955, p. 23), that is, groups willing and able to take on common community issues and problems now and in the future. The outcome of the work is that the community is organized and ready.

Extending this practice into youth work, moving from engagement to engaging signifies a shift away from a primary focus on short- and long-term (future) outcomes to a focus on current process and practices. It shifts attention from "the done" and the "to be done" to "the doing." What distinguishes engagement from engaging is seen in how each orientation provides a different answer to four essential questions that too rarely are asked about youth civic engagement: Who are young people? Why are we concerned? What should we do? How should it be done? Table 1.1 illustrates the distinctions between these two ideal-type orientations to youth civic involvement.

Engagement frames youth civic engagement as a family of practices to develop young people's capacity to become future active citizens in adulthood. In engagement, young people are viewed as having much to learn, from adults, with gaps and deficiencies in basic and necessary civic knowledge, skills, and attitudes. From the engagement perspective, young people are individuals who are not yet ready for prime time because they need more preparation by adults to be responsible citizens.

Table 1.1. Comparing Engagement and Engaging

Questions	Engagement	Engaging
Who are young people?	Citizens of the future Students "Not ready for prime time" "Going through a stage"	Civic actors Community change agents Citizens now Public workers
Why are we concerned?	Youth are apathetic, disinterested, and uneducated; they lack important civic knowledge, skills, and attitudes	Youth are disenfranchised and disconnected by existing structures
What should we do?	Train and educate; structure experiences to maximize the attainment of civic indicators	Provide opportunities to experience democracy and to live as a democratic citizen
How should it be done?	Focus on youth outcomes	Focus on democratic process and real change in community, program, or issues

This framing of the young person preforms the answer to the second question: why are we concerned? Given their not-yet-complete status (Konopka, 1973), concern is about their current deficiencies in civic knowledge, skills, and attitudes, and youth work practice focuses on preparing young people for future roles as active citizens. The engagement orientation frames the public concern as a problem of individual young people, not, in contrast, as a problem of access or disenfranchisement. Given this, what should be done for individuals to bring them to readiness to participate? The answer has been adult devised and has led much of youth civic and political education and training.

In contrast, the engaging orientation begins at a different place. It is grounded in two decades of work and examples that show that, indeed, young people are ready for actual civic work, public work, and political work (e.g., Boyte, 2003; Delgado & Staples, 2008; Ginwright, Noguera, & Cammarota, 2006, Hanna, 1936; VeLure Roholt et al., 2009). In the stories and examples that document this, examples of which are included here, young people are seen actually participating as citizens. Obviously, they can do that if we let them or don't block them. The engaging orientation is rooted in this image, understanding, and reality of young people, and in their history of doing citizen (work). This way of understanding the young person and young people leads to a contrasting question and answer to the issue of adult concern.

If some young people have demonstrated an ability to take on and perform the citizen role and have created public goods in so doing, the new question is, why doesn't this happen everywhere, more often, and with more youth? The engaging perspective poses this question: what prevents young people from living as democratic citizens in their everyday lives in their own neighborhoods and schools (and elsewhere), in part by addressing public issues they find personally compelling? This query moves concern from the individual level to the social, cultural, and political levels, and on these levels focus is on the realities—the values, structures, norms, and practices—that deflect and block young people from living their everyday lives as citizens. In this view, most troubling are the ways adult structures, beliefs, and practices actively disenfranchise young people's participation in civic and political issues. Adults keep young people disconnected from local and national structures of participation from community organizing to attending and speaking at school board meetings. They do this through simple acts (e.g., holding meetings at times when young people cannot attend) to more complex acts (e.g., creating environments in which young people's civic contributions are neither recognized nor supported). An obvious response to this disenfranchisement is to create opportunities for young people to become involved; to invite them appropriately; and to provide support for their active participation in everyday, ongoing political and civic activities (work), such as evaluation for community and city planning (chapter 5), community problem solving (chapter 8), and social change (chapters 2 and 4). Organizations, including schools, can also develop democratic decision-making processes (chapter 6) or work to create policy settings in which young people can find support when they choose to be involved (chapters 9–11). Indeed, many have already invited and supported young people to be able to successfully do this work.

In the engaging frame, adult support creates conditions for young people to actively discuss, work on, and act on their issues and concerns about their worlds, at all political and social levels. The chapters included here provide examples of how this has been done in a variety of contexts. Having young people actively working on civic and political issues, doing "public work" (Kari & Boyte, 1996), becomes the primary goal and an important criterion of success. Research, policy, and program evaluation shift from measuring individual learning and involvement to witnessing, documenting, and studying community, social, and political changes stimulated by and created by young people. This work is typically done in and through small groups, in large communities and in organizations, such as museums in Northern Ireland (chapter 3). These two different orientations—engagement and engaging—show the two different, major understandings and ways of civic work with young people.

This book is about the engaging orientation. It aims to deepen our understanding of this orientation by describing what youth workers do within this frame and how and why they do this. Their primary work is with young people in groups, opening and using spaces to experience and learn about and how to do civic (public) work. A result is the learning of a citizen role; another is enhancement of a citizen self (VeLure Roholt et al., 2009). This is what the cases, the stories, are about. They show the civic youth work craft orientation.

Why These Stories?

The authors invited are involved in a valuable practice, one that makes a positive difference to the youth and adults involved, and maybe beyond them. We selected projects because we believed that, at minimum, they make a good-faith effort to implement a perspective on young people and how to rightly and effectively work with them and/ or on their behalf to enhance their well-being and healthy development, as well as to make a positive difference in their larger world. Obviously and admittedly, our inclusion criteria are grounded in our own work, *Becoming Citizens: Deepening the Craft of Youth Civic Engagement* (VeLure Roholt et al., 2009), and our understanding of youth, the youth civic engagement process, youth citizen development, and civic youth work. Others could reasonably have used different criteria and included other, similarly worthy examples.

Second, we chose each project because we think that it can teach the field about understanding youth and working with them to enhance their positive development and to make their (and larger) worlds better places for themselves and others. What does it mean to say that a project has something to teach? This means that the project overall and all (or most) of its practices are ones we admire and that this project's particular way of understanding and working with young people shows how we believe such work ought to be done. Yes, our values again!

What we admire in a project is the joining of the technically correct and the morally good—as Benner (1984) puts it—in the project's work and in its and other's evaluation of the project. What we do not admire is project work or evaluation that is only (merely) technically correct in conception, implementation, and assessment. We are not about applied adolescent development. Rather, we propose active, authentic, right, meaningful, inclusive, just, and nonviolent youth citizenship, youth public work, and youth engagement. When a project embodies this ethos, we think that it has something to teach others who are working with youth or with any persons of any age.

Our editorial strategy aimed to ensure that each author's style and use of English was respected, but some were tweaked and added to with contextualization to put the story in larger sociohistorical and sociocultural terms, such as the Troubles in Northern Ireland as a contested space (Magnuson & Baizerman, 2007), and the adding of notation on a Native American youth media project because of the highly symbolic potency of the term *displacement* in the history of the US Army removing Native Americans from tribal lands. Finally, we added questions to stimulate analysis, reflection, and teaching while demonstrating our ways of making sense and working.

Organization of the Stories

The stories lend themselves to emphasizing our intent in at least two ways: by the different domains in which civic youth work is practiced, such as media, museums, schools, and community, and by a larger focus on the civic youth work enterprise—the civic youth worker; civic youth work programs and programming; policy making and program development in civic youth work; and teaching and training civic youth workers, whatever the discipline, profession, job title, field of practice, or job responsibility. We chose the latter because we wanted to focus on and emphasize the basic categories for understanding civic (and other) youth work.

We give primary attention to civic youth work and civic youth workers, and these are the lenses through which we view programs, programming, program development, and policy making. It is the civic youth worker's ethos, craft orientation (Bensman & Lilienfeld, 1973), skills, and everyday practices that transform work with youth and youth work into civic youth work. These things are what make simple activities and projects into meaningful civic youth work programs. It is more real, practical, and easier to think of practices as embodied in and carried out by persons (civic youth workers) than by policies or programs; to hold the latter is to invite the error of reification—the treating of an abstraction as if it were a concrete thing in the world. In our view, civic youth work practice with young people is what constitutes the core of civic youth work programs.

The book is divided into four parts. The first three parts focus on the civic youth work enterprise. Each chapter presents a different story of effective civic youth work. The fourth part examines strategies to further develop civic youth work.

In the first part, four civic youth workers tell stories of their work. Each chapter describes different civic youth work practices (broadly conceived), including participatory action research, participatory museum exhibit development and design, youth-led organizing and social change efforts, and youth participatory evaluation. These chapters present a range of practice methods and challenges. Most of these stories are personal and tell the story from the perspective of civic youth work or worker. All the authors are experienced in deciding what they can do to enhance young people's civic engagement and their citizenship. Together, the examples provide a rich introduction to the book and it main focus: civic youth work emerges when workers cocreate and co-sustain and work with a group of young people in a democratic space, when they commit to co-making democratic space with young people. They describe a way of doing almost any youth work in the family of youth work practice. The stories highlight this emergent democratic practice, rather than formal programming, as an effective approach to civic youth work, but their descriptions remain incomplete. To understand civic youth work more fully is to know how it is embodied in and lived as a craft by the worker.

We start with Katie Johnston-Goodstar and Joanne Krebs, who describe the Critical Media Literacy in Action project at an urban school for teen mothers and their children. Students in the project produced two digital documentary films in response to a school board decision to shut down their school. Using critical media literacy pedagogy, students and teachers critically interrogated the broader power structures and discourses that shaped their lives and the particular situation. Through this investigation, students came to understand how social structures render them invisible. The production of documentaries represented a concrete strategy to resist both their invisibility and the efforts of the school board to shut down them and their school.

The third chapter describes ongoing work with youth in Northern Ireland museums. Here young people are given wide breadth to create something that represents them and to put it in a public space. This generally entails an exhibit in the museum so that others can see it and understand more about them, their everyday lives, their communities, and the like. However, some groups took different approaches. One group decided to put on a rock concert inside the museum grounds to solve the problem of young people having nowhere to go in their town. Another group created a painted silk mural to represent their multicultural backgrounds and wrote a song about racism.

In chapter 4, Katie Richards-Schuster and colleagues describe the history of the Mississippi Safe Schools Coalition (MSSC). This youth-led organization was founded in 2008 by a group of queer youth activists. The MSSC works to create a safe learning environment for all students. The coalition has protected students' constitutional rights and has worked to address homophobia, transphobia, sexism, and all forms of discrimination. Using a dual strategy of public education and advocacy, MSSC aims to foster acceptance of students regardless of their actual or perceived sexual orientation or gender identity.

Chapter 5, the last chapter in this first part, has Rob Shumer sharing how youth participatory evaluation presents a model that can both capture the emergent learning of such youth work while simultaneously providing opportunities for young people to assume real responsibility and perform important social tasks, with benefits to them and others.

The second part of three stories is about civic youth work programs and programming. These cases illustrate how schools and community-based organizations have created structures that invite and support young people's participation and contribution to both the organization and the larger community. These stories tell how organizations can support young people's citizen involvement and development.

Schools have long had a civic mission, but this often is reduced to civics instruction. Terrance Kwame Ross, in chapter 6, describes the efforts of the New City School in Minneapolis to create a social and academic community in which all children feel understood, safe, valued, and respected, and in which they learn to value and respect others. The school uses the responsive classroom approach to promote, give structure to, and prepare students for leadership and service in the school, at home, and in the community. Rather than teach civics, teachers and students work together to cocreate a democratic school culture; that is, they do civics.

Mary Ann Steiner and colleagues present a brief history of Manchester Craftsmen's Guild in Pittsburgh, Pennsylvania, in chapter 7. The basic work of the guild is for young people to develop their artistic talents by working with resident teaching artists. However, it is much more than simple instruction in art. Great care goes into developing the culture of the guild in ways that promote democratic community and individual empowerment. There is an emphasis on dialogue, collaboration, building a community, and reflective practice that infuses all the work, from mastering the technical skills of ceramics to creating large-scale public art events.

In chapter 8, Ofir Germanic describes how an organization in Israel, Green Light, changed its programmatic structure to invite and support Jewish and non-Jewish groups of young people throughout Israel to help reduce teenage driving morbidity and mortality.

In part 3, the focus is on policy-level descriptions and the impact that different policies can have on youth civic engagement. In chapter

9, Professor Yun Jin Choi describes recent campaigns by young people in South Korea and the impact of their work on transforming South Korean society. As she describes, South Korean policies, norms, and traditions have all worked to reduce and lessen young people's civic engagement. The story she tells provides insight into what national policy changes can be made to support youth civic engagement.

In chapter 10, Jennifer De Maio surveys a variety of different conflict resolution programs that have been designed to address civic conflict in Africa. She documents the crucial role that youth play in peacemaking, preventing violent crime, and opening up dialogue among different tribal groups in several African countries.

In chapter 11, Emina Bužinkić tells the story of how the Croatian Youth Network became established. By creating a loose network of youth organizations throughout Croatia, several critical youth policies were created and enacted. These policies have provided some support for young people to become engaged in local and national civic work in a country recovering from decades of conflict.

The final part addresses the strategies for developing civic youth work as a practice. In chapter 12, we reflect on years of doing trainings for civic youth workers. We trace the process and techniques we use to teach civic youth workers. In the final chapter, we describe civic youth work orientations and practices that emerge from across all the chapters and pull these together in more abstract discussions of the ethos, craft orientation, practice, and skills of civic youth work.

A Note on the Chapter Questions

Questions at the end of each chapter are intended to stimulate and facilitate reflection, analysis, and teaching. That is well and good. Harder is to choose a philosophy, strategy, and practice in which to ground, formulate, present, and use these interrogatories for our and other purposes, such as policy making or program development.

Questions address us and may claim us, and if they do, they may call us to engage them. Questions can invite dialogue with their ideas, and with another text. They guide us to read and reflect and analyze and, always in these and other ways, to respond to. Address, call, and response are elements of dialogue and, in another way, elements of vocation. Questions can be vocational in their claim on us, what matters to us, what we give ourselves over to.

We say in our youth studies teaching, consultation, training, and writing that youth workers embody questions—indeed, they go to the world as questions, not as responses or as those responses that qualify as answers—because they close the circle opened by a (good) question.

Practice and research are joined in their reliance on the orientating and investigative powers of questions and questioning. Indeed, civic youth work is a questioning orientation and attitude.

It is difficult to know how best to find a particular strategy of questioning in these specific questions. One we used previously was directed at the deep structure of youth work in contested spaces (Magnuson & Baizerman, 2007). A favorite is in *Reading Zoos*. Malamud (1998) distinguishes five types of reading and questions about animal zoos: about zoos, through zoos (i.e., as a challenge to zoos), against zoos, beyond zoos, and zoos themselves (i.e., how zoos name themselves). Here, the strategy suggests questioning civic youth work and/or each programmatic essay as such to get at what is explicit and implicit, visible and less visible to invisible, included and excluded in the story and account, (over)emphasized and (over)minimized, seemingly accurate or inaccurate or even false, documented or implied, demonstrated or asserted, claimed or not, and the like.

Another useful approach is to frame questions in the categories making up civic youth work practice: ethos (philosophy), craft orientation (of workers), (worker) practices, and (workers') skills. This we show in the final chapter.

These are all viable, practical, and useful for the purpose of inviting analysis, reflection, and teaching about civic youth work. There are other appropriate, vital, and effective stances for constructing questions to guide reading and reflection, and to suggest how those examples could be used for training, programmatic decision making, and policy change. For example, stipulate a role (e.g., youth worker, program evaluator) and read the text and design and answer questions from that angle or space. For example, for a program evaluator:

- What data are presented to substantiate and/or document that the program, effort, or initiative was effective (in whomever's terms: youth, staff, management, funders, and community members)?
- Is there an explicit (program) evaluation design?

Another example is to take a theoretical stance and work from there to develop questions and in this way direct the reader. For example, for process emphasis:

- How did the worker go about talking with the youth?
- What words did the worker use to invite young people's reflection?

Or another example for constructivist theory.

- How did young people define *young person* before, during, and after the civic work?

- What did *young person* mean to them before, during, or after?
- How did these self-conceptions fit with larger community expectations for what is and how to be a young person?
- Were these self-meanings brought to a larger world, and if so, with what early reception and later acceptance?

Finally, for now, inviting and guiding reading, analysis, reflection, and teaching can be achieved by using questions that come out of each reader's reaction to what he or she is reading. This is the strategy we use.

We solicited, edited, read, and reread each chapter multiple times, before and after communicating with authors about our assessments, ideas, and suggestions. So we go a step beyond that now to read (again) each chapter and then simply ask questions about it stimulated by that reading. In this way, we are inviting first the text and then the reader to talk together about what is on the page and what the page stimulates us to wonder. Doing this, we make explicit only some of the questions each chapter discloses about itself and invites us to engage.

So be it! As a good civic youth worker, we invite you to read, construct, respond, and answer any question that grabs you. Each is a door to a deeper look at the text; all point the way, as in Martin Buber's (1957) idea about education: Look, what do you see where I am pointing? Where do you want to point to see?

OVERALL QUESTIONS

These questions can be used to reflect on the whole book and/or to help think about each chapter, along with the questions specific to that chapter:

- What does *cocreating with youth* mean, in general and in your context?
- What does *youth spaces* mean, in general and in your context?
- What does *democratic* mean, in general and in your context?
- What does *cocreating democratic youth spaces* mean, in general and in your context?
- What does *civic youth work* mean, in general and in your context?
- What similar terms to *civic youth work* can you think of that capture the practice as described in this book overall and in each chapter?
- What if anything is unique about civic youth work practice as presented in this book and in each chapter?
- What concept, metaphor, or term could be substantiated for (civic) space and enrich the ideas and practices described and discussed?

- How does space and/or time work in everyday civic youth work practice?
- How are the concepts, metaphors, and terms *youth, young people,* and *young person* used in general and in each specific chapter?
- What chronological age range is implied or referred to?
- How are these terms used against the scientific concepts of adolescence and adolescent?
- What, if anything, is ageist about these terms?
- Do these terms provide different images than *adolescent, teenager,* and *kid,* and if so, what are those images?
- What does *young person political agency* mean, in general and in your context?
- What should a reader think about when reading a chapter in this book?
- What questions should a reader ask him- or herself?
- How should a reader go about using what they learn from reading? What precautions, if any, should he or she take when applying what is read to his or her own context and situation?
- In the contexts of the international essays, what are the limitations, the culture-bound features of civic youth work as presented in this text?
- Is there a universal civic youth work ethos?

PART 1

Civic Youth Workers

Critical Media Literacy in Action

Engaged Space in Urban Public Schools

Katie Johnston-Goodstar
and Joanne Krebs

You received education through the music you heard,
Cafeteria tables enabled beats to occur,
Where students separated in cliques
The State of the Nation manifested up in high school politics.
History repeated, you repeat it to regurgitate.
Slave ownin', dead white men,
Folks you know they made curriculums to make obedient drones.
Bring your paper but please leave your lyrics at home.
—*Blue Scholars, "Commencement Day" lyrics*

At first glance, the notion of engaging spaces with young people seems a nondescript task. Surely, parents, teachers, and youth workers engage young people in spaces on a daily, if not hourly, basis. But as the Blue Scholars illustrate, engaging spaces in urban schools is hardly a simple task, especially when the complexity of our American society and its history reveals itself at every turn. Creating spaces of legitimate engagement in schools when and where the very notion of education is contested requires more than unlocking the door to an open gym, more than hosting an after-school group or teaching a class. It must be a mindful and arduous practice—a purposeful, critical, and continued cocreation of a space that opens possibilities and activates the agency of young people to explore the contexts of their everyday lives (Batsleer,

2008; Cammarota & Fine, 2008; Duncan-Andrade & Morrell, 2008; Gin-wright et al., 2006; Morrell, 2004; VeLure Roholt, Hildreth, & Baizerman, 2009; Weis & Fine, 2000).

In this chapter we introduce preliminary findings from our qualita-tive evaluation (Checkoway & Richards-Schuster, 2003; Cousins & Whitmore, 1998; Madison, 2005) of the project Critical Media Literacy in Action, a youth media project that we, the teacher, and the young participants have come to define as an engaged space. Our chapter articulates the theories and practices that informed the work and high-lights the importance and results of this engaged space for our young participants. It furthermore exemplifies that this type of practice, though difficult, is possible in public schools. First, we introduce our young participants, situating them in the context of their society, com-munity, and school. We then introduce the crisis that precipitated the development of their media project. We follow this with a presentation of the theories and a description of the practices used to create an engaged space with the youth participants. Finally, we present initial results from their engagement with this unique space.

Project Context: The Everyday Lives of Our Teen Parents

The Critical Media Literacy in Action project was located in an urban public high school designed exclusively for teen mothers (between the ages of fourteen and twenty-one) and their children. Nearly 400 stu-dents attended the school each year, including approximately 250 chil-dren, from infancy to kindergarten. Students represented the diversity of our urban core, including African American, Latina, Asian American, Native American, and Caucasian communities. In its original design, the high school was a beacon of relationships and supportive, holistic services. It included fully certified teachers, a school social worker, case managers, a licensed child-care center, a health clinic, co-located county economic assistance services, and a visiting nurse program. The school also offered comprehensive sexuality education programming; college courses; a General Equivalency Diploma program; and unique course offerings for credit recovery, including parenting support and prenatal programming. Students were able to attend school year-round in an effort to encourage their success and eventual graduation.

The school boasted many successes. More students graduated high school, attended college, and participated in job-training programs than before. In 2009, average attendance was at an all-time high of 65 percent. Students had healthier and fully immunized babies; approxi-mately 98 percent (compared to 47 percent citywide) of students' chil-dren were fully immunized. Subsequent births among students nineteen years old or younger, were reduced to 8 percent (compared to 22 percent citywide). Students were present more than 50 percent of the time, and they were more likely to graduate and be on track to graduate by credits and state standardized tests. The 2010 graduating class produced thirty-six students, more than half of whom were continuing on to postsecondary education.

In this holistically designed school, many of our participants were successful in navigating the simultaneous challenges of being young parents and students. All of our students, however, continued to face significant structural challenges and inequitable conditions in their everyday lives. Even in a supportive space such as the school, these societal challenges often went unengaged. Many students experienced homelessness, poverty, and substandard educational opportunities in other schools. They woke each morning to a hostile society that represented them in the local newspaper as welfare queens; lazy women of color who had no aspirations higher than producing children to augment their welfare checks. Fellow citizens habitually scoffed at them as they carried both backpacks and baby bags on public transportation. Even advocates in the schools and local agencies limited their political agency with public statements like "these kids aren't going to picket," further reinforcing the societal discourse that they were little more than "babies having babies." As of this writing, many were struggling against a wave of gang violence that had directly affected them and/or claimed the lives of friends and relatives. In a cruel and ironic twist, our young students also feared the police who were intended to protect them from this gang violence. In no small terms, issues like community violence, discrimination, economic inequality, and a pervasive lack of power shaped their everyday lives.

Amid these harrowing conditions, the students were thrust into the spotlight when their local board of education voted to demolish their school building. In collaboration with the city government, the board proposed to build a new district headquarters in its place that would help "revitalize" the neighborhood. What ensued was a rapid and devastating relocation of the high school program to a downtrodden local high school (which the school board also voted to close months into the relocation), a relocation that not only displaced the students but also drastically altered the school's original design. The previously mentioned holistic services were largely dismantled or relocated to an off-site location more than two miles away. While being heralded at national conferences as a model of success, the school lost more than half of its student body in less than six months; this included a significant number of the original project participants.

In a world of standardized curricula, conditions such as these could have easily thrown off even the most masterful teacher. However, the

combination of a reflective media-arts instructor, flexible school administrators, and the integration of critical pedagogy (more specifically
the theory of critical media literacy) allowed for the cocreation of an
engaged educational space in which a remarkable youth-media project
was developed. The students proposed to produce a film that would
document their school as it was, investigate the decision-making processes and social context that led to their displacement, document the
effects of that decision on their everyday lives, and advocate for themselves and the future of their program.

Critical Media Literacy as Engaged Space:
Theory to Practice

Contemporary discourse often positions youth as disinterested and
uninvolved. These descriptions further a moral panic about young people's "apathy" and, consequently, the future of democracy. But "what
may look like apathy to one observer may not in fact be considered
apathy to the person being observed" (VeLure Roholt, Hildreth, &
Baizerman, 2009, p. 6). Our youth claimed that they were not apathetic,
but rather not often invited to engage and/or already engaged in multiple ways in the fabric of their communities. They and their teacher
sought to cocreate spaces to critically integrate and apply their media
arts and civics education in their everyday lives. They proposed developing a deeper understanding of the structural inequalities that defined
their lives, as well as engaging in the immediate crisis they faced as a
result of their impending school transition.

The project we are writing about emerged from educational theories
and practices that supported the claims of our youth and assumed their
active engagement with the world around them. Critical pedagogy
(Freire, 1970) and youth participatory action research (Cammarota &
Fine, 2008; Canella, 2008; Ginwright, 2003, 2008) were identified as
bodies of scholarship that supported the creation of this project space.
Critical pedagogy is an educational approach that unequivocally binds
education and liberation, asserting that education is a "predictable site
of struggle" (Johnston-Goodstar, 2009, p. 27). It positions students as
cocreators of knowledge and as agents of change in the pursuit of social
justice and the transformation of unjust realities (Freire, 1970). It challenges the notions of authoritative, "banking models" of education, in
which young people are filled with "knowledge" by adult teachers, and
instead positions students as "critical co-investigators in dialogue with
the teacher" (Freire, 1970, p. 80).

Youth participatory action research (YPAR) is a related paradigm that
pushes the theory of critical pedagogy into spaces of active research. It

is a process of critical and collective inquiry conducted by youth in their communities. It manifests as a voice for those left out of the dominant research and decisions; it positions youth as capable and competent researchers. Through this methodology young people study social problems that affect their lives and determine actions designed to address and/or rectify them. Moreover, YPAR engages in critical scientific inquiry: students research questions, develop and implement methods to answer those questions, and analyze their findings. Inherently, YPAR embodies a component of political engagement—by engaging in collective critical inquiry, students learn about complex power relations, the history of struggle, and the consequences of oppression.

Critical pedagogy and YPAR allow for the creation of dynamic, engaged spaces pregnant with liberatory potential. Evidence of the success of these methods is found throughout the literature (Duncan-Andrade & Morrell, 2008; Ginwright, Noguera, & Cammerota, 2006; Johnston-Goodstar & Nagda, 2010; Morrell, 2006; Weis & Fine, 2000) More specifically, contemporary educator Amira Proweller uses these paradigms to cocreate engaged spaces with teen mothers, who are conventionally constructed as at risk and/or deviant and, at worst, abnormal. Her work on critical pedagogies of resiliency counters the pedagogies of deficiency that define young mothers' educational experiences. A pedagogy of resiliency, she states, assumes engagement and "attributes competency, resourcefulness, insight and vision to pregnant and parenting teens. . . . [It] writes/rights lives that have been underwritten as wrong" (Proweller, 2000, pp. 116–117).

In developing the focal project we are writing about and identifying appropriate engagement strategies, the instructor relied heavily on the theories of critical pedagogy and YPAR and their cyclical practice of theory, action, and reflection (Johnston-Goodstar & Nagda, 2010). More specifically, he used a critical pedagogical theory and practice called critical media literacy (Goodman, 2003; Kellner & Share, 2005). Media plays an influential role "in organizing, shaping, and disseminating information, ideas, and values" (Kellner & Share, 2007, p. 3). Media representations and coverage had largely rendered our students, their school, and their experience invisible. Critical media literacy provided a framework for exploration, analysis, and the production of counternarratives in which "people in subordinate positions [to] have the opportunity to collectively struggle against oppression to voice their concerns and create their own representations" (Kellner & Share, 2005, p. 371). Using a framework of critical media literacy, a research and production process that melded theory and practice was co-developed—the participants identified a relevant medium to investigate and engage in a situation they identified as unjust, socially constructed, and therefore challengeable and/or changeable.

Critical Media Literacy in Action: The Research and Production Process

As part of the preproduction process, participants defined what engagement meant for them. Together, they researched dominant definitions and strategies of engagement; they then discussed those strategies and explored what they meant in the context of their lives and community. They found that many typical definitions of engagement not only were inappropriate but also often posed significant risk to emotional and physical safety. Given stereotypes about urban youth of color, our participants reported that typical strategies such as public protests or rallies entailed physical risk (large groups of youth of color frequently encountered aggressive police response). In addition, they found traditional political processes limited in their effectiveness and elected officials and candidates unrepresentative of their communities and concerns (few officials represented or were familiar with the economic, racial, or geographic experiences of our young participants, and some were unaware that their school existed).

In place of these more traditional engagements, our participants and their instructor identified critical media literacy, particularly media production, as having the greatest potential to engage their immediate crisis: the closing of the school and their displacement. They claimed the media research and production project as engaged space of exploration, resistance and creativity, a cyclical practice of theory, action, and reflection. The project included formal research and production meetings held twice weekly with extensive time given to reflection and engagement with findings. It also included informal meetings and production consultations as needed with project staff. Further, the participants had unlimited access to production equipment during school hours.

The collaborative research and production process included the following (presented as a linear process for simplicity but in actuality, it was an ongoing, cyclical process):

- A historical review of the city and exploration of the development of segregation, gentrification and the concept of root shock (Fullilove, 2004) and dialogue about its impact on communities of color
- Multiple field trips to sites of historical and community significance, such as community murals and local political and spiritual sites
- A detailed investigation of the decision-making structures and processes of school, local, and state government
- A thorough review of elected school board members, including their educational and personal biographies and policy platforms

- A review of school board meeting minutes for the previous year, which led to the discovery and investigation of a city–school district collaboration for urban "revitalization" that precipitated the school closure
- A review of newspaper articles about the school closure, including lengthy and critical dialogues about the public commentary in these articles, which frequently included inaccurate and offensive statements about the students and their communities (the students worked to deconstruct these myths and identify who or what benefited from the perpetuation of these myths)
- Screened multiple documentaries and digital shorts on related topics
- Course work on filmmaking technique (e.g., shot list, shot angles, camera, sound, story board, editing principles)
- Course work on interview technique (e.g., question development, role-play, probing questions)
- Compilation of supplemental images for postproduction, including digital images and B-roll shots
- An examination of relevant educational policies such as No Child Left Behind, standardized testing, and a field trip to view and discuss the relevant documentary *Waiting for Superman* (including discussion on the content of the film but also an exploration of production details, such as story-line development and delivery of media messages)
- Informal meetings with elected officials and candidates
- Creation of an issues platform for delivery to policy makers
- On-camera interviews of school staff, faculty, and graduates about their thoughts on the program and the decision to dismantle and relocate it
- Development of interview questions for school board and superintendent interviews
- Multiple meetings with a consultant for the superintendent
- Participation in interviews with area media outlets
- On-camera interviews with school board members
- Private interview with the superintendent

The students are currently in the postproduction and editing process. They have produced two digital shorts, one documenting their school as it was when it was intact and another documenting the processes and decisions to relocate them and dismantle their services. They continue to work on the production of a final product documenting their school as it was and the effects of that decision on their everyday lives. They continue to use their film production process to advocate for themselves and the future of their program, and they hope to host a public forum and screen their documentary at a community theater in the future.

Transformative Possibilities of Engaged Media Spaces

Look me in the eyes and try to feel my pain
Do you know how it feels to be left out in the rain
Each and every day, there's someone judgin' me
Worry about my life and how I live in these streets
—Sean McGee, "My Story" lyrics
(soundtrack chosen for digital short)

As we evaluated the project and the unique space that was created, we came to the realization that the project serves as an exemplar for a rather simple reason: it cocreated a space that no longer marginalized the agency of the youth. The space worked to reaffirm prior claims that the participants had always, already been engaged. Through the co-creation of an engaged project space, they were able to achieve remarkable results and contest their invisibility. The students transformed themselves, engaged with and influenced the structures that held power over their lives, and developed new realities and positions of power that demanded space, which thereby works to shatter myriad perceptions of urban youth.

The project provided space for young people to transform themselves and their realities. They developed and embodied what we have come to call critical civic identities, becoming power brokers and stakeholders who demanded to be heard. They exhibited a growing awareness of hierarchies of power and came to a deeper understanding of racial, socioeconomic, and geographic disparities and their status as teen parents. In short, they developed a critical awareness of both their constructed and potential place in society, evidenced in statements like "I didn't think politics affected me until I started this project." Their confidence in advocating for themselves with power brokers like school district officials, teachers, and reporters grew exponentially; they refused to choose among the limited options provided by the district and demanded other realities. One young participant fearlessly probed the superintendent during an interview, asking her three times, "What is going to happen to our school"? Along the way, they consciously avoided re-creating inequitable patterns of dislocation by advocating for others and ensuring, as one youth participant said, that "changes [were] laid out for the next generation." Some even embraced new career aspirations and committed themselves to working with youth. Not only have they come to fully embrace their identities as capable, competent young women replete with personal agency; they have become community activists with an extensive political network at their disposal.

Despite the abundance of positive personal effects, as of the time of this writing, the young people's ability to transform the reality of their dislocation or influence the bureaucratic structure of their school district has been minimal. The participants have been afforded space by the bureaucracy and have been acknowledged in a way that they would not have been before, but it has, in general, been a tokenized or co-opted usage. The research process and production of the film legitimated a professional relationship with district stakeholders, but this did little to shift the system itself. Commitments to reunify the school have not come to fruition, and the students continue to experience the negative ramifications of the displacement. Although the students still do not occupy a literal space at the decision-making table, they occupy their own space, a critical space that they have cocreated and that cannot be ignored.

Although we found that the young participants had a limited ability to effect change in this arena, they have, through the production of their documentary, created a parallel power-political structure, and they are making visible the injustice and marginalization that they experience. Similar to Proweller's (2000) work among teen mothers, the participants have used their film to begin "the difficult work of reeducating the broader public from within the particular confines of school space" (p. 116). They have thrust private matters "back into the public arena in terms that bear the imprint of teenage girls hard at work reimagining themselves as participatory members of the larger social collective" (Proweller, 2000, 116). They have transformed themselves and embodied their potential, and they will continue to transform their realities.

Future Prospects for Engaging Space in Public Schools

Education can and should be dangerous.
—Howard Zinn (2009)

In addition to the transformative potential of engaged media spaces, our evaluation also found that there are significant risks involved. These spaces are not to be taken lightly; one cannot assume that education is neutral. Risk is inherent for both educators and participants. Youth workers and teachers may lose their jobs if people in positions of power take issue with the project, process, and outcomes. Questions will be asked about what appropriate engagement is: Is it too political for youth? Do they really have the capability to think like this? Should they be addressing such serious issues when mainstream society perceives them as too young? Shouldn't we be putting our energy into teaching students "real" subjects like math, science, and English?

Questions will be asked about whose agenda is motivating the project: are the educators co-opting, manipulating, and/or using participants to advance their own opinions? The final product of spaces such as these is that they may overtly challenge structures of power that do not welcome this commentary. For participants, staff and students alike, creating engaged spaces becomes an issue of ethics: At what cost must the story be told? Whose knowledge and experience counts as valid? What educational spaces and practices allow for these different kinds of knowledge and stories to emerge? This is a compelling and real tension.

Conclusion

This project illustrates the successful application of critical pedagogy in an urban, public classroom. Through the implementation of a critical media literacy pedagogy (Goodman, 2003; Kellner & Share, 2005, 2007) and the production of a youth-led documentary, the project space contributed to the transformation of self and structures and to the development of new realities and positions of power. Both participants and educators in this project experienced transformation; each emerged as unequivocally different people but both took real risks and dealt with subsequent consequences. Because of the high stakes involved in creating critical educational spaces, it is not always ideal to establish space within the confines of public education, but it is imperative that spaces be established. Students deserve nothing less than an opportunity to engage authentically with their worlds.

Reflection Questions

- What does the phrase "spaces of legitimate engagement" mean in this specific school context?
- What spaces of illegitimate engagement can you imagine existing in that school (and in your program, agency, project, or everyday life)?

- What do the phrases "mindful and arduous practice" and "a purposeful, critical and continued cocreation of a space that opens possibilities and activates the agency of young people" suggest to you in terms of a practice ethos, skills, and practices in your own context?
- What ethos, knowledge, attitudes, values, and skills do you think the youth workers possessed and used to carry out the work they reported? How do you name and categorize this set of philosophical ideas and practical skills? Does the term *civic youth work* capture what you think the workers knew about and knew how to do? What term would you use?
- What do you think the youth got out of this experience? Do you believe that this is valuable learning for them? What do you think the youth workers got out of this experience? Do you believe this is sufficient for them?
- Given the status of the school at the end of the case study, was the project successful? How would you defend your assessment?
- What more does this chapter need for it to teach you about cocreating with youth democratic spaces for their involvement?

CHAPTER THREE

Northern Ireland Museums as Sites of Youth Engagement

Lisa Rea

Youth work in Northern Ireland is in transition. During the Troubles, the most recent period of conflict, work with youth focused on keeping them off the streets. This was optimistically called peacekeeping (Smyth, 2007). With the signing of the Good Friday Agreement on April 10, 1998, and the disarmament of the Irish Republican Army, work with youth shifted from peacekeeping to peacemaking and finally to democracy building (Smyth, 2007). This chapter describes democracy-building work with youth in an unlikely setting: Northern Ireland museums. I first describe the context of this work and then provide background as to how this work began. Then I provide two examples. I finish by reflecting on these examples and sharing what I, a youth worker facilitating this work, learned about youth work through participating with young people creating museum-quality exhibitions in several of Northern Ireland's public museums.

Working with Youth in Northern Ireland

Young people in Northern Ireland grow up in a contested and divided society (Magnuson & Baizerman, 2007). The legacy of violence continues to shape their neighborhoods, youth clubs, and schools. Schools remain segregated (Gallagher, 2004), as do youth clubs (publically funded, community-based youth centers) and neighborhoods. The young people involved in these projects come from ethnically homogeneous neighborhoods (Catholic or Protestant, and increasingly neighborhoods of ethnic minorities and immigrants) and attended religiously separated schools (what are called controlled, primarily Protestant; maintained, entirely Catholic; or integrated). Controlled schools remain almost completely Protestant, and Catholic schools, not surprisingly, remain almost entirely Catholic (Gallagher, 2004). Integrated schools are growing and typically have fairly even student enrollments from both religious communities.

Education for mutual understanding (Smith & Robinson, 1996) in schools and the initiative Joined in Equity, Diversity, and Interdependence (JEDI) in the youth sector (Youth Council Northern Ireland, n.d.) were both created in response to the community, school, and geographical separations that young people in the two major communities (Unionist and Republican) encountered in their everyday lives. This work is referred to as community relations, in reference to building a better relationship across the separation, and it also responds to the legacy of violence on both sides. Within the larger effort, cross-community contact remains a primary goal. With young people this often means adults facilitating contact either in or outside of school, where young people both learn about the other community and share what is unique about their own community. The youth work described in this chapter has its roots in these initiatives. It too seeks to address the legacy of division and violence in Northern Ireland by creating and sustaining spaces in which young people from diverse backgrounds can come together to talk about issues that matter to them. But the work did not follow a typical community relations strategy, which often emphasizes cross-community contact. Instead, it created its own process, which I describe next.

Young People Creating Heritage

Over the past five years, I have worked on several similar youth-involved museum projects that have used heritage as a tool and a resource (*heritage* here means simply what we inherit from our ancestors, such as language, ways of life, sense of place, and physical artifacts). They were inspired by the work done by the Science Museum in Minnesota that embraced working with young people in an inclusive way and allowing young people to develop research skills and projects that had positive effects on their communities and the museums. These projects can support youth, museum, and community development simultaneously (VeLure Roholt, Baizerman, & Steiner, 2002). The idea for the Northern Ireland projects I describe and reflect on in this chapter was created through collaboration between Public Achievement Northern Ireland, a nongovernmental civic youth organization, and a curator at the Ulster Museum. Because heritage has such a broad definition in the Northern Ireland context, some projects have been drawn from the physical landscape, whereas others are focused on history. All the projects included young people using museum resources (e.g., archives, oral histories), to research and develop their projects.

The Northern Ireland version of these projects differed from the work done at the Science Museum of Minnesota in that they were based in history museums and facilitated through a partnership of the participating museums, Public Achievement, and local community groups. However, the premise remained the same: to open up the museum as a space in which young people could learn their voices, hear them, practice them, and have their voices heard by others, and as a space in which they could contribute to the institution and in turn to the community in positive ways. In this way, the project partners hoped that the young people, who were not traditional users of the museum, would begin to have a sense of ownership over the museum and exhibition space and to encourage others from their communities, adults and young people, to become users of the space.

This work received funding from the Heritage Lottery Fund and the Department of Education for Northern Ireland. Both funders had different reasons for supporting the work. The Heritage Lottery Fund wanted to support ways to increase access to heritage for nontraditional users, whereas the Department of Education was primarily concerned with other issues, such as ensuring that the groups participating were from both Catholic and Protestant backgrounds, that the project enabled cross-border work with groups from the Republic of Ireland (and Northern Ireland), and that a high enough number of young people were participating. For the Department of Education, heritage was secondary. As the youth worker on the project, I had to find a way to meet these two different aims while also supporting the particular methodology of my employer, Public Achievement Northern Ireland, which I describe next.

Approach to Engaging Youth

The methodology of the projects stemmed from Public Achievement's work in communities and schools in Northern Ireland. It is an approach that puts dialogue at the center of work with young people and encourages them to identify issues important to them and to take actions that have positive results for their communities and others.

In non-museum community-based youth groups, the work is less constrained by the aims of outside stakeholders. Typically, the youth worker begins by asking young people about their communities and brings in tools, such as community mapping and issues identification, to facilitate further reflection on where they live and what issues they notice in their neighborhood. Often, these activities support conversations among group members, who come to agree on what really matters to them as a group. Once they agree on an issue or topic to address, the youth worker coaches the group to set its own aims and to identify stakeholders who may help or hinder their project, and then the youth worker may provide skills training that relates directly to the work the youth need to do to complete their project, such as information technology, public speaking, interview techniques, and photography. The overall goal is for the group to develop an action plan that incorporates all they have learned to address their issue or topic and then put that plan into action.

The work based in museums followed a similar pattern, but it was slightly different because the aims of the worksite and funder put additional restrictions and boundaries on the projects that the young people could undertake. The young people continued to have the opportunity to create something that represents them and put it into a public space, a museum, so that others could see it and understand more about them. Typically, this has resulted in an exhibition that displayed aspects from their lives. In several of these projects the young people took an anthropological view of their own communities, choosing to display everyday scenes, whereas other projects critiqued their cultural landscape by analyzing public art, murals of the Troubles, memorials, and graffiti. However, not every group working in museums chose these foci.

For example, one group took the pragmatic approach of putting on a rock concert inside museum grounds. In holding the rock concert, the group was addressing the limited youth activities available in their community. Another group created a mural painted on silk to represent their multicultural backgrounds and wrote a song about racism. I provide a more in-depth description of these two examples next.

ROCK CONCERT IN THE MUSEUM

When I started working for Public Achievement as a youth worker, one of the first museum sites was the Fermanagh Museum, in Northern Ireland. I entered the project after it had already begun, and there were already two fantastic coaches in place. The coaches were museum staff who took on the role of supporting a weekly youth group at the museum. My role was to support the coaches and to work directly with the young people. I supported the coaches with advice about funding, group work skills, and project planning, although I was very lucky because the two coaches were very capable and needed little direction.

The group met weekly after school in the museum. The coaches had decided to allow the young people a level of freedom within the museum that was not afforded to the general public. This included use of the staff kitchen to help themselves to tea and coffee, as well as the use of computers in the office area. These small gestures appeared to create a sense of ownership in the museum for the young people. Taking the young people to the storerooms of the museum on several occasions enhanced this. By doing so, the museum workers demonstrated that they trusted the young people to be responsible with the museum's collections, many of which were irreplaceable. In response, the group expressed trust in their opinions as museum staff by asking for their advice in creating new exhibitions or evaluating existing displays.

In supporting the young people in coming up with a project, we discussed what they were interested in and what resources they had at their disposal. It was important to be open and transparent about the expectations of different stakeholders in the project. The initial funding application stated that the young people should work on a project that helped remove the perceived barriers between young people and museums, so a rock concert in the museum grounds was an exciting way to bring a new group of people into that space.

However, there was also an expectation that the work should have a heritage aspect, so the coaches had to encourage the young people to consider how they could address this issue. The group responded positively with an idea to create an exhibition about different styles of music found in their country (Northern Ireland). This also met the expectations of the museum that was hosting the project, because it would have an exhibition to attract a new audience over a longer period of time than one concert. Once the project was decided, the focus in the group shifted to creating a plan and then putting that plan into action.

During the weekly meetings, youth group members discussed their project and how they might make progress. Weekly conversations were reflective, evaluative, and functional. The group often talked about what they wanted to achieve, how they would do it, who in the museum and community would support or hinder them, what resources they had, and how they should plan the project to ensure that it was completed by a particular date. The role of the coaches and youth worker in these sessions was to ask questions and provide feedback using their knowledge and experience. The youth worker supported the work.

For instance, if a coach knew something about hiring a marquee and the group was discussing this, the coach would share with the group his or her experience and knowledge but not do the work for the group without their prior consent. The group decided what should be done, by who, and when. It is important to note that the coach was not always considered the person who knew best, as often the young people would have more knowledge about something, such as the best bands to book. Planning the rock concert was done by a group of young people who all came from the same community. In the silk mural project, young people came from several different communities, and this therefore required a different strategy from that of the concert.

THE SILK MURAL

In working on the project to create a silk mural, there were many other considerations to make. In this project the young people didn't use space within a museum to such a great extent. Their group included young people of different faiths and ethnic backgrounds, and when they met, it was important that everyone would feel at ease expressing themselves and their similarities and differences with one another. During this project we tried to meet in places where the young people could have access to resources they needed and would feel that everyone was in a neutral space (given the tensions about space following the Troubles). We met at the city hall, the central library, and in a community arts building in an area of the city that was equally unfamiliar to group members. We felt that this was the best approach, as it meant that the young people would be having the same experiences and that no one would feel more comfortable than any other because of the space.

In preparation for creating the silk mural, the young people did exercises based around art, conversation, and critical thinking to explore what made up different aspects of their (cultural) identity. In this project we also focused a lot on how objects can tell a story, and we asked the young people to pick objects that said something about them and could communicate an aspect of their identity. The groups met regularly at their individual sites and came together as a larger group every five or six weeks. My role in this was to facilitate group work, ask questions, and develop different exercises that would help the young people explore their identity without fear of judgment or repercussions (also part of the legacy of violence in Northern Ireland). In doing this we had to develop trust with the young people by spending time with them and by delivering on the things we said we would do. Sometimes the basis of successful youth work is showing up on time and doing what you said you were going to do. I think by proving this over time, the young people will trust us to take them on an emotional journey in which they may be looking at things that make them feel uncomfortable, such as labeling themselves in a public setting as different from other group members.

When it came to working on the silk mural, we booked an artist to come and deliver the session. After discussing this process with the group, we all admitted that we didn't possess the artistic skills to create the mural alone. Fortunately, the artist chose to work with the young people in creating the mural. The artist encouraged the young people to think of some of the objects, images, flags, and symbols (all basic to group and community identity during the Troubles) that they had thought about through the previous sessions and how they would like to incorporate these into a communal piece of art. The young people decided to create a forest scene in which some of the trees, flowers, and animals would be in symbolic colors or would be the chosen objects in clever disguise. It was a successful aspect of the project, as the young people could see their individual identities represented in the forest but they all worked together to make an interrelated scene.

Engaging Youth Work Practice

Through working with young people in museums over the past five years, I have begun to develop my own practice wisdom on how to create engaging spaces for young people. In my practice, I aim to introduce young people to spaces and places that might be unfamiliar to them; to encourage them to critique the curatorial voice and to develop their own voice; and most important, to support dialogue with young people.

OUTSIDE THE COMFORT ZONE

The projects took the young people outside of their comfort zones and into spaces in which they didn't always know how to act or what to say. This had to be incorporated into the project to ensure that young people felt comfortable enough in a museum or archives settings to keep them involved. Often, this meant providing an orientation to the museum and arranging for the youth group to meet different museum staff. In these projects, the participants were invited behind the scenes at the museums; they talked to curators and designers to understand what makes a good exhibition and how to tell their stories using appropriate words, pictures, and objects.

THE CURATORIAL VOICE

Personally, seeing a young person learn to question the curatorial voice has been a rewarding part of the program. The young people in the various groups have come to realize that the people who create exhibitions in the museum are just people with opinions and a particular political, social, or religious viewpoint. In that respect, their own voices have as much validity in the museum space as what they have seen on their site visits.

DIALOGUE

The most important aspect of this work is the use of dialogue. Dialogue is more than talking; it represents shared respect and equality among participants. If I were talking to new youth workers about the nature of conversation and dialogue, I would recommend that they read *Pedagogy of the Oppressed*, by Paulo Freire (1970). Freire emphasizes the need for respect among parties involved in the dialogical process and the need for them to work with one another rather than having a teacher-pupil relationship in which one participant imparts knowledge to another.

I have learned a lot from young people through my interactions with them. When going into a different geographic community or a community of interest, the young people are the experts and hold the knowledge about what issues affect their daily lives, as well as about who holds power in their communities and who are the stakeholders and gatekeepers. Learning this information helps the youth worker in supporting the youth in whatever they decide to do. As a youth worker in this situation, I have learned that I have a lot to bring to the conversation: the skills to ask the right questions, the skills to listen, and knowledge of comparable situations. I have also learned that young people also bring a lot to the conversation. By engaging in conversation with young people, we can find out what is really important to them rather than assuming and imposing our own program and ideas on them. When they have ownership of an idea, they are much more likely to stay involved.

Another important aspect of using dialogue as a tool for youth work is to try to build up trust with the group before embarking on asking questions that may seem intrusive or personal. This might seem like common sense, but when a youth worker has constraints around time and money, it is easy to get carried away and want to get at the issues straight away. I have found that it is important to remember at moments like these that the work will suffer if the group members do not trust one another. This includes the youth worker. Giving a bit of yourself can go a long way. Appropriate personal information and time spent playing pool or another activity can mean a lot to group participants, and for me these things have made work conversations with them more successful. This means that in icebreaker exercises, it is important to join in, even though most youth workers I know dislike them. But if you are going to ask a young person to participate, then you should too, as this is important in building the mutual respect needed for authentic conversation.

In these types of projects, in which it is important to build relationships, understand young people, listen to them, and work on issues that matter to them, dialogue is fundamental. There are many exercises and activities that a youth worker can use to draw out dialogue and provide a safe environment for the project to flourish. By working in this way, I have learned several things about working democratically with young people.

Conclusions

There are several things I learned in the process of delivering these projects that would make repeating the process smoother and hopefully more successful. I learned that it is really important to build time into the program for relationship development among group members, but especially between the person who is "delivering" the project, often the youth worker, and the group. This is especially important because the program takes young people into a space they are not familiar with or comfortable in. It is important for the young people to trust the person who is taking them there. This can be done by meeting with the young people consistently and regularly in a space they are comfortable in before taking them to the unfamiliar space (all of this is especially so when working in a contested space; Magnuson & Baizerman, 2007).

It is also important to take the time to get to know the group both as a group and as individuals through dialogue, games, and icebreakers. This is imperative when it comes to the stage of the project in which the group is trying to decide on the project's focus. If you have some knowledge of the group, it is easier to suggest things that members hadn't thought about before, and that might grab their attention and get them excited about doing a project.

It is also important that the partnership with the museum is a strong one and that the relationship between the organization running the program and the museum is equitable—that both are aware of the mutual benefits of participating. This can result in the museum allowing the young people to stay inside once the doors have been closed to the public or allowing the young people into the storerooms to see objects not on public display. To achieve this, it is useful to have a key contact in the museum, and it is especially useful if that person has some authority to make decisions, as museums are quite hierarchical organizations (in Northern Ireland at least), with little communication between departments. Learning to navigate the power structure of the museum can take time and can be energy sapping, so it is especially useful to have an insider who is committed to the project and its ideals.

I found that honesty and transparency are very important when explaining the project to the young people. They need to know what is expected of them and what they can expect from the project worker in return. Negotiables and nonnegotiables should be set out early on to avoid false hope over what can be achieved. This is important because a lot of the project can be directed by the young people in terms of their subject, how they want to represent themselves, and so on. However, certain things have to be achieved to make the project successful in the eyes of the stakeholders, including funders. It is important to be realistic and to be as transparent as possible not only so the young people know that they can trust you and don't get disappointed but also to maintain an environment of exciting possibilities. Although we want young people to know that they can achieve anything they want to, it is important to do this in a way in which they learn how to best negotiate their surroundings and other people. Again, this is crucial in a conflict or postconflict space.

Sensitivity to insider-outsider dynamics must also be considered. Certain groups in Northern Ireland can be suspicious of people from outside their (own ethnic, racial, religious) communities. This is very much a legacy of the Troubles, and it takes time to build trust to the extent that quality work can be done. Therefore, it is also important to be aware of the issues that may arise surrounding religious-ethnic divides. In the case of some of the groups I have worked with, certain ones had never traveled the single mile from home to city center because they did not feel it was a safe space for them, or they felt that they had no need to travel outside their own community. In the case of working with ethnic minorities, especially the Muslim community in Northern Ireland, it was important to make arrangements so that male and female participants were not sitting together and to be aware that, for this particular community, overnight trips were not an option. This may not be the same for other Muslim communities elsewhere. There is no way of finding these things out except by asking those who have worked in these communities. Again, dialogue becomes an important aspect of this work. It is important that the youth worker not be afraid to ask "stupid" questions.

Working with young people in museums to create public exhibitions has been very rewarding. Through doing this work, I have learned that young people have much to offer, not only to their local communities but also to public institutions. Inviting and supporting their contributions takes dedication and commitment from the youth worker to learn about them, individually and specifically, and to work with them so they can make the difference they understand to be valuable.

Reflection Questions

- What is the history of the past fifty years in Northern Ireland?
- What are or were The Troubles?
- What might it have been like as a child or youth to grow up in this divided and contested society in the 1960s, 1970s, 1980s, and 1990s in a Protestant, Catholic, Jewish, or Muslim family?
- What does each of the following terms mean, in general, in Northern Ireland and in your context: *peacekeeping, peacemaking, democracy building*?
- Imagine what youth work could be and what everyday practice could look like in a community so fully divided by religion and/or culture. What could be the goals of youth work? What could be its ethos, practice, and skills? How could such workers be trained? Would these workers need protection for their safety?
- Should youth work be done under conditions of continuing violence?
- Why was the museum a reasonable site in which to take on this work? What other sites in your community might also be good for this work?
- How does the author use dialogue as her basic strategy in her museum work? What skills constitute dialogue? Is dialogue different from conversation?
- What values are implicit in a dialogue strategy of youth work?

CHAPTER FOUR

Creating Spaces for the Next Generation of Civil Rights in Mississippi

Youth Participation in the Mississippi Safe Schools Coalition

Sarah Young,

Katie Richards-Schuster,

Anna Davis,

and Izzy Pellegrine

Most historians would agree that Mississippi was the hotbed for civil rights organizing in the mid-twentieth century. Facing incredible injustice and rights violations, Mississippians—including many young people—were at the front lines of voter registration drives, mobilization marches, sit-down protests, and boycotts. Many looked to Mississippi to assess the direction the movement was taking.

The legacy of the civil rights movement remains a critical issue in Mississippi. Issues of racial, economic, and environmental justice continue to be the focus of activism across the state. Young people remain a critical part of modern civil rights organizing efforts in communities across Mississippi.

Among the ongoing civil rights battles is the modern-day issue of rights and equality for lesbian, gay, bisexual, transgendered, and queer-identified (LGBTQ) youth. These young people face harassment and bullying in their schools and communities across the country, but nowhere is this experience more exacerbated than in Mississippi. According to the Gay Lesbian Straight Education Network's (2004) "State of the States" report, Mississippi is the most hostile state in the nation for LGBTQ youth: the state has a score of -3 out of 100 points, and Mississippi was the only state to receive a negative score.

Although many national organizations have viewed Mississippi as the state least likely to change in this area, many living and working in Mississippi on queer issues and youth issues realized that no change was just not an option. In addition to the experiences of youth and adult allies, the recent national media spotlight on LGBTQ youth justice focused on Mississippi and the South has provided the framework through which youth-led efforts to affect policy change have emerged.

Youth-led organizing involves young people identifying issues that affect their lives, developing strategies to address those issues, and engaging in action to create change (e.g., Checkoway et al., 2003; Finn & Checkoway, 1998). Youth organizing is an emerging field in social work and much of what is known to date has focused on case examples of youth and community change efforts in urban communities (e.g., Checkoway & Gutierrez, 2006; Ginwright, Nogura, & Cammarota, 2006). Among the types of examples that emerge in this growing area of practice are those that focus on LGBTQ organizing. Many of these examples focus on youth and youth-adult partnerships to address LGBTQ rights in urban and suburban schools and communities. However, to our knowledge, little if any work has been done to examine efforts by young people in rural communities and in the South to organize around LGBTQ issues. Given the climate around LGBTQ issues, it is important for the development of community organization practice that more knowledge of this work be documented, analyzed, and diffused.

A primary vehicle for this change has been the Mississippi Safe Schools Coalition (MSSC), a youth-led organization founded in 2008 by a diverse group of queer youth activists. The mission of the MSSC is to ensure that all students have a safe learning environment by protecting students' constitutional rights; ending homophobia, transphobia, sexism, and all forms of discrimination; and fostering acceptance of students regardless of their actual or perceived sexual orientation or gender identity through public education and advocacy. The MSSC remains dedicated to its youth leadership model; today it is led by the Queer Youth Advisory Board (QYAB), which comprises eight members who range in age from sixteen to twenty-eight years old.

Over the past two years, the MSSC, largely with the leadership of the QYAB, has achieved historic progress for queer youth in Mississippi. The MSSC hosts the annual Queer Youth and Allies summit, which draws more than one hundred LGBTQ-identified youth and supporters from around the state. The organization gives a voice to marginalized youth and collects data about queer young people through its Stories Project and through statewide surveys. It has successfully advocated for students' rights in several dozen school districts around the state and has mobilized youth around many high-profile cases. In 2010, it drew nearly five hundred queer youth and allies to its Second Chance Prom.

The success of MSSC has brought it significant media attention from outlets including CNN, *USA Today*, and the BBC. Boasting a membership of more than five hundred people, most of whom are youth, the MSSC plans to continue its groundbreaking work, which is rooted in community mobilization, grassroots education, and youth participation and leadership in policy change.

Getting Started: Origins

Community organizers and attorneys doing LGBTQ advocacy work in Mississippi and other parts of the Deep South had been discussing the need for an organization focusing on queer youth rights in schools and communities since 2004. There was a clear need for some sort of coalition to begin to build effective community advocacy strategies at the grassroots level, to bridge the gaps between a civil rights violation and a lawsuit. In addition, many of the initial planners were connected to the national safe schools movement through an organization called the National Safe Schools Roundtable. Through this connection, organizers in Mississippi learned that safe schools coalitions had been effective nationwide in bringing diverse stakeholders to the table to advocate for long-term change.

Initial conversations and planning meetings brought together the few young people known in Mississippi who had experiences starting or leading gay-straight alliances (GSAs) in their communities. At that time, there were three established college GSAs and only one in a middle or high school. From this small yet extremely talented core group, others joined in initial conversations about the vision until the group grew to five or six dedicated individuals.

As can be the case in working with communities living under intense oppression, there was a tight network in which queer youth seemed to know other queer youth to bring into the process. This series of conversations, which usually happened late at night or on the weekends to accommodate the busy schedules of the youth involved, were aimed at generating ideas and themes about queer youth experience in Mississippi. Although this type of networking can be detrimental to the creation of diverse organizations, the organizers made active efforts to bring everyone's voice to the table.

In the beginning stages of formation, the vision was open and flexible enough so that when youth were assembled as initial visionaries, they could truly and authentically form their vision for what the work and the coalition would become. This was facilitated in large part by meetings that were open to everyone. Youth were encouraged to bring a friend or two. Brainstorming and open-ended questioning were tools used to generate ideas. There was an unspoken commitment not to rush into any decisions without having conversations with the youth planners. Another tool that assisted in maintaining open and flexible planning was that the youth themselves organized the planning meetings. Youth co-facilitators, formally and informally, helped shape questions in an authentic way and helped find common themes among youth from across the state. When it became evident not only that there were common experiences of oppression and discrimination among queer youth in Mississippi but also that this core group of talented people could actually begin to address those issues through organizing and advocacy, the focus became to find funding and build a sustainable organization.

The MSSC officially began to coalesce in the fall of 2008, and the small core group (including community partners) organized the first LGBTQ youth-focused conference in the state. This conference happened at an Episcopal church in Jackson, Mississippi (the state capital), and seventy people (mostly youth) attended. The conference further solidified the need for and interest in MSSC. This work, however, was happening with little funding, apart from support from the American Civil Liberties Union (ACLU) of Mississippi. The ACLU of Mississippi, which had helped start the coalition, became its fiduciary home and provided staffing, space, and legal and technical support.

Following the conference, young people and the adult allies focused on building a sustainable organization. Youth took the lead in identifying funding sources, drafting grant proposals, and participating in meetings with funders. The vision was for an organization to focus primarily on mobilizing and training youth around the state to address issues of oppression and inequality in schools. Membership was intended to be voluntary, solicited through outreach at events and by existing members, and free to anyone interested in furthering MSSC's mission.

In April 2009, the newly formed Mississippi Safe Schools Coalition was notified that it had received a $100,000 grant over a period of three years from the Queer Youth Foundation, the first investment in queer youth in Mississippi and significant national funding for LGBTQ advocacy in a state and region that is often deemed a "lost cause" for change on this issue and subject.

Formalizing the Role of Young People in the MSSC

From the very outset, young people were at the core of the vision and development of the MSSC. Not only were young people key in the founding of the organization; there was also a recognition that it would be impossible to make schools safe without giving young people a voice in the decision-making processes of how to do this.

In the early stages of the MSSC the members discussed the need to create a formal structure to ensure that young people were always central leaders and participants in the coalition's decision making. The coalition formally established the Queer Youth Advisory Board (QYAB) as its governing body and board of directors. Although *queer* is used in the LGBTQ rights movement nationally to reclaim the derogatory connotations it has held, it is not a term widely used in Mississippi or in much of the South. Youth felt that adding the word *queer* to describe the advisory board served two purposes. First, it said that there was no doubt that the members on the board were themselves queer or allies. Second, it served as a public insertion into and assertion of the word *queer* to the movement in Mississippi.

The QYAB currently is made up of eight diverse high school and college-age youth activists from across the state, between the ages of sixteen and twenty-eight. The QYAB defines *youth* loosely, as members leave the board at thirty years old. Thus far, the QYAB has been made up of youth between the ages of fourteen and twenty-eight. Elections to the QYAB happen annually in December to fill any spots. Terms at present are unlimited, and many of the members of QYAB have been on the board since its inception. The MSSC is the only LGBTQ organization in the state of Mississippi that is entirely youth led, and it serves as a model to other organizations that youth can indeed create, direct, and envision meaningful policy change.

The QYAB has four retreats every year, which allows the board to make the financial and programmatic decisions of the organization, much like any other board of any other nonprofit agency. The QYAB, however, serves another important purpose. It is grooming the next generation of queer leaders by offering them tangible skills to lead, direct, and participate in social justice work in Mississippi. As such, the QYAB is an essential vehicle for youth leadership development in the MSSC and in Mississippi.

Engaging Youth Policy Leaders

The QYAB was founded on the basis of a train-the-trainer model of organizing, in which youth themselves support the development and leadership training of other youth. This is seen in a number of the QYAB's activities.

During retreats, QYAB members learn how to facilitate meetings, balance budgets, write grants, talk to national and local media, and plan major events, among many other skills. These retreats are organized by senior QYAB members or those with an interest in learning how to plan and conduct retreats. Often, the youth themselves lead the retreat. In places where there is no one on QYAB with expertise in the specific skill needed, a member of the community is asked to train youth participants. The QYAB members also attend trainings held by allied groups to further develop and refine their leadership and policy advocacy skills.

Discussing queer issues in Mississippi can be dangerous, invoke hostility from many adults and young people, and at the very least can make communities and policy makers uncomfortable because of the deeply conservative and often religious social context of the state. Strategically, having youth speaking directly to those in power about their lived experiences of oppression has proved effective in deescalating many potentially difficult situations and has been quite effective in forging meaningful relationships with individuals and groups and in creating lasting policy change.

The QYAB has also become an effective recruiting tool for new members of the MSSC, because it allows other queer youth to see themselves as leaders; peer-to-peer communication has been the best way to get the word out among queer youth in Mississippi. The organization has grown quickly, and it is likely that with adult leaders, its growth and development would have been slower and smaller.

The MSSC in Action

Over the past two years, the MSSC, led by the QYAB, has worked to engage young people in identifying policy issues in their local schools and communities, to provide spaces for LGBTQ young people to address common concerns across the state, and to work with state and national coalitions to address policy issues at the state and national level.

Although QYAB is the decision-making body of MSSC, its members are key in determining the priority policy issues for the organization. Policy actions are generally targeted at addressing a specific want (e.g., equal access to high school prom and other traditions, specific antibullying protections) brought forward by LGBTQ students on the front lines of change in their schools. Further, MSSC recognizes the crucial need to work in coalition with other organizations to achieve legislative and administrative policy change. However, there is even more to MSSC and its work.

Annual Queer and Allies Conference

The MSSC has hosted a statewide conference every year since 2008, and it uses this opportunity to bring together youth, teachers, parents, and other community allies to discuss queer youth issues in Mississippi and to train participants in how to make their schools, colleges, and communities safer and more inclusive of queer youth needs and wants. In 2008 about 70 individuals attended the conference, in 2009 there were approximately 150 attendees, and 2010 saw the greatest attendance yet.

The QYAB is responsible for event planning. Workshop topics have included policy advocacy training, gender 101, how to start and run a GSA, LGBTQ rights training, ally training, and other relevant topics. The conference trains youth and allies in skills that can help them bring about policy change in their local communities.

The MSSC has found that the annual conference is a fruitful place to network on a statewide level. This has resulted in an increase in active members and in policy change at the grassroots level. Once youth have been trained at the conference, they often have a keener sense of identifying when their rights have been violated, and they also seem to feel more empowered to do something to remedy such violations.

Stories Project

The MSSC, in partnership with the University of Michigan's School of Social Work, launched the Stories Project in 2009. This encourages LGBTQ youth and allies to share stories about any discrimination, bullying, and harassment they have experienced at schools or in college. The purpose of the project is to raise awareness about LGBTQ youth and ally experiences and to identify policy recommendations aimed at creating safer schools and communities for young people.

To date, the MSSC has trained youth to interview other youth and to capture stories in written or video form. These youth also edit the footage and compile it into a format that they can share with policy makers at the school and state legislative level. Since 2009, the MSSC has involved nearly thirty young people and adult allies in this work. The ultimate vision for the project is to create an educational tool that is relevant in Mississippi and can be used as evidence for why policies need to include explicit protections for LGBTQ youth.

Local and State Legislation

Since 2009 the MSSC has focused more intensely on state and local policy change for queer youth in Mississippi. The MSSC partnered with Gay Lesbian and Straight Education Network (GLSEN) and played a key role in advocating for a comprehensive antibullying bill being introduced in both the Mississippi House of Representatives and Senate.

The members of MSSC had face-to-face meetings with key legislators and told stories sharing why such legislation was necessary. Members also met with seasoned lobbyists and learned how the legislative process works in Mississippi and how to build coalitions for social justice reform and change. This led to a statewide antibullying law in 2010 that required every school district in the state to have policies and procedures in place to address bullying. The MSSC also played a supporting role in the passage of an antibullying policy that is inclusive of LGBTQ students adopted by the Jackson Public School District (the second largest in Mississippi).

Prom Watch

The MSSC, largely because of the influence of the American Civil Liberties Union of Mississippi, a founding member of the coalition, has its roots in defending youth civil rights in schools. In 2008, after a public high school in Jackson, Mississippi, prohibited students from bringing a same-sex date to prom, the MSSC successfully intervened to change school policy. This case, in addition to youth across the state expressing that prom season was hostile and unwelcoming for queer youth, inspired a project called Prom Watch.

Prom Watch sends youth leaders to communities to present and train youth and their allies about the legal right to bring a same-sex date to prom and the right to wear appropriate attire that expresses one's gender, and it trains participants on how to stand up when these rights are violated.

In 2009, the Prom Watch trainings combined with media coverage of MSSC-sponsored events and the group's vast networking and presence across the state led two young people—Ceara Sturgis and Constance McMillan—to contact the MSSC and ACLU of Mississippi for support. Ceara had been banned from appearing in her high school yearbook because she refused to wear the traditional black velvet drape for her senior pictures. Feeling more comfortable in a tuxedo, Ceara's choice ignited a national discussion about gender and dress codes. Constance McMillan also received national attention when her desire to bring her girlfriend to the prom violated a school policy that banned same-sex couples from attending school dances. Both turned into lawsuits that garnered national media attention.

There is no doubt that the two major court cases of Ceara Sturgis and Constance McMillan have provided both momentum and resources to MSSC and its work. Following the filing of Sturgis's case and the resolution of McMillan's case, youth seem even more empowered to stand up for themselves and assert their rights in their schools and communities.

To date, both McMillan's and Sturgis's lawsuits have been used as a vehicle for talking about discriminatory policies at schools and colleges.

Second-Chance Prom

Much like the annual conference, Second-Chance Prom has been a key MSSC event since its founding. The goal of the prom is to create a safe space for students and allies who were excluded from prom at their own schools because of their gender identity or sexual orientation. The QYAB is in charge of organizing the event and assembles a prom committee of MSSC members to assist. This committee shares the intense workload but also aims to bring new voices and talent into the planning process while involving members who want to be active but are less attuned to nonprofit management and legislative work.

Second-Chance Prom is the clearest indicator of the progress MSSC has made for students in Mississippi in its two-year existence. In 2009, the first Second-Chance Prom was held in a small bar in central Mississippi. About forty students were involved and the event ran on a $100 donation from the ACLU of Mississippi. In 2010, the Constance McMillan story began to receive national attention. The McMillan case was significant because, although MSSC was aware of students around the state experiencing similar situations in their schools, Constance was the first person who came forward publically. The QYAB used this press recognition to recruit major donors and to involve students who were not yet aware of MSSC. The 2010 Second-Chance Prom involved nearly five hundred students and allies, raised more than $50,000, and was the subject of a documentary and a brief report series on the national cable television network CNN.

Easily the most labor-intensive event for MSSC, the Second-Chance Prom is a pivotal event in increasing MSSC's name recognition in the LGBTQ community, in involving students deterred by traditional perceptions of activism, and in recruiting donors who want tangible change and direct action on GLBTQ issues in Mississippi communities and schools.

Impacts on Young People and Policy

Although the MSSC is in its early stages, its work has had a clear impact on the members of the QYAB and has influenced policy and practices in Mississippi. In discussions with QYAB members, most of the young people believed that they have learned to have a voice and, as a result of their participation, that they do have a voice. Through their work, they have learned to develop civic skills such as speaking out, planning, organizing, and advocacy.

Also through their work, they have helped influence organizational development and policy change at the state and community levels across Mississippi, including antibullying policies at the state level. The MSSC has also provided resources to support GSAs across the state through its summit and outreach. The MSSC's involvement in the two court cases helped students to connect and raise awareness of their work. The MSSC has come to serve as a convener and resource for young people around the state, and as a result, it has become a voice at the national level for young people in Mississippi. Members of the QYAB have attended national summits, participated in discussions of LGBTQ issues with national organizations such as the GLSEN, and most recently were invited to represent Mississippi at a White House conference on LGBTQ youth issues.

Creating Spaces

The MSSC often talks about its work as creating spaces. The QYAB members talk about QYAB and MSSC as safe spaces in which they can come together to discuss their experiences and as an activist space in which they can work for change across the state. They also talk about the importance of their activities, such as the Second-Chance Prom, conference, and support to local GSAs as creating spaces for others.

The concept of creating both safe and activist spaces is critical for MSSC. Given the politically conservative and religious context of Mississippi, LGBTQ youth take a huge risk in coming out and in organizing with others to do so. The work of the MSSC is often viewed as outside the mainstream and as challenging mainstream norms. The youth who participate often operate at the margins of spaces, "disrupting" the culture of the communities, schools, and universities in which they are studying and working. For these reasons, the idea of creating a space in which young people can come together to discuss their ideas and experiences and then draw on those in working for change is crucial and effective. Young people create the space for themselves and then, through their activities, work to create such spaces for others.

Given the statewide nature of the work, finding times and transportation to come together face-to-face can be very difficult. Often MSSC grapples with how best to create physical and virtual spaces for its work. Compounding this are the challenges of technology and access to technology, which have slowed the work and limited some QYAB members from participating as much as they might like to.

The work of MSSC provides a few lessons learned. First, MSSC is still struggling with how to do outreach in the context of Mississippi. Building on relationships, creating opportunities for face-to-face interaction, and creating a structure for young people to get involved have been critical. Second, MSSC has realized the importance of acknowledging the realities of LGBTQ young people in Mississippi. Through Second-Chance Prom, the Stories Project, and various media pieces, the QYAB members have confronted a belief that LGBTQ young people do not exist, but through these activities, the MSSC has both validated their existence and helped give voice to young people's experiences. Although policy change is an ultimate goal of MSSC, this cannot happen without opportunities for young people's engagement and empowerment. The MSSC is working to use these activities to help build a broader youth network for organizing. Last, MSSC is helping engage in dialogue about how to create a statewide organization that allows for active youth participation and engagement given the challenges of access, transportation, and the risk of participating. It has a long way to go, but the MSSC uses face-to-face retreats, conference calls, web technology, and small meetings as a way to move its work forward. Slowly, the MSSC is showing other organizations and organizers that a youth voice not only is critical in social change work but also is effective, efficient, and creative in bringing about change at the grassroots level.

In many ways, this notion of creating spaces is part of the legacy of the civil rights movement. In the history of the movement, young people and college students used freedom schools, movement safe houses, and local homes to talk about issues, raise awareness about injustice, and organize for change. This was dangerous work, and these spaces served as critical spaces in bringing people together. Almost fifty years later, young people still work to create and sustain these spaces of safety and activism.

Future Work and Closing Comments

Today, the Mississippi Safe Schools Coalition looks very different from in 2008, when a small group of GSA leaders met over tacos to address a need that was obvious but difficult to engage. The organization faces many of the same challenges as any new nonprofit, ranging from fundraising and incorporation to membership management. What may set it apart from other youth organizations is that its leadership is defined by, motivated by, and affected by its mission. The youth who run MSSC did not come together with the specific hope of creating a nonprofit organization. Rather, they brought forward the issues that they knew students were facing and developed the necessary social change model along the way.

As the MSSC's work continues, the QYAB will be tasked with keeping Mississippi at the center of the discussion of LGBTQ youth issues nationwide. No area is as poised for change, or as desperately in need of it, as the Deep South. With an unwavering commitment to diversity, visibility, and the rights of all students, MSSC is developing not only youth but also an entire social and political change movement.

Reflection Questions

- What are some similarities and differences between civil rights organizing in the 1960s and 1970s and civic youth work as described and discussed in this chapter?
- What are some legacies of young people's involvement in the civil rights movement?
- What is a coalition? What characterizes the type of interorganizational relations involved in a coalition? What are some other similar forms of organizing?
- What is a youth advisory board? How do these work? Do you have one? How does it contribute to your work? If you don't have one, would one work in your context?
- What does *marginalized youth* mean, in general and in this specific case study? Are there such young people in your context?
- What is community mobilization? Is this a civic youth work strategy, practice, and skill set?
- What is networking? Is this a civic youth work strategy, practice, and skill set?
- What are the practical values of holding retreats with young people?
- Are helping young people facilitate meetings, write grants, plan major events, plan retreats, and plan for conferences considered civic youth work activities? Why or why not?
- Is public and agency policy a legitimate civic youth work focus? What about municipal and state legislation?
- What makes a space a safe space? What makes a space an activist space? Should creating such spaces be goals of civic youth work in every context, regardless of program or project?

CHAPTER FIVE

Engaging Youth in the Evaluation Process

Rob Shumer

Youth participatory evaluation is a relatively new field. Although young people have always been involved in community work, their entrance into more formal evaluation work has been seen only in the past two decades. For example, in a review of more than five hundred participatory studies (Cousins & Earl, 1995), no study involved youth as evaluators. Just a decade later we find an entire field of youth engaged in evaluation at different levels, from school-based to community-based settings (Checkoway & Richards-Schuster, 2003; London, 2000; Sabo, 2003; Sabo-Flores, 2008; Shumer, 2007). The paradigm of youth-led and youth-engaged work is gaining momentum in the twenty-first century (Delgado & Staples, 2008).

As a new paradigm of youth activism and learning, youth participatory evaluation involves the combination of two fields: youth development and evaluation practice (London, 2002). In parallel to the fields of positive youth development, believing that young people can be contributors to society and can demonstrate and model responsible behavior—and combining this with more participatory evaluation practices, such as utilization-focused evaluation (Patton, 2008), empowerment evaluation (Fetterman, Kaftarian, & Wanderman, 1996), and participatory evaluation (Whitmore, 1998)—places young people in a position to actively engage in programs in schools, communities, and other areas where youth live and contribute to society.

Although there is much being written about the theories and outcomes of youth-led evaluation, the more critical issues revolve around how it is implemented and what contexts and conditions allow it to develop and thrive. This chapter addresses that point: what examples of youth participatory and/or youth-led evaluation demonstrate its potential and its practice so that all can learn from the experiences of the early adopters and practitioners.

Much has been written about the theories of youth development and youth participatory evaluation. From mapping the field (London, 2002) to an entire Wingspread Conference on impacts and outcomes of such work, doing youth participatory evaluation has important value for both youth and communities. In some cases it is transformative (Whitmore, 1998), making dramatic changes in both the communities studied and the youth themselves. Results of a symposium on youth participatory evaluation (Checkoway, Dobbie, & Schuster-Richards, 2003) identified several outcomes that resulted from good practice:

- Transformation of participants
- Promotion of youth empowerment
- Building of mutually liberatory partnerships
- Equalizing of power relationships between youth and adults
- Inclusive processes recognizing democratic leadership
- Involvement of youth in meaningful ways
- An ongoing process of youth involvement

Thus, youth-led evaluation has the potential to affect youth in many positive ways. Although it will not necessarily have impact in all areas, youth participatory work certainly can make dramatic changes in the way youth think and in the way they approach interactions with adult society.

Goal of the Chapter

A primary purpose of this chapter is to describe several youth-led evaluation projects and explain how those initiatives produced positive changes in youth and contributed important information to the evaluation process.

Many of these outcomes relate to increased knowledge of critical-thinking skills and engaging reflective work. In many ways this is the essence of evaluation work: developing the capacity of young people to ask questions, organize information to answer those questions, and analyze and make sense of the information collected to use the process to change or improve a program and/or a community.

CITY SCAN

Perhaps the concept of youth participatory evaluation is best understood in context. For the sake of example, I examine a program in Connecticut that addressed all the issues connected with youth participatory evaluation. The City Scan program provided high school students with digital cameras and personal digital assistants (PDAs) to examine the community needs of Hartford. Students literally scanned every street in Hartford; recorded information on their computers and PDAs; and created an entire information system that identified abandoned vehicles, graffiti, abandoned buildings, blighted lots, and the dumping of waste on the streets and in the green spaces of the city.

Youth in City Scan were enrolled in a summer-school program that covered government and social studies, as well as technology. The courses were designed to support the scanning activities and to promote technological knowledge and skills, as well as to involve youth in the active study of civic engagement. The courses were held in the afternoon, usually after the youth had completed their scans for the day. The courses were taught by Hartford-area teachers and assisted by City Scan program directors.

Included in the overall program was a youth participatory evaluation component. Because the City Scan organization included youth in separate groups (e.g., Alpha, Beta), one or two youth evaluators were selected from each group to study evaluation techniques and to process data collected throughout the week. A college student with special training in evaluation directed the youth evaluation component. She met with the youth once a week in the afternoon, usually during one of the two class sessions. The goal of the meetings was to enhance the youth evaluators' skills and to produce a final report on the City Scan program. The trainings involved having the youth initially learn how to conduct participant observations and self-reflections, which included covering some of the basic steps as they worked weekly to analyze and discuss the data collected. The college student provided feedback each week on the data and then helped the youth to set goals for the ensuing weeks. They repeated this process throughout the duration of the program, producing a report that complemented the more formal evaluation conducted by an outside professional evaluator (Shumer, 2003, 2004).

Youth evaluators collected their data through a participatory observation approach, in which youth observed their group conducting the various scanning activities during the week. They interviewed peers as they conducted their work and wrote about their own personal experiences with the project. They discussed their findings with the college mentor-instructor and produced short reports on their findings. The evaluation experience culminated in a half-day interview and discussion with the professional evaluator to determine what they learned from the evaluation experience and to summarize the important findings from their work during the summer.

The youth report included many different findings about the City Scan experience. Although adults involved in the program thought youth learned a lot about technology, for example, the youth evaluators reported that much of what they learned they acquired in the first few weeks and that they didn't feel that they learned as much as they could have. They mastered learning how to operate the cameras and PDAs in a short time, and much of the instruction occurred when one youth helped another with the equipment. Teachers were also helpful, but much of the actual training came from the youth themselves.

Youth evaluators also reported more student-teacher tensions than the adult supervisors acknowledged. The majority of youth were of color; the majority of teachers and youth supervisors were white. Youth said that although there weren't many acts of opposition, they felt that the teachers and supervisors didn't relate to them as well as they had hoped. Although there was no outright racism, there were some racial and cultural differences that bothered several of the youth. Youth also said they had a different attitude toward the civic engagement solutions to the community problems of blighted lots and dumping. Rather than continue to work with the city to clean up unkempt lots and dirty areas, youth thought they could have been more effective if they used some of their scanning time to actually organize local residents to help share in the responsibility for keeping the blighted and dumped areas clean. They wanted to meet with local residents, many from the communities in which the youth actually lived, to organize cleaning teams, thus rotating responsibility for cleanup among the residents after the youth had performed the original work. The youth thought that because the teachers and supervisors didn't live in the neighborhoods where the scanning took place, they didn't have the connections to actually pull off this transfer of responsibility to the local community. Thus, the youth evaluators presented some different perspectives on several issues related to the study, demonstrating that they can provide a point of view that was important to finding good solutions to problems.

An evaluation session (focus group) was held with the youth evaluators at the end of the summer program (Shumer, 2004). They discussed the City Scan program and their role as evaluators. They reported that the evaluation role made the program different for them than for their peers. They discussed having to take on a different perspective while experiencing the City Scan program—they were constantly asking questions (both of others and of themselves) while doing their daily work. They saw students acting responsibly and effectively. They also saw some youth wasting time, with individual effort in the group scanning quite varied. There were always some youth who were engaged and busy; there were also some who weren't involved and who socialized as they walked.

The bottom line was that their new role as evaluator and participant made them more critical of actions and more appreciative of the good work that was done by both youth and adults. It changed their perspective—it made them continuously ask questions about whether things were working and whether they were making a difference. In summary, it produced some of the very changes discussed at the Wingspread Conference on youth participatory evaluation—it empowered the youth to take an active role in the program; it changed their approach to the program by making them more critical; and it changed their relationship with the adults, thus making them more equal in their roles in the program. The youth evaluation work had impact and was considered important by the adults, and it gave the youth permission to work toward improving the program from a positive point of view. The evaluation was always couched in the spirit of improvement, so the adults listened to what the youth had to say. They didn't always agree, but they listened.

Perhaps the greatest impact of the youth evaluation project was the developmental growth of the youth evaluation team. They felt that they matured because of their work and were functioning in more adultlike roles. Being an evaluator is a serious role, and the youth believe that their function in that role made them more mature, more responsible, and more effective in asking questions for the evaluation team, thus demonstrating that youth can perform as adults.

YOUTH ENGAGED IN SERVICE

The Mississippi Commission on Volunteer Service (MCVS) developed the statewide program Youth Engaged in Service (YES). The purpose of the program was to involve secondary youth in volunteer activities that led to civic engagement and service learning in their communities. Students met periodically in Jackson, the capital, to discuss program activities and to plan events and programs that would promote service learning and community involvement by other youth. After Hurricane Katrina, they focused their attention on hurricane relief and assisting those who suffered great damage from the storm.

The director of the program engaged an outside evaluator who was studying YES in the development of a youth-led evaluation project. The focus of the evaluation was for the youth to develop their own participatory observation knowledge and skills to track the activities of the members and to engage YES members in collecting data on their own involvement. These activities were supported by the external evaluation consultant, who helped document some of his own information on the program and its impact on the community. Included in that evaluation was an assessment of the youth-led evaluation component, collecting data on how the youth participated in the evaluation activities and what impacts they made as a result of the YES initiative. Not all youth engaged in the evaluation work; only a select few had some additional training and guidance in maintaining the personal participatory reflections that constituted the youth evaluation component.

Youth received short training sessions, conducted by the external evaluator and supported by the local YES program director. The training involved actually walking the youth through some participatory evaluation activities, helping the youth describe their YES activities, and showing how they could compile them into a report. They practiced short evaluations during some of their monthly meetings and received reinforcement at a December 2005 meeting to verify their understanding of the process.

Results of the youth involvement provided great insight and descriptions of what youth actually did in YES and how the program affected them and the communities they served. After attending the evaluation training in December, several youth worked as participant observers in their own program, assessing the impact of the program on themselves and on those they served. They described what made the program important and how it affected their lives.

Youth evaluators were asked not only to evaluate their programmatic activities in the Gulf region but also to assess their youth summit and the general impact of the program on their learning and service activities (Shumer, 2006). One report included here, written by a high school senior, captures the feelings and comments of most of the YES participants and highlights the Gulf trip as being the most important and enjoyable activity they performed:

> This year has been my first time in the YES program, and already we have done service projects that have meant more to me than hundreds of service activities that I have done in the past. The feedback that was collected from each of our service projects has really made me realize that our volunteer efforts are definitely worth everyone's time. The service project that I would like to focus on the most is the YES trip down to the Gulf Coast. Entering into such a destructed, chaotic place, I was ready to get down and work hard to help the

couple and their house. What I did not realize was not only did we help physically, but emotionally, everyone was affected as well.

The thing that I liked most about our service to the coast was that everyone worked together so well and that owners of the house appreciated it so much. Our YES group is an amalgamation of people with numerous diversities, but we all share one passion—service to our community. When we were working on the house, it was obvious to me that everyone wanted to do his or her part. Not one person acted like they were too tired to do the work. There was no time to be lazy—the couple's house withstood a ceiling-high storm surge, but not without paying a price. Parts of the floor were ruined, the sideboards were molded, and the ceiling had to be entirely redone.

My job was to pull the tiles off of the ceiling, but not only did the tiles come off[;] dust came with them every time. We all had to wear face masks as well as goggles, but this stopped no one. In fact, I observed people actually wanting to take the people's dirty job who were on the ladders. When my shift on the ladder was up, it was my job to collect the dirty tiles on the ceiling and place them in a wheelbarrow that someone else would take to the street to be picked up by the garbage truck. Meanwhile, some of the stronger guys ceaselessly worked on tearing up the floorboards in the kitchen. What I liked most was that every once in a while, someone would start singing a song and the rest of the group would join in, which made our work so much more enjoyable. In my describing everyone's jobs, I mean to show how our group works in a team so well. No one was discouraged although it was obvious that a ton of work was necessary in the damaged house. It was amazing what our group of non-skilled workers could get done within just several hours.

The part that I did not like about the activity was the fact that we did not have enough time to spend working on the house. In my opinion, the service itself was flawless, but I wish that the YES group could have made it longer than a day trip. Ms. Bristow, director of the youth service program in Mississippi, did take a group previous to the trip that I attended, and worked on the same house that we did. Hopefully another trip will be planned soon, so that our service to the couple can continue.

The YES group helped the young couple in tearing down their newly bought house but built up their spirits while doing it. Our service to the community was in helping out a friend who was in need and taking the rebuilding of the hurricane's path one step at a time. Without our help, solely the two owning the house probably would have done the labor, because the neighbors were suffering the disaster just like they were and were not inclined to neglect their houses. In fact, the house across the street was forced to be bulldozed because it was in such bad shape. In such a chaotic environment, our group came to lift their spirits as well as physically aid the gutting of their house.

It was obvious to all of us that our work to the house on the coast was effective. Not only did it occur to us though, but the couple that we helped continually recognized how much we had helped in building their house back. The woman of the house constantly thanked us as we worked. At the end of the day approached, they both talked about how much they appreciated our helping them in such terrible disaster. They told us that what the coast really needed were volunteers like us, not just giving supplies and clothing. We also got to talk to their parents, who live down the street from their house, and they also complimented us on our work and how much it meant that volunteers were willing to do so much for them. By observing their attitudes toward us as well as their direct acknowledgments, it was obvious that our work truly affected their lives.

The YES program is a group that incubates new and ready volunteers for the world. I absolutely love spending time with the people whom I have so much in common with regarding service work to our community. Specifically working on the coast with them, I learned so much on how to appreciate what we have, but at the same time, we worked hard to make the couple feel better about their situation. The fact that there were volunteers ready to spend their precious time in solely helping them really encouraged the couple in their time of need. Due to the YES program, I have realized that being involved in the community is both a privilege and responsibility.

This report, similar to others, indicated the importance of the group work and the feelings of accomplishment from seeing the results of their volunteer efforts. It also represented the personal connections in the group and the fact that the YES experiences "meant more" than hundreds of previous service activities. The report also highlighted the value of conducting evaluation activities as part of the process: it was the feedback the student received that helped her to realize the value of the service experience, both physically and emotionally.

Perhaps the most inspiring comment came from a youth about participating in the evaluation process. She wrote about the impact the evaluation training process had on her learning and development:

> Ever since I did the first evaluation with you, I really don't look at things how I used to. Every time I do a project I look back and watch what other people are doing and I have learned a lot from watching others. Thanks for teaching me something that I will not only be able to use as a member of the YES program, but in my everyday life.

Thus, the training in evaluation, coupled with the power of the program, helped youth to see the connection between evaluation and monitoring the impact of youth work in community service. The evaluation training helped youth develop a keen sense of purpose and critical reflection, one that had important ramifications in their everyday lives. It, like the previous example, changed their frame of reference in analyzing their lifework and helped them to develop the knowledge and skills to prepare them for their critical role as citizens in a community. Evaluation became the mechanism that helped them grow in intellectual ability and in the willingness to become self-critical in understanding the impact of their work on community development and change.

Conclusions

These two examples demonstrate how youth participatory evaluation can change the perspective of young people and help them move into more adultlike, responsible, reflective roles in their communities. Participatory evaluation is more than just monitoring and assessing programs and activities; it is about the personal, intellectual, and civic development of young people as they move from roles of program participants to program assessors and people who begin to actually change and analyze the world they live in. It is about personal and professional development, about changing young people from program actors to program planners. Youth participatory evaluation is, in many ways, the embodiment of positive youth development. It changes the perception of youth from role of passive, quiet, accepting child to that of active, engaged, and responsible citizen who assumes real responsibility for the assessment of personal programs and personal actions. It moves the young person along the path from dependence to independence, to a cause of the problem, to the solution to society's problems.

Just as important, engaging youth in the evaluation process provides a perspective on the world that is simply impossible to create through adult experience. Young people need to have their voice heard and their lived experience registered for evaluations to be complete and comprehensive. Youth, engaged in youth programs, must have their point of view voiced and activated so that they can make decisions and develop policy and programs that have stakeholders invested in the production of education and social initiatives in which young people are the primary clients and actors. To do so is to violate the basic principles of democratic society and to withhold vital experiences from young people that are important to the overall development on the road to adulthood. As mentioned at the beginning of this chapter, youth participatory evaluation combines two major fields: youth development and evaluation practice. The outcomes of this connection make for better, stronger young people and for a better, more engaged society.

Reflection Questions

- Why did the author join youth activism and learning? What does this suggest about his take on civic youth work as pedagogy?
- What does *diffusion of innovation* refer to, and what is its place among early adopters?
- How do the outcomes for good practice referred to here map onto civic youth work outcomes?
- Why should young people not be involved in evaluating activities, programs, or projects in which they are participating?
- Is evaluation a civic practice and skill? Is it a political practice and skill? How do these relate to it being a scientific practice?
- What are some problems and liabilities of having youth-led and youth-involved program evaluations from a civic youth work perspective?
- What is the place of group work in civic youth work practice?
- What skills might youth develop by learning about and doing evaluations that can also be developed by doing civic youth work?
- In what ways is civic youth work, like participatory evaluation, about the personal, intellectual, and civic development of young people?
- What is the place of youth voice in both participatory evaluation and civic youth work?
- What would an engaged society, community, and group look like? How does each of these fit into your (emergent) conception of civic youth work?
- Is civic youth work a pedagogy?

PART 2

Civic Youth Work Programs and Programming

CHAPTER SIX

School as a Site for Civic Youth Work Practices

Terrance Kwame Ross

The US public school system is by far one of America's greatest experiments. The vision to uphold the ideal democratic government, "for the people and by the people," compels the country to use schooling to socialize citizens on how to be lifelong participants, members, and citizens of this society. The very core of the idea of school in the United States embodies the ideas, values, and traditions of a democratic society. Recent social reform in the Middle East shows that there are other ideas, values, and conceptions of democracy, too.

John Dewey (1909, 1916), who is acknowledged as one of the preeminent educational theorists of the twentieth century, presents one of the most compelling arguments linking democratic values and education, arguing that schooling is an opportunity for students to develop social responsibility in and through action. He states that for students to learn how to act in a democratic society, schooling should be structured so as to allow young people the experience of developing rules and living in accordance with those rules. Here, schools can be a legitimate domain to live the ideas and ideals of democracy. Although Dewey's insight into the connection between civil society and a literate public was groundbreaking, his vision of what and how schooling could be used for training youth to become adults and to be full members of society has not been realized.

School as a site for civic discourse and for acquiring the skills, knowledge, and attitudes of civic work is in competition with other societal
agendas for schools. School reform efforts and educational social policies, such as the enactment of the No Child Left Behind legislation of
2011, have put extreme pressure on schools to give preferential treatment to an academic achievement discourse and practice that reduces
schooling to cognitive mastery assessed by test taking and to a culture
of individualism, which leads to individual, not group or communal,
success. As a result of this current sociopolitical narrative, the goal of
doing well on high-stakes testing at the cost of providing a well-
rounded education for all children has set the tone, educational agenda,
and pedagogy for too many schools across this country.

The other pressures for academic achievement have marginalized
civic as well as human development discourses about what it means to
be a citizen and human being. The idea of school being a place to teach
the young how to live well and to live as citizens has been pushed aside.

Schools also are increasingly expected to make up for the failures of
other social institutions. Comer (1980) puts it this way: "The American
public schools have also been expected to take leadership in every
national inequity our federal government has addressed in the past
generation. This includes the inequalities associated with poverty, racism, and sexism" (p. xiii). Comer's keen observations bring clarity to
the fact that schools have always been a core site and space for America
to work out its constitutional creed of "a more perfect union."

It was in this context of seeing school as a place in which we could
open opportunities for our community to become more inclusive and
to help us live up to the moral imperative to be of and for the whole
community that we started New City School.

History and Context of Work

New City School (NCS) is a public charter school in Minneapolis, Minnesota, established in 2002. It began after three years of planning. As
described on its website (http://newcitycharterschool.org), the NCS
vision was and continues to be "to create a supportive community
which actively engages students to build knowledge, ask meaningful
questions, design creative solutions, open their minds, care for others
and their community, and become skilled, responsive citizens of the
world."

I and several other educators set out to establish a learning space
grounded in the understanding of schools as socializing institutions
that mirror and feed the larger society's culture, values, and social
norms. Schools reflect both the positive and the negative aspects of our

society. We took on as moral necessities the patterns of racism, sexism, poverty, and homophobia that are manifest as unequal educational opportunities for a large segment of American children. These pressing social wrongs propelled the founders of NCS to see this school as a microcosm of the broader society's struggle to appropriately address and enhance greater and equal participation and engagement by all the members of the school community. The NCS was to be a space in which children learned about the world, evaluated this larger context, and learned to make both school-world and larger-world better places, that is, places that are more just, equitable, and caring.

New City School's goal was to create a school world in which student apathy was not an option. The founders wanted the school to be a place in which all students could thrive socially, emotionally, academically, and as citizens. Social-emotional integrated academic learning would be the touchstone of this belief and its pedagogy, sparking student engagement throughout the school environment, curriculum, and pedagogy itself. Given the historical times, the founders of NCS were very aware of the challenges in trying to create a space in which students would be listened to, cared for, challenged, and given the opportunity to take on real responsibilities in and outside of school.

The NCS was being founded at a time when talk of "failing schools" and the "crisis of the American educational system" were the most prominent educational discourses. Superficial media coverage about the failure of schools to meet the needs of society was everywhere. This moral panic and confusion of the real issues surrounding American public education forced many schools to strengthen their already highly authoritarian, highly formalized academic programs and learning environments and to emphasize even more "teaching the basics"— reading, writing, and arithmetic. This approach was suspect in the past and had not worked for many children and youth then: what would be so different now?

Founders of NCS saw the coming disappearance of progressive ideas and innovative teaching and curricula that had been created over the previous two decades to engage students as whole persons and members of society. The objective of most of these was to educate the whole person—the social, emotional, moral, psychological, and civic person— not just the intellectual person. The methods proposed include opportunities to learn by doing; art-infused lessons and experiences; service-learning opportunities; and with the aid of mature adults, the exploration of democratic values in an open, receptive school environment. Yet it was these very subjects and ways of working that took time away from teaching the basics. To some, these "soft" skills and experiences were a continuing cause of declining scholastic achievement, as measured by standardized tests. The founders of NCS rejected this traditional claim of schools and opened a space that was developmentally appropriate for children and adolescents, culturally responsive (Gay, 2000), and grounded in a humanizing pedagogy (Bartolome, 2008); that valued social interaction with the aim of co-constructing knowledge (Vygotsky, 1934/1986); that scaffolded reflection and guided participation (Rogoff, 1990); and that provided opportunities for community service and social responsibility (Youniss & Yates, 1997).

The NCS was to be a space in which there was a diverse learning community—racial-ethnic, social class, family structure—and diverse, too, in knowledge and thinking styles so as to serve as a demonstration space for the integration of social, civic, and academic learning, the mastery of these, and their use in the everyday lives at school and in neighborhood and community.

The NCS was designed to build strong connections between and among school, community, family, and children, and among formal, informal, and nonformal learning. The school as a world was also the curriculum—so, too, the students themselves and their learning, growth, and development.

Program Model

Learning and succeeding in school and life requires active engagement in these. A disproportionate number of children and adolescents think that learning in school is boring, a waste of time, and not relevant to their everyday lives. This sentiment serves as a powerful source for students' choice to disengage from their learning, their school, and their communities, and it can produce alienated, apathetic, and disengaged children and youth. Our pedagogy of choice had been shown to respond well to these very issues. New City School's program model is built on the Responsive Classroom, a nationally recognized, social-emotional integrated academic learning strategy and method with a comprehensive set of highly practical ways to improve and promote students' engagement in their own learning mastery.

In using the practices of the Responsive Classroom approach, we at NCS held to a set of ways of thinking, learning, and acting that, at its core, speaks to social justice issues. There are ten practices: morning meeting, interactive modeling, democratic rule making, teacher language, working with families, room organization, guided discovery, logical consequences, collaborative problem solving, and academic choice. All are ways to get honest student buy-in to the school, its mission, and its practices, including strong participation in all aspects of the school world. We take our work with children and adolescents seriously, and by that we mean that we constantly adjust our everyday practice so as to build an environment and create spaces wherein both student and teacher together deal with problems and situations.

The overall NCS program model has eleven elements:

1. A social and academic curriculum that is developmentally appropriate for learners
2. Differentiated instruction that meets a variety of learning needs and modes
3. A constructivist approach that is built on active, exploratory learning in areas of interest to students
4. Academic choices so that students participate in the design of their own learning
5. Discovery-based approaches to learning about materials and routines
6. Inquiry-based approaches to the content of both social and academic classroom experiences centered around a group of core essential questions
7. An integrated curriculum that allows students to weave understanding from subject to subject, with a special focus on urban life and other forms of community living
8. An approach to building relationships that is based on social-emotional learning research
9. A system of positive discipline that is based in respect, relevance, and realism
10. A system of classroom and school physical organization that supports learning and relationship building
11. Multiple, balanced assessment approaches that help us see students from many perspectives and includes not only what they know but also what they can do with what they know

New City School's program model promotes, gives structure to, and is committed to preparing students to become and to be responsible citizens in their school, peer group, family, community, and broader world.

Opportunities for action and service are important at NCS. Service learning in and out of school is an integral component of the program model. At the beginning of each year, teachers co-plan with students schoolwide service-learning projects. Students are asked to think about how they might contribute to the school community. Students engage in walks around the school looking for opportunities to serve. Some examples of projects generated, designed, planned, and initiated by students have included planning and preparing snacks for schoolwide meetings; planning and coordinating schoolwide special events such as peer tutoring; setting up a process for students to recover lost items from the lost and found; designing, writing, and distributing schoolwide newsletters; and designing a student survey to gather data on students' perception of school and presenting the surveys to the principal. These activities are metaphors for responsible social behavior, public work, and civic and citizen work.

In addition to using service learning as a means to invite and teach the skills of how to be a responsible member in a variety of worlds, NCS places a high value on human interactions and intentionally gives daily opportunities for students to engage in effective community life. Each student is trained in conflict resolution and encouraged to use those skills with their peers and adults to problem solve and resolve conflicts peacefully. Through participatory structures and methods such as conflict resolution, role-play, and problem-solving meetings, students have many tools and opportunities to problem find and to problem solve individual, group, and school issues. Opportunities for individual and group reflection are also available as structures in daily sharing and representing meetings, a way to practice effective communication skills, basic to citizen life and citizen work. All of this was formalized as outcomes and impacts.

Our outcomes and impacts:

- Teach an ethnic and socioeconomic mix of students in an urban setting.
- Focus on a core curriculum that students will address critically and with depth.
- Use instruction that is differentiated and challenging, active, arts infused, interdisciplinary, and inquiry based.
- Model applied civic, social, and academic skills in collaboration with the larger community.
- Launch students into the world as confident, competent, socially responsible citizens.

In addition, we seek to increase youth's social skills and social and academic engagement, to establish positive school and classroom climates, to increase learner investment in all of these, and to increase children's and adolescents' independence in order to give them a sense of initiative and self-efficacy.

Engaging children and adolescents is not an easy task, but the program model sets the stage for greater student involvement and participation. Students at NCS come to feel a great sense of pride in their school and do not want to miss being there; absenteeism is very low. Students feel a strong connection to one another, to their teachers, and to the school's physical space, as demonstrated by Maya, a fourteen-year-old eighth-grade student. On a dreary, cold, rainy spring morning,

Maya walked into the school building two hours after the start of the school day gasping for breath. She was tired and wet. I asked her why was she so late to school. She told me her story of missing the school bus and having to walk to school. Maya couldn't imagine missing the day's activities with her peers and teachers and decided to walk more than ten miles in the freezing rain to join her community. This same sentiment is common among other students who beg their parents to be allowed to attend school even though they have a fever, cough, and a runny nose. They don't want to miss anything.

Students consider the school a place for interesting, engaging, and enjoyable learning. "We not only learn about the civil rights boycott, [but] we also research some of the characters, discuss what we learn, and then use role-play to reinvent the history," one said.

"Our voices are heard" is another theme of students' reactions. At the beginning of each academic year, NCS uses the democratic rule-making process for setting classroom and schoolwide rules. Students in each grade level, from kindergarten through eighth grade, cocreate rules in their individual classrooms. Then, representatives from each grade level meet with the principal and negotiate and consolidate eight sets of school rules into four or five schoolwide rules. This process involves representatives from kindergarten through eighth grade advocating for their classroom rules while also working on the larger task of forming rules for the entire school community. This is citizen work; these children and adolescents learn valuable lesson of negotiating to get something for the common good of the whole school. The rules developed in this way are used to make schoolwide decisions about practical realities such as lunchroom behavior, recess, and throwing snowballs. The whole student body discusses, debates, and votes on all decisions. All year long, staff lead students through the process on how to monitor and reflect on rules and on decisions made, and how to modify these for greater equity and safety, if needed: this is civic learning in action.

New City School is a good place for children and adolescents. What makes it a great learning space is that we know children and adolescents as persons and as individuals. We know them developmentally, culturally, geographically, intellectually, and personally. But at the same time, our pedagogical approach to being with kids allows us to bracket our knowing and to be responsive to the individual standing right in front of us, as a unique person in the here and now. This is one form of our embodied youth work practice.

We know them as children and youth. We know them as students. We know students as children and youth and as this child and this young person. We also know about teaching and learning. We know how to set up a learning environment that respects cultural diversity among students and is responsive to and supportive of their different learning styles. Our teaching methodology has depth and flexibility. Faculty at NCS spend a considerable amount of time thinking and planning each learning experience. We have a set of operating goals that each learning experience should embody. We plan choice, personal connection, reflection, sharing, and fun into each lesson or experience. We believe that these elements engage students in ways that support their independence and interdependence, including participating fully in their learning and in the world—as responsible citizens.

So far we have presented NCS from the point of view of an educationalist, that is, as a new and better type of effective school. Next, we approach NCS from youth development and youth worker points of view. Here, the same facts and programs are highlighted differently.

The NCS Program Model Seen from Youth Development and Youth Work Perspectives

Youth development as we see it is an ongoing process in which young people are engaged through processes and other ways to meet their basic physical and social needs and to build the competencies and connections they need for survival, success, and joy in their school, family, and community worlds. All youth at NCS are engaged in the process of their own and others' personal development through the acquisition of a broad range of competencies and the demonstration of a full complement of connections to self, others, and the larger community.

New City School is a space for promoting healthy youth development in that it seeks to contextualize young people in the positive—as fully flourishing human beings. We cocreate with them spaces and learning experiences and pathways whereby they become motivated, directed, socially competent, compassionate citizens in and outside of school.

YOUTH DEVELOPMENT

New City School is the community's organization. Its aim is to assist a community in raising its young. The students at NCS are the community's young people. We have a moral compact with them, their family, and the community. New City School assists children and youth in their process of growing up and in developing their capacities in positive ways so as to be full community members in school and in neighborhoods and community. This membership includes citizenship, such as doing citizen and/or civic work, the public's work.

New City School as a domain for youth development balances the school's academic goals with positive social values, such as respect,

responsibility, caring, and civic responsibility. Pittman (1991) conceptu-
alizes these as five basic competencies:

1. Health and physical competence—good current health status plus
   evidence of knowledge, attitudes, and behaviors that will ensure
   future health.
2. Personal and social competence—skills for understanding self and
   having self-discipline; working with others, communicating, cooperating, negotiating, and building relationships; coping, making
   good judgments, evaluating, making decisions, and problem
   solving.
3. Cognitive and creative competence—useful knowledge and abilities to appreciate and participate in the areas of creative expression for thinking, seeing, tasting, and hearing.
4. Vocational competence—understanding and awareness of life
   planning and career choices, leisure and work options, and taking
   steps to act on those choices.
5. Citizenship competence—understanding of personal values,
   moral and ethical decision making, and participation in public
   efforts of citizenship that contribute to the community and the
   nation.

Although these five competency areas are usually associated with nonformal and informal youth development education, they are central to
NCS's curricula and program model. Table 6.1 presents and summarizes
how NCS meets the criteria of positive youth development.

Here we have made some connections between youth development
and NCS's program. Now we will see what type of worker it takes to
work inside of a school as a teacher who sees and acts to enhance positive youth development in the classroom, in the school as such, and in
preparing children and youth for community life.

YOUTH WORK

It has been proposed elsewhere (Baizerman, 1994) that youth work is
that vast family of practices, occupations, and settings that are given
over to positive youth development. The term as well as the idea of
youth work is mostly associated with nonformal and informal education. So, too, is the term *youth worker* and the role of youth worker.
However, as we have shown here, NCS is a space in which an educational program aligns with the goals of positive youth development and
youth development programming.

By far, most schools are places of traditional learning that reflect formal ways of organizing human interactions, teaching materials, and

Table 6.1. How NCS Supports Youth Development Education

Criteria for youth development education	NCS program elements and practices
Health and physical competence	• A nutritious school breakfast and lunch program • Multiple, balanced assessment approaches are taught to students so they can monitor, correct, and reflect on their progress toward a certain goal or competence
Personal and social competence	• An approach to building relationship that is based on social-emotional learning research • Discovery-based approaches to learning about self, school materials, and social routines • A social and academic curriculum that is developmentally appropriate for learners
Cognitive and creative competence	• Differentiated instruction that meets a variety of learning needs and modes • Inquiry-based approaches to the content of both social and academic experiences centered around hands-on and arts-infused learning
Vocational competence	• A constructivist approach to learning is applied that allows students to take on a variety of learning roles in active, exploratory ways to rehearse the many modes of being in the world • Academic choices about what to learn, how to learn it, and how to evaluate the learning are given to all students
Citizen competence	• An integrated curriculum that allows students to weave understanding from subject to subject, thus enhancing perspective taking, with a special focus on urban life and other forms of community living • A system of positive discipline that is based on respect, relevance, and realism • A system of classroom and school physical organization that supports learning and relationship building

instruction. These traditional ways of organizing schools generally go against the everyday lives of children and youth. Children and youth are spontaneous, curious, vibrant, risk takers, and they like to explore their surroundings. Formal education and teachers sometimes find it difficult to meet those needs and wants inside of a school. This we sought to engage by making the learning space (the school) a site of many spaces in which the ways of being a child and youth were not merged (only) into "student" as in a typical school but could be lived authentically.

As one of New City School's program guideposts, a developmentally appropriate social, academic, and physical environment is at the heart of the school. This is what NCS has in common with nonformal and informal educational settings. Paying attention to, and being intentional about, how the environment is cocreated with youth and what goes on in that environment to enhance civic, personal, and cognitive competence is what good youth work and teaching are at our school. New City School practices receive influence from both formal and informal education theory.

Doyle and Smith (1999) outline eight bread-and-butter concerns that informal education and educators are concerned with: an aim for democracy, a commitment to mutual aid, work for a clear focus, attending to people's feelings, encouragement of positive interactions, development of structures, knowing the place of special activities, and attending to reflection and learning. Table 6.2 describes how New City School also supports informal education.

In another way, NCS is also similar to youth work. Typically, teachers teach content to students. A teacher working like a youth worker teaches students content, teaches children and young people content, views the children and young people as content (curriculum), facilitates children and youth in their learning. These shifts in perspectives and practices are real, observable, and consequential—for kids, teachers, parents, school, and community. It is a small step from vocational competence to supporting and seeing students as citizens of the school, where they participate in creating the rules and doing the work of a school. In this view, school becomes a youth space and a youth agency, with teachers becoming youth workers. The teacher embodies an ethos of youth work as he or she works with young people who make up the class.

That all of this is done in the name of both learning and of youth development shows how we at NCS are a site of youth work and a school. Table 6.3 illustrates this.

New City School is successful using classical educational criteria as well as youth development and youth agency criteria, and it has been for almost ten years. How did this come to be? This mix comes from

Table 6.2. NCS Outcomes and Impacts and General Goals of Informal Youth Work

NCS outcomes and impacts	Concerns of informal education and educators
Teach an ethnic and socioeconomic mix of students in an urban setting	• Aim for democracy
Focus on a core curriculum that students will address critically and with depth	• Work for a clear focus
Utilize instruction that is differentiated and challenging, active, arts-infused, interdisciplinary, and inquiry based	• Attend to reflection and learning • Know the place of special activities
Create positive structures to model applied civic, social, and academic skills in collaboration with the larger community	• Encourage positive interactions • Develop structures • Attend to people's feelings • Commit to mutual aid
Launch students into the world as confident, competent, socially responsible citizens	• Aim for democracy

our own multiprofessional education in education, youth development, and youth work. What have we learned about designing, implementing, sustaining, and evaluating NCS that can be reduced to lessons learned?

What a school can be:

- A space for teaching and learning, with shared responsibilities by teachers, young people, parents, and the larger community
- A youth agency serving young people where they are at
- A space for rehearsal and show, for the school world and for the larger world beyond

Table 6.3. Parallel Worlds of Schools and Youth Agencies Lessons Learned

Youth agency	School
Youth development	Schooling
Youth work	Teaching
Youth worker	Teacher
Curriculum as learning experiences, outings, sports, and the arts	Curriculum as subjects such as math, reading, writing, science, and social studies
"Youth"	"Student"

- A space to learn how to negotiate and have conversations about shared goals and common interests

What a teacher can be:

- A student of learning
- A youth worker who values human relationships over methods as the way to work, that is, to facilitate learning
- A facilitator of learning who uses a variety of learning activities and experiences to capture the imagination and interest of youth
- An ambassador for a democratic education based in social justice and youth development
- A social and academic educator

Who students can become:

- Competent youth, adults, and citizens in the school, family, and community
- Metaphor for the continuation of democratic values and traditions
- Our present-past, present-present, and present-future
- Fully flourishing persons in the world
- Our neighbors, friends, teachers, youth, and community workers

How to evaluate our school and our work:

- Use both quantitative and qualitative evaluation methods
- Use both types of methods and place equal value on outside evaluators and inside evaluators, such as researchers, teachers, students, and parents
- Teach youth how to review their learning, reflect on its strength, and improve on its weaknesses through authentic assessments such as reflection protocols and inventories, portfolios, and learning journals
- Demonstrate learning of teachers, students, and parents through sharing of meetings, art, simulations, and public discussions and conversations about the success and challenges of teaching and learning
- Involve students in all these evaluations

Conclusions

New City School is unique and replicable, not in exact ways but at least in ethos, goals, and pedagogies. It is unique and innovative (and effective); the ways it became a learning space and how it works as a learning space are not hard to see, hear, or touch. Can NCS as a model go to scale, for example, with thirty of them seeded and later successful in the United States and internationally? As with any innovation, there is much that is unique, and much of what is unique may not be fully replicable, but much can be. Innovations in school are too often adaptations of models proven elsewhere or pedagogies new to a particular school or, typically, curricular changes. Too infrequently ethos is taken as the crucial core for understanding success and for using this as seed corn to grow crop.

For us, it is our ethos and how it is embodied and lived that is the crucial mix that must be understood if one is to understand NCS, that is, to understand that we both are and are not a school. We are an engaging and engaged space for young people.

Reflection Questions

- How does civic youth work fit the ideas, values, and traditions of our democratic society?
- How can civic youth work be thought of as a practice toward developing students' social responsibility?
- What is some of the resistance to a school-based practice of civic youth work? To the place of civic youth work in fostering and co-sustaining civic discourse in schools?
- How might civic youth work practice contest student and/or youth apathy? When is apathy really noninvolvement by those who may be passionate? Why does this distinction matter to civic youth work practice?
- How does the Responsive Classroom learning strategy map (and not map) onto civic youth work practice in general and for each of the eleven points?
- Is service learning a civic youth work practice? What would make it so?
- What are the pertinent family relations involved between and among student engagement, youth engagement, and civic engagement?
- What are some competencies that young people might begin to master through a civic youth work practice? Which of Pittman's (1991) five categories of competence might a civic youth work practice enhance?
- Is civic youth work as a pedagogy and a practice more or less formal, informal, or nonformal learning?
- Where might civic youth work practice help realize the author's suggestions of what a school can be?

CHAPTER SEVEN

Manchester Craftsmen's Guild

Art, Mentorship, and Environment Shape a Culture of Learning and Engagement

Mary Ann Steiner,
Tracy Galvin,
and Joshua Green

As a teenager growing up on the North Side of Pittsburgh, Pennsylvania, during the 1960s, Bill Strickland was not much different from other kids in his working-class, multicultural neighborhood. The social upheaval of the civil rights era was taking place, exposing inequities in the world-view of many people, and Bill was not immune. Disengaged and uninspired at school, he was unable to grasp any sense of a hopeful future. In one moment, that all changed. Awestruck at the sight of a skilled artisan raising and shaping the clay form, Strickland entered and approached the teacher, Frank Ross, who was working on a potter's wheel. Over the coming months, the relationship that Ross and Strickland initiated around a still, plastic vessel gave life to Bill's future and his vision of Manchester Craftsmen's Guild (MCG).

Ross was not a typical teacher. He brought records to class from his personal collection to play and shared stories about the legacy of Pittsburgh's jazz community. Through music, he drew connections to the clay artist's essential challenges: balance, harmony, intuition, improvisation, flow, and structure. While visiting the home of Ross and his wife, Strickland experienced how the family's way of life was enriched by aesthetic sensibilities. Hand-woven tapestries adorned the walls, and crafted objects were in daily use. As he gained mastery over the potter's art, Strickland began to experience success in school. Other teachers could recognize that his newfound self-confidence transformed his self-image and affected his willingness to persevere and learn in all of his classes.

A few years later, in 1968, while completing undergraduate studies at the University of Pittsburgh, Strickland established Manchester Craftsmen's Guild, operating the nascent center in a pair of adjacent row houses in a North Side neighborhood named the Mexican War Streets. At the time, Pittsburgh was a city racially divided and economically distressed. Strickland's vision for MCG was to develop a neighborhood center to provide a safe haven for youth while combating the economic and social devastation experienced by the residents of the now predominantly African American community. Strickland and his father built a kiln in the garage of the center and acquired a few potter's wheels. Photography was soon added to address the interests of community members and because Strickland understood that artists needed visual representations of their work to promote and help sell it. Many decades later, with the addition of adult vocational programs, a jazz program and an international replication of the Manchester Craftsmen's Guild model, the youth studio arts program sustains its founding vision and story. In an interview with *Fast Company* magazine, Strickland spoke about his passion and single flash of insight on that long-ago Wednesday afternoon outside of Ross's classroom: "You start with the perception that the world is an unlimited opportunity. Then the question becomes, how are we going to rebuild the planet" (Terry, 1998, p. 173).

The primary purpose of this chapter is to give the reader an insight into the daily routines and practices of youth and teaching artists at MCG. A number of vignettes and observations from the three authors attempt to draw in the reader to witness and experience what makes MCG a success and identify three overarching themes: the physical environment, the culture, and the empowerment of youth and staff experiences. These are discussed in terms of how MCG provides space for these themes to have a direct impact toward promoting positive interpersonal relationships and trust, individual learning opportunities, reflective practice, and the key values incorporated to support active citizenship. These all underpin the success of the organization over a forty-year period in which young people shape their futures. Pseudonyms are used throughout the text for both staff and youth.

Introduction to the After-School Youth Program

Manchester Craftsmen's Guild's after-school program, known as the Apprenticeship Training Program (ATP), is the cornerstone of its service to youth and the community. From three o'clock to five-thirty in the afternoon, from Monday to Friday, Pittsburgh high school age youth are able to access free art instruction; individualized advising; and visits to cultural institutions, colleges, training schools, and local professional settings that help students develop their vision for careers and for what and where they want to study beyond high school. Enrollment takes place at three times during the school year, and a continually renewing set of courses are offered through the MCG's four studios: ceramics, photography, design arts, and digital arts. All who come are welcome. There are no formal entry requirements, such as demonstrations of prior talent, experience, academic ability, or complicated applications. Accessibility is also maintained through a partnership with Pittsburgh Public Schools that enables any student attending one of the school district's high schools to attend without fee for instruction, materials, or supportive services.

Physical Environment

Numerous studies have examined how the physical environment has an impact on the learning of youth of all ages, particularly with respect to behaviors, attitudes, and achievement (Earthman, 2002; Kumar, O'Malley, & Johnston, 2008; Maxwell, 2007; Young, Green, Roehrich-Patrick, Joseph, & Gibson 2003). The learning environment should be planned, programmed, and designed to support the intended learning activities to contribute to the social and physical development of youth (Lippman, 2010).

The structure at 1815 Metropolitan Street houses the anchor operations of Manchester Craftsmen's Guild, which opened in 1987 and was designed by architect Tasso Katselas, a student of Frank Lloyd Wright. The design shows Wright's influence in its sense of materials, proportion, light, and the integration of interior and exterior space. Circular and arched window and door openings, along with warm terra-cotta-toned exposed masonry inside and outside the building, call to mind a modern interpretation of indigenous African mud-wattle structures. Quilts, paintings, and hand-wrought furnishings, vessels, and sculptures are everywhere in this structure, creating a palpable sense of warmth, inspiration, and hope. In Safe Havens, a 1993 study of the Manchester Craftsmen's Guild by Project Zero of the Harvard Graduate School of Education, MCG is described as "a place of cultural and educational renaissance where the futures of urban youth are transformed from risk to promise[,] . . . a place in the sun." Strickland states, "My vision of a school is that it looks like your house. . . . [P]eople feel comfortable and they feel at ease. You feel safe psychologically. That is a very important thing" (Davis, Soep, Remba, Maira, & Putnoi, 1993,

p. 82). The theme of safe havens recurs throughout the building. Nearby spaces such as the youth area, the fountain outside the building, and the hallways near the studios that act as galleries for professional and student art are some of the destinations where youth go to be alone or with one another. In our observations, the youth seemed to flourish and respond to the open responsibility and trust that the staff have in them as they sat among unique furnishings designed and built by Tadao Arimoto, a designer and craftsman who worked under the great George Nakashima. Nakashima was a Japanese American architect and wood craftsman who was a leading innovator in modern furniture design and an important early figure in the revival of the American fine craft movement.

Strickland has always added to the craftsmanship showcased throughout MCG that represents all members of the community, locally and internationally, so as to allow people "to get comfortable with art" in providing "a perfect human shelter" to all who enter the premises, which adds another layer of softness and beauty to the space (Strickland, 2007, pp. 12–14). This creative space has a strong resonance among youth and staff members alike:

> It's different than in business because there is so much art and there is so much physical space that it lends itself to this notion that you really are here to create and that creative process is valued because it's really mirrored and reflected around you—that is one thing that really contributes to the artistic culture. It suggests massively that there are no limits; it suggests that the possibilities are truly limitless. When you walk into the rotunda and you look up and you see giant tapestries or giant pieces of art, you think, "[W]ow that must have taken a really long time to create[,]" and, "[W]ow, and you must have a space large enough to hold it." And your eyes elevate to the top of the building and you see through the building and into the sky. I think, but maybe I'm over-analyzing and being entirely too cerebral, but I think that environment suggests quite strongly that we want you to think beyond the boundaries, that we want you to engage not only in realistic possibilities but in those possibilities that might not be so readily apparent or obtainable—it lends itself to creativity—the physical environment does that. (Teaching artist interview, December 1, 2009)

This building shows the role of creativity and craftsmanship of staff and youth alike. Public and private spaces in MCG create model environments for education, exhibitions, performances, professional gatherings, and social events for local and wider audiences in the Pittsburgh area. Youth and staff inspiration are found in photo exhibitions, ceramics, paintings, handmade objects, furniture, and artworks by youth and adult artists (resident and visiting), which are shown throughout the hallways and two galleries. One teaching artist spoke of the effect that the building had: "when you walk in here or you're walking up to the building, it's a warm feeling, it's not a cold feeling. . . . [T]hat definitely affects the mentality of people's thinking" (teaching artist interview, October 22, 2009).

A youth described the physical environment in this way:

It's just friendly and easy to work with. The building is spacious and has room for everybody to do what they need. Like, there's three or four kilns in the ceramics studio just inside the building, then we have one outside. There's artwork everywhere from various mediums that people do, that are submitted by students and instructors. So it's sort of hey this is what I can do, but it influences you. And then you can implement different works into yours. You see different shapes or patterns you want to try that might work in different ways. (Youth participant interview, November 17, 2009)

The youth's work is showcased throughout the four studios and exhibited at the end of every trimester, which provides occasion for young people to invite friends, family, and neighbors to celebrate their efforts, to network with peers from other studios and with community members and other art enthusiasts, and even to sell some of their pieces. According to Strickland (2007), "making a big deal out of showing the youth's art is mostly a new experience for most of the youth that shows support and recognition and does wonders for their souls" (p. 15).

The event has a significant effect both personally and socially on how young people communicate with new people, how they respond to constructive criticism of their pieces, and how these activities make them think critically and reflect about their pieces in relation to themselves and others. This dialogue and discussion happens every day in the studios, so the youth are well prepared to talk about the art process and about how other pieces inspired and influenced. The mission and educational philosophy of MCG clearly identifies a value system that endorses Bill Strickland's vision, focusing on the personal and social development of every young person to achieve meaningful success.

Manchester Craftsmen's Guild Philosophy and Culture

Strickland (2007) passionately talks about what he has learned from life experiences that became the essential ingredients of the philosophy of MCG:

> Every human being, despite the circumstances of their birth, is born full of potential, and . . . the way to unlock that potential is to place individuals in a nurturing environment and expose them to the kind of stimulating and empowering creative experiences the feed the human spirit. . . . [Y]ou cure poverty by understanding that poor folks are human beings before they are poor, and by providing them with access to the fundamental spiritual nourishment every human heart requires: beauty, order, purpose, opportunity—the things that gives us a meaningful human. (p. 194)

In Bill's narratives about MCG it is clear that culture is what drives the center to achieve this philosophy. Anna Craft, an expert in creativity in education and learning futures, commended Strickland's work at MCG, stating that Strickland fundamentally believes that "what is going on is self-expression, finding a unique voice for each person . . . and once people develop their voices they can develop as human beings" (Craft, 2005, p. xvii). A senior MCG staff member stated that "impacting lives and communities has a domino effect, as students define their own culture of learning" (management interview, November 11, 2007).

During youth interviews on the culture of MCG, two youth summarized their understanding and conception. The first said, "We are on an equal playing field here. We have the same opportunities to create something, and we're not singled out as the new kid or as a different ethnicity. You're just another kid who goes to MCG who wants to learn something and make something of ourselves (youth participant interview, November 13, 2009). The second said, "If I look at MCG I think peace, culture, artwork. So when I think of the culture of MCG, it's like someone took a whole bunch of fruits, threw them in the blender, put it on high, poured it out, made a fruit smoothie and was like ahhh" (youth participant interview, November 17, 2009).

Teaching artists spoke about the MCG culture in a positive manner:

> MCG has the equipment, materials and process knowledge in addition to artist instructors to follow a kid in any direction they are interested in as they become interested in it. I don't really know many places in the world where you could go where the answer to your question is yes. Like can I do

this? Can I try this? Can I think this? And it's like yes, yes, yes, yes, yes, yes. It's crazy. . . . The environment that Bill wanted to create wasn't a "no but maybe" environment. We've created we're going to do it. You're going to do it. We're going to do it the best we can. It's going to be wonderful. (Teaching artist interview, January 14, 2009)

Another artist commented:

Having a nice environment is very important, definitely people that respect themselves and respect the students, I think that's very important. Having top of the line equipment and materials, that's definitely very important. I think these are things Bill has said as well. I think it's instilled in the staff and what he's trying to create. He's trying to create that culture—having the nice building, having the passionate staff, making sure we have all the equipment and materials we need. Those are probably the main factors; everything else just falls into place. (Teaching artist interview, November 21, 2009)

VALUES FOR LIVING, WORKING, AND LEARNING (THE BANNERS)

A series of banners created by youth and staff are repeatedly encountered in spaces and studios throughout MCG, each highlighting a single word along with a corresponding metaphorical photo image featuring hands. The featured words are *respect, listen, influence, shape,* and *embrace*: "I will Listen with the intent to understand to be responsive. I will be aware of how my work Influences others. I will acknowledge my limitations and Embrace life-long learning opportunities. I will Respect others and conduct self with reason, focus and belief. I will Shape solutions to problems." The corresponding meaning of each banner is woven into an honor code that each participant signs as part of registration with MCG, and the youth sign collectively during their first class meeting in each studio. The overt message of each value has a dramatic effect on the attitudes of young people and staff members, as they explicitly declare what MCG represents.

The values are at the core of the MCG culture as staff and youth respect and appreciate what the banner words enforce. The words not only are used within MCG's walls but also seem to have significant consequences during external visits and field trips, and even in school and home life:

It's something you can implement into your life and help to form relationships with people you wouldn't think possible

because it gives you a different perspective on things and
how people may think. (Youth participant interview, November 13, 2009)

I think they're a good idea. It's not the rules, but the environment that you want to create. So we do talk to the students
on the first day of classes about the values and how important they are. It's how people should act in the building and
beyond the building. It's like life sort of, keep these things in
mind as you're making decisions with your life. . . . It's all
about keeping an open mind and how they behave with
other students and how they can affect or influence other
students. They're definitely a good thing; thumbs up. (Teaching artist interview, November 21, 2009)

For the most part I think they are really good core values
to hold. Especially the honor code, those are all super legit,
especially because it's about respecting each other, that's
one of my favorite things, just respecting one another, your
personal belongings, your space, your time, respecting all of
that. . . . For as long as I've been here, I think the traditions
have been up held pretty well. I think we're all on the same
page. (Teaching artist interview, November 15, 2009)

The studio culture and values are established from the start of the
first day for each course in each trimester. The teaching artist intro-
duces the banners and honor code to those young people returning to
MCG, and particularly to those who are there for the first time, so that
all have an understanding of the expectations and cultural aspects of
MCG. Each member of staff has their own way to use, develop, and
discuss these values with young people when the need arises, through
open discussions, informal chats, peer explanation, or individual
consultation.

One day in the ceramics studio, a teaching artist mingled and chatted
with youth, greeting them at the door and suggesting particular tasks,
such as cutting clay plugs and patting balls to throw on the wheel later.
The experienced youth immediately started up wheels and began to
throw pots. After about sixteen young people were in the room, the
teaching artist began to look around and asked another young person,
"Where's Jeremy?" Shortly thereafter, Jeremy, a young man with a few
years' experience, arrived with a smile, and the teaching artist turned
over the task of presenting the honor code and banners to him.

Jeremy begins, "You are now at the Manchester Craftsman's Guild
and people here, well, they basically trust you. We live by a few rules

but they trust you. There haven't been any fights, any graffiti. You just have to use your common sense and to live by these rules while you're here—and hopefully outside of here too!" In talking about the banners and values, Jeremy provided personal examples: "This is a studio. Wipe your feet on the mat before you go, especially in this studio, when new students are here there's often a big mud path down the hallway." This wasn't on the list, but the staff members in the room agreed it was a good one to mention. "That's part of respect!" one of the veteran girls shouted out. "Don't wear headphones because once this guy had them on and the teacher was trying to tell him something and he couldn't even get the advice. We try to keep it social here and be open to each other." "Oh and don't eat or drink in here, because of all the chemicals." The list went on, with Jeremy stating something, and the staff or other kids piping in with embellishments, stories, and reasons for the rules. The new kids listened and looked from person to person. "Use time wisely and work to your ability," Jeremy kept saying. "You know, basically, just be appropriate!"

STUDIO AND WORKSHOP VIGNETTES

Manchester Craftsmen's Guild has also established itself as a professional-level artistic center, attracting accomplished artists and musicians who through residencies produce new works and public programs as they engage the broader regional arts community. These artists make use of the same studios, galleries, and supports as the youth, essentially working alongside them. Sometimes this takes place through intentional workshops and sometimes, less formally, as part of the daily environment.

During the 2009–2010 season, the artist Julia Mandle led a residency on performance art, civic action, and urban revitalization. Working with the MCG youth, Mandle aimed in the workshop Paths to the Park to engage the artistic process as a form of civic activism.

Mandle and the youth produced chalk shoes, the soles of which were composed of massive casts of bright green-pigmented chalk. The performance would enable the group to achieve a sense of agency as they worked to reclaim a public-city space by drawing people's attention to the striking visualization of bright green (chalk) lines throughout the park. Adult leaders from eleven different cultural organizations accompanied the youth. The purpose of pairing the young people who had made and first learned to walk in the shoes with adult leaders who were learning to use the shoes for the first time during the performance was to transform traditional teacher (adult) and learner (young people) roles. The deliberate process of teaching and learning to walk during the performance created a situation that slowed the pace of urban life, opening space for contemplation and discussion among the pairings (Mandle, 2009).

On entering the youth area at MCG during the first day of the work-shop, there was a sense of enthusiasm and appreciation for the artist and her work. Two short videos were shown of performances that incor-porated the process of making the chalk shoes, with emphasis on the background and meaning of what previous projects represented. Immediately, the young people were intrigued with what was happen-ing and were asking whether they could go beyond the project plan to record video and make music for their performance. Others offered and promoted their skills and talents to the artist about doing the project and the final video.

Originating from their strengths and interests in music composition and editing, interview skills, project management, and photography, the young people were delighted to take on these critical secondary roles to enhance the project. One had written a piece of music and was willing to use it for the final video clip because he thought it was perfect for the project's particular message. Another then offered to edit the video and to include subtitles. The artist knew about the culture and philosophy of MCG, so she went along with the ideas and developed them further throughout the week. The degrees of commitment, resil-ience, and passion toward the project revealed self-confidence in those willing to take risks and be open to criticism. Expressing a sense of responsibility for their own learning and empowered to get involved in a new project, the young people took on additional work roles, thus ensuring the best result. This confidence was highlighted with excite-ment when one youth said, "This is going to be good, man." This kind of experience, regularly created at MCG, encourages innovation, young people's engagement with possibilities, and critical thinking as inherent in the process of creation. Awareness of peer knowledge and transfer-able skills among youth are exactly what is meant by MCG's culture in action, a culture expected and promoted at MCG in multiple ways. In this example, young people were given a voice and a strong sense of agency; they responded by embracing the opportunity for project con-trol, responsibility, and ownership, and ultimately, they directed the workshop. All their suggestions were used in some form in the final production of the performance.

Youth Experience at MCG: Ethos

On entering any of the four studios at MCG, you are hit by color, inspi-ration, warmth, and noise. Your eyes do not know where to look first—at the wonderful art pieces being produced or at the selection of showcased art scattered around the room. There is a sense of calmness (almost a slow-motion feeling) among the chaos and noise, and everyone (youth and staff) manages to find their own space to work, reflect, and develop the concepts they are working on. From informal conversations to deep engagement about an art process, lightbulb moments of euphoria occur, as when a young learner exclaimed, "Why was it never explained like that before?!", or "I get it. It's that simple when it's explained like that!" The noise and energy draw you in and make you want to roll up your sleeves and start working on an art piece. In these creative spaces you can get lost in thought as you are inspired by the work that surrounds you.

On entry to any studio, an immediate friendly smile greets you from both staff and youth. Conversations initiated by youth can spring from curious questions about who you might be, your artistic background, or why you're interested in MCG. It is standard procedure at MCG to have an entourage of local and global visitors to observe in the studios, whether new researchers, board members, university students, other teaching artists, administrative staff, or an international group tour.

One youth mentioned how MCG makes people feel:

[It allows for] a good opportunity to express yourself and learn different disciplines of art and also learn more about yourself and further yourself in ways you don't think of at the time; you can educate yourself in a way that school doesn't provide. Discipline and patience, stuff you can learn through like physical activity and repetition that you can't learn out of a book. (Youth participant interview, November 13, 2009)

Another said:

Learning at MCG is like being thirsty and having a glass of water in front of you. . . . In school, the glass of water is in front of you, but it's further. Here, it's kind of already there for us, all we have to do is drink.

And another youth in the same interview agreed:

There ain't no beating around the bush. The water, at school, you lose that water, you knock it over or something. But here, you keep the water and it keeps you hydrated for a long time. (Youth participant interviews, November 15, 2009)

YOUTH STORIES: EXPOSURE TO MATERIALS AND ART CULTURE
AND THINKING

Celine was a diminutive and talkative ninth grader when she first came
to Manchester Craftsmen's Guild at the encouragement of an older sib-
ling. Of Vietnamese descent, her family settled in Pittsburgh following
a paternal grandmother who had married an American GI. Her parents
soon separated, and Celine, along with four siblings, remained with
their dad, who worked in building maintenance. Vince was a shy and
quietly thoughtful boy from a different school who lived with his dad
and two siblings in public housing. He began to attend ceramics classes
at MCG the same year as Celine. Although their social styles and cultural backgrounds were different, they soon became friends in the studio. Celine began to master the basic steps of the potter's wheel, which
enabled her to produce shallow bowls and modestly sized plates. Many
days she devoted large amounts of her time to talking with peers and
teaching artists. Initially, the focus of her work was to produce as much
as possible as quickly as possible and turn it into cash through selling
her pottery.

The problem was that after developing some initial skill, she was not
pushing herself to make more challenging or distinctive pieces. Teaching artists could often be heard talking with her about the sloppy bases
of her plates, which might easily break after firing or at least require a
lot of physical effort to file smooth. She would shrug it off and say, "I'll
make more!" Vince was almost always focused on his work, and on
helping others with theirs, but he seemed to struggle with expressing
his thoughts and in the playful social interaction that comes naturally
to many teens. One day while an observer was trying her hand at a pot,
Vince came over to her and asked whether he could help. When his
advice was welcomed, he reached in and pulled the pot himself, losing
control at the end because of his standing position and then apologiz-
ing with some embarrassment. Assuring him that this was not a problem, the observer asked how long he had been working at MCG. He
responded, "Oh, a long time . . . three weeks." This deep sense of
belonging, sense of confidence in trying, and willingness to reach out
to teach others is the general ethos of MCG, and it is taken in by teens
who are learning to understand and who are growing their own abilities
and skills.

In the winter of 2008, Hiromu and Mieko Okuda, Japanese artists
and a married couple, came to MCG from the historical pottery center
of Shigaraki to participate in a six-week residency during which they
executed large-scale collaborative works to be exhibited during the
annual conference of the National Council on Education for the
Ceramic Arts. Celine and Vince had each been studying Japanese in

their respective schools. Celine also had a deep-seated fascination with Japanese pop culture, especially the storytelling and graphic expressions of anime and *manga.*

Hiromu embodied the traditional understandings of materials that were part of his heritage as a fifth-generation potter of an important artistic dynasty. While continuing to make traditional tea bowls, he also broke from tradition by making large sculptures that integrated ceramic forms with steel and wood. Mieko, who had come to ceramics through an interest in textiles, had a method of working with clay that often expressed the detailed texture of fiber-based works. One of the ways she accomplished this was by using a cutting wire tool held tightly between her hands to make gestural reticulated slices through clay, producing delicate leaflike forms that called to mind exotic sea creatures or flowers. Mieko's project involved interacting with hundreds of community members, from preschool age to the elderly, to teach them the technique. Her vision was to incorporate thousands of elements made by many hands in the community into a constellation-like arrangement that would transform a nearby greenhouse into an environment that expressed the diversity of the community while drawing implicit connections to the seas and heavens. Over the course of a few sessions in the ceramics studio, two researchers observed the way Mieko's presence in the studio moves through the young people and through both their personal work and their role as leaders in the studio.

> The Japanese artist arrived with two bags of white clay and a board. Moments later I look over and Celine has a wire with paper flowers on either end and she and the artist are cutting pieces of clay off the edges of the clay blocks and then twisting them into interesting shapes. The artist is showing her how to make a zigzag cut using the wire and pulling it up and down as she pulls it across the clay. Each time they peel it off a little surprising fish-fin like creation appears. Celine shows her what she has made and the artist takes it in her open palm and considers it, pointing out beautiful parts of it and saying, "Very nice."
>
> Vincent arrives and watches. The artist gives him her wire. He cuts some with very large zigzags and she shows him how to tighten up the cut to get more finlike results. The two of them pull one slice after another off the blocks, give them a little bend or twist and place them carefully on the slab. No one really notices what they are doing or seems to want to join them. The Japanese artist is with them for about 15 minutes and then she and her husband leave and the two young people continue to make the pieces.

Two days later a second researcher observed this experience take on a new form:

> The artwork by the visiting artists seems to be taking over more space. The teaching artist and a student carry a tray of small pieces by the visiting artist into another room. Another tray of small pieces is sitting on a nearby table. One of the guys with short brown hair asks the teaching artist about the pieces that are sitting on the table. He explains that the visiting artist will glaze them and lay them on the gallery floor in an installation. The student asks how the pieces were made. He says they were made with a wire tool. Vincent must have said something to the teaching artist after that exchange, because the next thing I noticed was that the teaching artist told the boy with short brown hair that Vincent offered to show him how to make one. Vincent got a lump of red clay and a wire tool. Without saying a word, he worked the wire tool through the clay, wiggling it up and down, to slice off a couple of wavy slices. He pinched them together into this little wing-looking piece that looks very much like the ones the artist made.
>
> A visitor who was working at the table commented that it was a good demonstration. The teaching artist picked up the piece and said that it would make a nice handle—that it could be attached to the kind of pots they were making today. Vincent continued to silently pull a few more wings and added one more to his piece.

In this way, Celine and Vince often greeted visitors and demonstrated and assisted them in the technique, whereas Mieko increasingly became the artistic director of the work. This transition of roles, subtle at first, enabled Mieko to devote greater focus on relaying her vision behind the work and to share information about her culture and its influence on creative production. By the time of the conference, the works were ready to install. The Okudas, with the assistance of MCG staff and youth, transformed the greenhouse and filled another gallery in downtown Pittsburgh with related works, some of which they had shipped from Japan. The national conference took place in the large David L. Lawrence Convention Center in the heart of the city's business and cultural districts. Vince and Celine accompanied and assisted the Okudas as they demonstrated their work before the thousands of conference visitors. The young people's prior knowledge and interest in the Japanese language also enabled them to provide some simple translations for observers.

Following the Okudas return to Japan, Celine and Vince both contin-ued to share the wire-cutting technique with visitors and other young people at MCG. Their works also grew more ambitious in scale and creative vision, pushing materials and process in new directions. They each became active participants, delivering artists' talks at their exhibi-tion openings. Celine's talks ceased to focus so exclusively on the price she wanted for her work and shifted to critical analyses of successes, failures, questions, decisions, and directions. Vince began to work more with ceramic figures and larger vessels.

The role of authentic art making, collaborative relationships with vis-iting artists, and opportunities to contribute to public art happenings are an authentic art-practice base that supports the strong culture of youth empowerment and ownership at MCG. But in daily interactions, young people have emotional, conceptual, and skill-building support from teaching artists. This combined youth work and art mentoring is both instinctive and intentional. The MCG attracts artists with a passion for supporting the ability of individuals to follow their interests, but the community of educators also structures the approach to art making and social development through a very intentional reflective practice.

Teaching Artists' Story

Without formal training in the process of drawing language-based evi-dence of learning from their students, many teaching artists initially feel most adept focusing on the technical aspects and production stages of the art-making process. Because MCG aspires to use the studio envi-ronment and the mentoring relationship that develops between young people and artists as a pathway to social, emotional, and academic development, building the ability to express ideas, feelings, challenges, and goals are key concerns of the instructional process. One youth said, "I like MCG cause . . . the instructors, they are really helpful and they really teach you a lot and they care about your learning, so as long as they care, I care" (youth participant interview, November 15, 2009).

One teaching artist stated, "In the beginning I was kind of resistant. I didn't want to talk so much in studio, just make art, but now I'd rather have meaningful talk about art than just make it. It lets me know if the students are picking up on the ideas, [and] it's helping me as a teacher" (teaching artist interview, December 1, 2009). To develop beyond tradi-tional practices of craft and to push learning to higher cognitive levels, MCG's teaching artists have participated in biweekly meetings dedi-cated to reflective practice. One staff member described the goal of these meetings as to find ways to create "feedback between staff and youth in order to inform studio activities, help young people realize their potential by reflecting on their thinking and work." In turn, it is hoped that the overall program will continually improve by providing youth and adults alike with time dedicated to explaining the value and meaning of their learning. It is further believed that the information exposed in these art-based discussions will help MCG explain the extraordinary strengths of the program to others, including funders, the school district, family, and friends.

For some instructors, the reflective practice routines enabled them to see successes in courses that they felt were not going well. In the context of a course on observational drawing, the teaching artist initially encouraged young people to talk about what they liked and what they did not like about their work. He shifted the discussion to attend to the kinds of activities and decisions they made in the process of creating the drawing. Some of the youth talked about how they used their fingers to form a viewfinder or frame, to determine the composition of a sketch. Others talked about how their drawing experimented with compositional strategy, like the rule of thirds, wherein important elements of the image are located along the imagined guidelines that divide the picture plane into nine equal parts to create a more interesting, off-center composition. Being able to recognize the rule applied in other artists' work generated much excitement among the group. Such discussions ultimately led to the kind of thinking and personal choices made on the basis of this framing of experience.

The leader of a course on functional pottery has been teaching in the ceramics studio at Manchester Craftsmen's Guild for about six years. College educated with a studio focus, she had no formal teacher training before coming to MCG, other than what she had developed through previous instructional experience in a museum-based program. As an artist, however, she describes herself first and foremost as a maker of useful pots for daily living. Rather than sketch out plans for a new piece or body of work, she makes a series of related forms and works through variations of decoration, handles, and lids until she arrives at a new and satisfactory solution to the problems associated with integrating form, surface, function, and visual appeal.

As her instructional practice at MCG evolved, her engagement in reflective practice meetings with other teaching artists deepened. She recognized how the meetings provided a space to develop specific routines to support shared studio practice. To make more apparent the effects of teaching and learning, teaching artists use these meetings to share breakthroughs and to wrestle with barriers to teaching and learning. If what was so important in her own creative practice was for her to quietly and mindfully work through subtle variations and evolutions in a body of work, how might traditional pedagogical strategies like quizzing, testing, and critique affect her ability to create a nonthreatening environment without editorial intervention? Rather than provide the group with model examples and expect them to replicate their elements, this artist wondered whether there might be different ways to elicit thoughtful and divergent explorations of traditional pottery forms.

To learn more, she began to bring to class each week at least one piece of pottery from her personal collection of other potters. After working for an hour or so, she would call the group together and invite them to handle the piece, think about it, formulate an observation, and pass it on to the next student. As the next student was handling the work, the previous handler would share her insight about it. During one course meeting early on in the term, she brought with her a favorite serving piece, a shallow stoneware bowl about fourteen inches in diameter. The bowl was thrown on a potter's wheel and the marks of the throwing process, known as rings, were visible through a glaze surface that broke from blue to brown depending on the relative thickness of the surface, as it flowed into the indentations left by the potter's fingers or crested thinly over the ridges between. In the center of the plate, the potter rendered a gestural decoration of a fish. Turning the plate over, one could find a surprise—another layer of glaze on the underside of the bowl with a decoration of smaller fish, which one would never see without taking the time to patiently admire the piece from all sides. The piece required a high level of personal interaction to take it all in.

The bowl had thin, uniform walls, a lightweight and elegant contour. As the bowl passed from hand to hand, some young people commented on the technical expertise of the potter. The glaze was smoothly melted, without defects, and had a rich and variegated color. Others commented on the quality of the firing and the pleasant tone the glaze might give to the food that it would contain. The decoration was delightfully energetic. Some commented on the skill of the drawing. As the conversation continued, the nature of the responses began to shift from the facts of the object to speculations as to the maker's intention and imagination. One young man wondered whether the potter intended users to serve a fish-based dish from it. Another young woman began to ponder the meaning of the large fish inside the bowl in relation to the smaller one hidden on the underside. She speculated that when the fish was removed from its environment and became a meal, it was important to recall this; it was once part of a larger life system. Even in this early course discussion, the levels of attention to detail, meaning, analysis, and synthesis were remarkable. Moreover, the teaching artist was able to listen and observe with awe and delight in the young people's capacities to observe, describe, and imagine. They began to teach one another that day.

Transformations: Today's Youth and Teaching
Artists Who Model Their Founder's Story

In his middle teens, Jonah was caught in an act of public graffiti that authorities called vandalism. Arrested, fined, and sentenced to community service, he soon found his way to Manchester Craftsmen's Guild after hearing from friends that it was a cool place to spend time. Although he enrolled in several courses on painting and drawing, Jonah continually gravitated toward producing his work not on canvas or art paper but on discarded cardboard and clothing. This piqued the interest and curiosity of the teaching artist and studio coordinator Thomas. Once Thomas and Jonah began to talk with each other about their motivations and sense of excitement when creating art, they began to find surprisingly common ground in nineteenth- and twenty-first-century ideas about the creation and appearance of art in the open. Over the coming months, this dialogue developed into a concept for a new type of course for the design arts studio: art for social change. The pair used the MCG course development guidelines to create a plan and curriculum for the new course. Jonah began to do research on other contemporary artists working on social activism and prepared PowerPoint lectures for the course. Although much of the work began in the studio, it became public in intervention art events, an art form developed in the 1960s to refer to an artist's conceptual and performance events engaging public space and communities.

The first work created during the course by a group explored the idea of a perfect moment. Each young person recalled and wrote a brief memory of a perfect moment and shared it with another person in the group. These brief narratives were then transferred to sheets of cardboard with stenciled letters similar to those used on billboards in the predigital era. They then wore these cardboard panels like walking advertisements while occupying a public park one afternoon in Pittsburgh's Cultural District, a loose network of galleries, performance spaces, and arts organizations. The youth made efforts to interview and record passersby's comments about their perfect-moment memories. One youth documented the event using digital video. Once the class returned to MCG, the video and audio were edited and the cardboard panels assembled into a large-scale, collaborative text-based artwork.

Jonah and Thomas had bridged a gap in artistic traditions from different eras to build a new relationship while creating, collaborating, mentoring, and leading. Jonah had the opportunity to design and teach a course, and in this course more than any other, the young people in the course experienced and shared their memories, hopes, fears, and dreams. This facilitation process and codesigned course resulted in an engaged experience for the teaching artist, the youth instructor, and the other participating youth. The design and implementation of the course corresponded with the initiation of reflective practice, and Thomas's enthusiasm for the practice allowed the space for Jonah's ideas to be the center of a new course. During the semester Thomas continually brought moments from the course back to reflective practice. Early on, Thomas shared his surprise and delight when Jonah took on the instructional role for the first class, setting the tone for the course:

> Then the group went to the youth area for a slide show presentation—Jonah did a slideshow he created and Thomas said, "He crushed it! He wanted to do it and loved it and he was able to relate to the youth and brought great examples— the best slide presentation. Best part of the day—he took questions at the end. He was like an adult—talking about art legalities and the lines you might cross." (Reflective practice notes, April 16, 2009)

A big idea that the teaching artists had been working on was creating space and time to discuss ideas together. As the program unfolded, Thomas had new examples of youth leadership to share at every session, including a story about a young woman in the class asking whether she could lead the transition discussion: "A teen asked about the transition discussion and I asked her if she would lead it. She said 'something short maybe.' She started the discussion and was the one the group looked to if they wanted to talk. She kept the conversation going" (Reflective practice notes, May 15, 2009).

During this reflective practice session, Thomas went on to talk about how the issue of race came up during the teen-led discussion and how hard it was not to have an answer. Building on this experience, the teaching artists discussed how to allow space to be vulnerable as an instructor, how to be OK with no answer or silence and yet not cut off expression. By sharing this process with his colleagues, Thomas gained strategies, support, and excitement about the process, which in turn gave him confidence to keep broadening what was possible in his studio.

The survival of MCG is closely related to its learning culture and the dramatic effect this has had on the many youth who attended. The relationships and friendships formed among youth and staff are the core of MCG. Informal interactions among staff and youth have led to trusting relationships and lifelong friendships. This social networking provides a respectful, supportive, and caring environment that has a direct influence on self-discovery and the retention of young people at MCG. A young person discussed how a teaching artist has influenced her to look for a career in which she can be passionate about her work:

> I think the teachers are always pushing you to learn some-
> thing new. Usually in every class every day, they're teaching
> you something new. And it seems like most of the people
> that come here are really interested in their artwork. . . . A TA
> influences me because she loves what she does[;] she loves
> being here and helping everybody out. When I'm older I
> want to have a job like that. . . . [H]ere I love what I'm
> doing. . . . [S]he influences me the most because she has a
> job that she loves and wants to get up to do it everyday . . .
> and that's the kind of job I want to have, even though I don't
> know what that is yet. (Participant interview, October 30,
> 2009)

Bryk and Schneider (2002) discuss values education in terms of
"trust relations as a dynamic interplay among four considerations:
respect, competence, personal regard for others, and integrity" (p. 23):

> Trust relations culminate in important consequences at the
> organizational level, including more effective decision-
> making, enhanced social support for innovation, more effi-
> cient social control of adults' work and an expanded moral
> authority to "go the extra mile" for the children. Relational
> trust . . . is an organizational property. . . . [I]ts presence (or
> absence) has important consequences for the functioning of
> the school and its capacity to engage fundamental change.
> (Bryk & Schneider, 2002, p. 22)

The freedom to be creative and trust extended to young people also
builds among staff a sense of confidence and risk taking that does not
exist in more formal learning organizations:

> And if I want to try something new, I have the liberty to do
> things and it's not like I'm supposed to be doing this or that
> at a certain time. I have a lot of freedom, too, just like the
> students so that's pretty cool. And everyone trusts everyone
> that they're working with 'cause we're not watched over, we
> don't have punch clocks, we do our own times and every-
> thing. I'm pretty OK with that. (Teaching artist interview,
> November 15, 2009)

Fielding et al. (2005) discuss the "considerable investment of time,
resources and commitment" (p. 11) needed for "joint practice development" (p. 16), which is based on trusting relationships. This is seen at
MCG, where staff members often collaborate informally with young

people to learn about the youths' home or school life and to offer guidance and direction, particularly to those disengaged from the formal school system. Staff members often collaborate with youth to provide feedback on studio projects or guidance on future courses. There is an exchange of ideas and knowledge about what worked and what needs improvement. Fewer curricular demands, the lack of high-stakes assessment, and the absence of focus on external, competitive learning allow for focus to rely on a culture of personalized learning, innovative teaching, interpersonal relationships and reflective practice. Manchester Craftsmen's Guild provides a safe and supportive environment in which staff members provide educational guidance, peer coaching, mentoring, advice on creative work and college applications, and in which they share their passion for art and transmit the core values of MCG.

Conclusion

The informal approach of MCG does not happen casually. It begins with a vision for the potential of people to learn and create, it supports that vision with a beautiful and well-equipped environment, and it nurtures that vision with a culture of trust and mentorship. The empowerment and freedom afforded through respect for the youth and staff sustains Bill Strickland's vision. The personalization and intimacy of Strickland's story about making a simple connection with a mentor artist remains the present-day driver of teaching artists at MCG. Their belief that every young person who walks into the studio embodies the potential to make the impossible possible is echoed in their daily choices and efforts to support a creative process, to make a safe space to talk about that process, and to build relationships. Their care and concern in this endeavor is echoed in turn by the young people who return again and again to enjoy the relationships and express themselves.

Reflection Questions

- In what specific ways can the context of work, site, and agency influence actual day-to-day civic youth work practice?
- Can one do and be a civic youth worker without knowledge of this practice, a relevant vocabulary, or training in this practice?
- What makes civic youth work practice a type of youth work? What would have to change in civic youth work ethos, practice, skills, and knowledge to use this approach with adults or the aged?

- How might the guild's banners be framed in a civic youth work ethos?
- Why might experienced and effective civic youth workers want to talk about their practice with teaching artists? What might they have in common in their ways of thinking, seeing, and working with young people? What about their philosophies and conceptions of their praxis?
- How might young people's engagement with possibilities in an arts world oriented to the process of creation fit philosophically and existentially with their civic engagement?
- When a new student asks an experienced student how a pot was made, the latter can tell how. Can young people involved in civic engagement tell how they failed (and succeeded) in their group work?
- Why is reflection basic to civic youth work practice?
- Is mentoring a practical civic youth work practice?
- How does the craft metaphor work in discussions and analysis of civic youth work?
- Are classical craft mentoring strategies and practices in the arts useful approaches to mastery in civic youth work?

CHAPTER EIGHT

Leading the Way

Young People Cocreating a Safe Driving Culture

Ofir Germanic

In Israel, as in most places in the world, automobile accidents are the leading cause of death for young people between the ages of ten and nineteen (Knishkowy & Gofin, 2002). Israel's fines and penalties alone have not changed youth driving culture or youth behavior on the road. More and different approaches are needed. To that end, Or Yarok (Green Light) invited and supported young people in developing alternative strategies. This youth strategy built on Israeli youth culture and theories of youth and adolescent development in our context.

As a nation and a society, Israel is a contested space, culturally, religiously, and politically. Growing up in Israel, young people are often divided into sociopolitical, socioreligious, and sociocultural groups. Young people in Israel come from a wide variety of national, ethnic and/or cultural, and religious groups (e.g., Arabs, Bedouins, Christians, Druze, Jews from more than forty countries) speaking more than six languages, in addition to Hebrew, the national language. Israeli youth are not homogeneous. Belonging to these groups has real and immediate consequences for young people, their families, their communities, and the larger society. For example, after high school or university, Jewish young people are required to join the military full time for three years, followed by twenty years of reserve duty. For other Israeli citizens (e.g., Arab-Israelis), military service is prohibited. This is just one example of how national policy makes a distinction based on ethnic, cultural, or religious background. As in most contested spaces, daily life about such existential issues as arms conflict and simmering (and often seething) intergroup tensions are experienced as real and immediate. Adolescence and youthhood in this context is often described as contested. In this contested space, young people go through similar rites of passage as in other places.

In Israel, earning a driver license is a rite of passage signifying one's movement from childhood to youthhood, even to adulthood, from dependence to new forms of interdependence, even independence. Among the interdependent others of youth are friends and peers. Israeli youth driving culture is part of both the larger Israeli adult driving culture and the culture specific to one's ethnic and/or religious group.

The leading killer for young people around the world is car crashes (Knishkowy & Gofin, 2002), yet we found that the general public and young people are apathetic to road-safety issues. Our organization Or Yarok (Green Light) has worked to reduce road fatalities among young people.

Or Yarok (Green Light)

Or Yarok (Green Light) Association for Safer Driving in Israel was founded in 1997 in recognition of the critical need to prevent and reduce traffic accidents, and of the importance of community involvement in this effort. The goal is to minimize the number and rate of youth and adult morbidity and mortality from traffic accidents and to do this by changing Israel's youth and adult driving cultures.

Green Light's annual budget of US$8 million comes from one philanthropist who lost his son in a car accident. Since its founding, Green Light has sparked a genuine social revolution in public awareness about road crashes and has become a leader in the sociocultural movement to prevent car accidents (e.g., a 2010 study by Policy and Public Analysis shows that 43 percent of Israelis believe that Green Light contributes to the reduction in car accidents, whereas only 38 percent believe that policing does). The work supported by Green Light has always been cooperative. In all its programs, Green Light staff work to involve other organizations, such as the Israeli Army, the Education Ministry, the police, and other national and community formal groups and organizations.

Until January 2011, I headed the Youth Department of Green Light and was responsible for youth programming, including school programs, after-school programs, collaborations with the juvenile court, and training of Israeli military officers on road safety. As the head of the department, I worked to create road-safety projects for young people that supported them in driving safely. The program used a participatory action research project philosophy and practice. The program goal was to explore how peers could contribute to safer driving practices among teens. The project is based on a broad understanding, called the three circles of influence, of why young people drive recklessly (Taubman-Ben-Ari & Mikulincer, 2007).

Reckless driving is situated within three circles of influence: the individual, family and friends, and the larger context (figure 8.1). The theory describes the multiple factors involved in supporting young people's safe or reckless driving practices. According to Taubman-Ben-Ari and Mikulincer (2007), a deeper understanding of youth driving practices emerges when the individual characteristics of the driver (e.g., personality, attitudes toward risk, experiences, driving skill and ability) are considered along with how their parents drive and talk about driving; peer pressure (either positive or negative, such as being supportive of safe or risky driving practices); and the larger context of driving laws, driving norms, and driving cultures.

The project I describe here is called Leading the Way. Its focus is on the second influence circle: the young person's family and friends. It is commonly understood that during adolescence, peers and friends can influence individual young people's behavior both positively and negatively, often referred to as peer pressure or positive peer pressure.

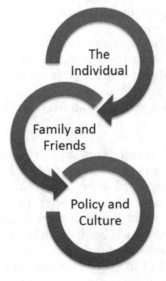

FIGURE 8.1. *Three Circles of Influence*

Often, friends have an influence on the driving norms that the young driver will adopt (Allen & Brown, 2008).

Why Do Young People Drive Dangerously?

Peer pressure is a common explanation for dangerous driving by youth. Arnett, Offer, and Fine (1997) refer to this as a conspiracy among young friends. As a way to "have fun," peers push the driver to take risks when driving. Many times, the driver's willingness to take risks is related to wanting attention and prestige from others in the car. Our intervention drew from this understanding and supported teens in bringing about changes in their friend's driving behavior. We tried to formulate a working model of how friends could influence safer driving practices that worked among all populations, with appropriate cultural adjustments.

This project is built on a participatory action research cycle. Young people have the option to join social youth groups and are asked to reflect on their and their peers' driving practices and norms. These groups create a space in which members' voices are heard and in which their ideas about how safer teen driving practices can be supported are developed. From this beginning, the group expands their understanding of safer driving practices through learning about road safety, doing field studies, and building projects based on what they have learned and discussed in hopes of leading to changes in road safety among their friends.

The program goals are the following:

- To raise public awareness about road accidents
- To develop positive attitudes toward road safety
- To learn about safe driving behavior
- To become agents of social change and a model to others
- To provide practical tools to volunteers working with groups in the community

The basic idea is to recruit, train, supervise, and monitor local youth coordinators, who recruit local youth to become members of a local advocacy group for teen road safety. The youth coordinators are typically university students who receive tuition scholarships, and in return, they engage in four hours of weekly community work. Green Light offered these students the opportunity to facilitate a road-safety group in their community as part as their required hours of community work. In the first year of the project more than sixty scholarship students showed interest in facilitating a youth road-safety group in communities throughout Israel. Youth workers in these communities were all familiar with road-safety problems, but in the absence of professional knowledge they did not build road-safety projects that young people wanted to join. It was necessary to bring in another knowledgeable person, the youth coordinator, to begin the work.

The youth coordinator is required to attend a training course that includes the following:

- The Green Light approach to road safety
- Familiarity with the youth world
- Building a road safety group
- Ways to engage young people, using group processes
- Skills to work in public

The project works as follows: First, the group operates out of a local community center, youth club, or a high school. A youth director in each community recruits a group of boys and girls who then learn the process and skills for building innovative and meaningful road-safety projects. University student volunteers recruit and train youth and facilitate group activities. The group meets weekly to develop and implement road-safety field research and an action project on youth road-safety promotion.

During the first year of this model, we worked in several community centers and schools and different regions of the country to test the feasibility of working in collaboration with local youth agencies within and across religio-ethnic groups. All the community centers contacted agreed to try the project. Although having good youth coordinators facilitate the groups is important, the coordinators also needed to understand the local community and its particular culture, history, and language.

Making Cultural Adjustments

We wanted the program to be community based and therefore decided that it would be run by volunteers and university student scholars. To create the necessary unique cultural adjustments for each population, it was decided that a group facilitator had to come from that community; for example, in a Bedouin village, the scholar must be Bedouin. This was done to ensure that the unique culture of that community was respected and that the work was culturally specific and appropriate. It also reduced any tension that might have existed if we had introduced a coordinator from outside of the community. In a contested space, outsiders are not immediately trusted.

The youth coordinator is close in age to the teens, and the youth in the group often view him or her as a role model. Because the youth coordinators come from the community, we have found that they are familiar with local community issues and have an understanding of young people's everyday lives—because of this, they are not considered foreigners or "old" people who try to tell the youth that reckless driving is dangerous. Also, we train youth coordinators in how to better understand the everyday lives of young people and in challenging local and national adolescent and teen stereotypes, and we provide youth coordinators with accurate information about young people today. In most cases, youth coordinators know how to speak the "language" of the local youth. An important part of the youth leader training is to teach them about the youth world and ways to engage young people.

Training was done in several regions and is offered in several languages—in Arabic for the Arab, Bedouin, and Druze workers. We invited, encouraged, and supported youth coordinators in using their own materials and ideas. In addition, youth coordinators translated the resources written in Hebrew that we developed, as well as programs and activities, into their language and cultural practices. We gave them somewhere to begin but also supported them in working cooperatively and creatively with one another and with the youth group they facilitated.

What Is the Program?

The program consists of twenty weekly sessions. The program begins with youth learning about road safety through different and innovative activities, such as driving simulation, team building, meeting with a parent who lost a child in a car accident, debates, presentation of different approaches to road safety in other countries, and so on. As their knowledge of road safety increases, the youth are asked to begin learning about local road safety and issues, norms, and practices in their own community that support or hinder safe driving among young people.

In their local area, young people carry out practical field research on topics such as observations of adult and youth driving behavior, as well as peer surveys about road safety attitudes so as to enhance knowledge about the causes of road crashes. They also use these data to design an effective, preventive initiative around safe driving practices.

Do Youth Participate?

Despite the importance of adolescent road behavior, the very image of road safety may keep youth from participating: road safety, we thought, is simply not cool, and this, for young people, might prevent active participation in our work. We were surprised! During the first year of the project in 2009, we managed to establish sixty youth groups, with an average number of fifteen young people per group, and nine hundred Israeli youth participated in the first year. The figure that was most surprising was that among minority populations of Arabs, Bedouins, and Druze, the participation rate was even higher. Of all youth groups, more than a third came from these populations (twenty-four groups). Most groups met regularly and participants attended regularly.

The program was implemented as planned, and youth began to make, design, and plan monthly tasks: a survey conducted among friends about attitudes toward careless driving, observations at busy street intersections, writing letters to local authorities on behalf of youth, and more. The group carried out all of these activities in their local area, and many began to include their friends in the group project.

After a few weeks of activities in the classroom, some field observations, and the survey, the youth group started to design and create projects to reduce the number and rate of road accidents. Examples from 2009 to 2011 include the following:

- Establishment of a youth pavilion where young people received special eyeglasses to play a racing video game that simulated how perception changes after drinking
- Building of a bench made from crashed cars, which was placed in the lobby of the local city hall
- Distribution of candy and balloons to children who crossed the street at legal pedestrian crossings (positive feedback)
- Presentation on road safety to their peers at school
- A Road Safety Day with activities at school
- A bicycle parade in the city in memory of victims of road accidents
- Creation of a musical competition for young bands to create new songs about road safety
- The writing and performance of a play about road safety and car accidents
- Creation of a road-safety film
- A poster design competition at school about various road-safety topics

Given the breadth of approaches young people developed and the skills they demonstrated in creating these projects, Green Light wanted to showcase the projects to a larger audience. In 2009, we organized a national conference that brought road-safety youth groups from around Israel together to share what they had done in their local communities.

National Conference

National meetings, with cross-ethnic religious groups, were held in 2009 and 2010. In Israel such meetings are rare because of intergroup tensions in society as a whole and in some local contested spaces. Even with these tensions, the conference attracted large delegations from five different ethnic groups. A one-day event was held with four hundred youth participants who belong to the Green Light Association. Because they believe that the issue of road safety is important and indeed common to all, irrespective of religion, race, or nationality, they worked together, a reality also rare in Israel.

In 2010 we made adjustments to the program and created a new syllabus for the road-safety youth groups that was based on our experience running the project for two years and with young people's input. We added ten activities, including a simulation of a road-crash court trial. We succeeded in recruiting ninety groups, 50 percent growth over the previous year.

Does This Model Work?

Nonscientific evaluation data suggest that the project is effective with participating youth: they changed their driving behavior and rate of auto morbidity and mortality by 10 percent. There was also a positive effect on their friends, classmates, and other local youth. Youth who participated in this project reported that they changed their views and behavior toward road safety and dangerous driving, with more than 90 percent saying that they would try to influence road behaviors of friends and family.

Can This Model Be Replicated?

The core elements of this model can be adapted to other national sociocultural and sociopolitical contexts as a community-based project that uses local community resources, such as university students from the community who reach out to youth. The model does not enforce one way of thinking, and each community is encouraged to find a way to address the issue of youth road safety. This project has taught us that there is more than one way to address road safety for young drivers and that the best solutions are those supported by the local community.

In addition, young people from various cultural backgrounds typically respond positively to a challenge when they believe the subject is authentic. Young people want their voice to be heard, especially when it has to do with their lives. We do not tell the young people what to do or what is right or wrong, we help them to understand the reality, and with them we find ways to address that reality. Because young people want their voice to be heard, road safety, like other everyday issues, can be a subject that can be used to engage young people to take active roles in their community, no matter where they live.

Road safety serves as a metaphor, as a way to bring youth into participating in civic issues and positively contributing to their local communities. However, youth obviously have the capacity to engage in real-life issues that matter to them, and with coaching they can engage in these on their own terms, not because we want them to do so or have to seduce them to do so. They engage because they want to, because the issue pertains to them and they are compelled to respond: this is their vocation—active citizens who want to make a difference.

Reflection Questions

- In what ways is driving safety both a reasonable and a counterintuitive space for civic youth work?
- What makes Green Light a civic youth work effort and not simply just good youth work?
- Is civic youth work a universal process with a universal ethos, practice, knowledge, and skills, or is it culture bound? If the former, how does civic youth work practice respond to cultural, social, political, and related differences? If the latter, can civic youth work be practiced as envisioned in this text in vastly different cultures?
- Is it expected and is it reasonable for civic youth workers to be surprised by the young people they are working with? When and under what conditions?
- What does the author mean by "road safety serves as a metaphor"? How does your answer fit in your and our conception of civic youth work?
- Do you and the involved youth have to know that they are engaging in a civic youth work process for the work to be civic youth work?
- In what vocabulary and with what insight should young people who have been involved in a civic youth work process talk about that experience?
- If you adapted this project to your context, what would you change from how the work was done in Israel, and why?

PART 3

Policies Supporting and Challenging Civic Youth Work

Youth Civic Engagement in Korea

Past, Present, and Future

Yun Jin Choi

The concept of youth civic engagement is still a foreign concept in Korea. Under the influence of Confucianism, youth in Korea are perceived as a subordinate part of the family and of society, dependent and reliant on the older generation. These ideas were further reinforced after the liberation of Korea from Japanese colonial rule in 1945. During this period, Korea began to adopt Western, modern capitalism. Thus, education at all levels was considered crucial for national economic and social development, as well as to support improved economic status for young people. As a result, youthhood in Korea became a period during which young people were expected to study day and night to prepare for their future adulthood. Young people were expected to set aside their role as citizens until adulthood. They became citizens-to-be. Consequently, young people in Korea had, and continue to have, few opportunities to get involved in civic matters and to put forth their own opinions or participate in any decision-making process.

Nevertheless, young people in Korea did not simply stop being civically engaged. Instead, there are numerous historical events that demonstrate how Korean youth have engaged in and contributed to Korean society, especially during times of social change and development. This chapter describes the challenges to youth civic engagement in Korea and examples of how young people have chosen to remain

politically and civically engaged. I end by offering some practical recommendations to improve youth civic engagement in Korea.

Youth Civic Engagement in Korea

Young people have been active citizens at different moments in Korean
history. Young people have consistently fought against totalitarian
regimes in Korea. During the Japanese colonial period from 1910 to 1945,
youth were part of the national liberation movement against Japan.
They fought for liberation and resisted the colonial power. After the
Korean War, young people continued to fight against the totalitarian
government and for a more democratic society and government. As a
result, many young people were victims of what is now called the
Bloody Revolution, of April 19, 1960. The harsh treatment they received
did not dissuade youth from political activism, as the Bloody Revolution
was followed by the Gwangju Democratization Movement and the June
Uprising, which resulted in the announcement of the June 29 Declara-
tion in 1987. These were significant events that shaped Korean society
and moved it toward a functional democracy.

As democracy took hold in Korean society, middle and high school
students also began to advocate for their own rights—abolition of hairstyle restrictions, the elimination of after-school compulsory study,
greater religious freedom, lowering of the voting age, and the elimination of excessive college entrance competition all became major issues
of the youth (student) rights movement. The efforts of youth in advocating for their own rights has had a significant impact on society. As a
result, a few local governments enacted students' rights regulations to
ensure students' rights.

From an online signature campaign for the repeal of schools' hair
code, which gathered 160,000 signatures in 2000, to an enormous candlelight vigil opposing US beef imports in 2009, there are increasing
numbers of youth aware of and active in current social and political
issues. With the growth of the Internet, there are more and more cases
of social movements starting as online engagement and evolving into
substantive social movements and protest. These efforts have been successful because they overcame the many barriers that hinder youth
civic engagement in Korea. They also demonstrate the possibilities of
youth civic engagement in Korea.

The Economic, Social, and Political Context
for Youth Civic Engagement

Korean society has experienced three critical changes since the
Japanese liberation: economic, political, and cultural. First, Korea

experienced rapid economic development. In the 1950s, the country had significant numbers of people living in poverty. Today, the country has one of the highest standards of living in the world. During the 1950s, the factories built to support the Korean War effort contributed to economic prosperity. In the 1960s, the Vietnam War allowed Korea to profit by exporting war supplies to Vietnam, thus helping make the country one of the world's leading economic powers. Other events, such as the opening of a high-speed railway in 1964, the hosting of the Olympics in 1988, and the joining of the Organization for Economic Cooperation and Development in 1996, led South Korea to become an economically advanced country.

Eventually, the per capita income, which was barely $1,000 in the 1960s, surpassed $10,000 in 1979 and $20,000 in 1989, reaching $28,000 at the beginning of the twenty-first century. This rapid growth of the economy, however, has created societal problems, such as social conflicts between the rich and poor, as well as what I see as a general dehumanization attributable to the hypercompetitiveness of society. As the traditional farming communities disappeared, the urban lifestyle expanded. These changes also brought with them new expectations for young people. Today, young people are expected to focus on school and future.

These changes in Korean society have had an impact on young people and youthhood in Korea. The economic changes have created a greater need for highly educated workers. University admission is extraordinarily competitive, and young people are expected to sacrifice everything else in pursuit of higher education, which is believed to support Korea's economic development. Their lives are dominated by school. Up until recently, this was not considered troubling.

Second, there have been rapid political changes. Since liberation in 1945 the country has been divided in half, North and South, and has become two separate countries. South Korea, as a democratic republic, tried to adopt and implement democracy, but establishing a true democratic society caused a great deal of hardship and sacrifice. The tension between South Korea and North Korea became worse after the Korean War in 1950, and this tension strengthened the anticommunist political faction in South Korea. The anticommunist ideology led to a period of repressive military government in South Korea, which made democratization even harder and greatly restricted citizenship activity for everyone, not just young people. Surprisingly, young people took the necessary actions to strengthen democratic traditions. After several bloody revolutions, and as a result of resistance movements led by college students, in 1987 the first direct presidential election in sixteen years took place. This supported the evolution of South Korea into a more liberal and open democratic society. Although young people have been leaders in creating the new democratic state of Korea, they are still not formally invited or supported to engage civic and political issues.

Third, from a cultural point of view, Korean society has experienced an immense confusion in values. As the traditional Confucian values faded away, Western-oriented individualism took over, creating generational conflicts. In addition, the core values of the 1960s and 1970s were sincerity, diligence, endurance, and preservation, to focus on achieving a better future by sacrificing today. Ever since becoming a consumer society in the 1980s, however, the value of immediate consumption, which focuses primarily on current well-being and achievement, has dominated society. Young people are expected to focus on their own academic achievement and their own well-being.

Since the enactment of the UN Convention on the Rights of the Child and European Union policy developments to promote social participation of youth in the late twentieth century, awareness and interest in youth rights has increased in Korea. Policies for involving youth in the government were introduced at the same time as the appearance of various human rights movements and the spread of the Internet. Korea is now among the most wired countries in Asia. Korean youth have led the trend of the rapid spread of information and globalization, and they use new media to communicate and to learn about social issues. These technologies have allowed young people to see beyond the boundaries of school. This has supported young people's civic and political engagement in recent years.

Young people continue to face many barriers that challenge their civic and political involvement. Although these barriers certainly exist, some young people have always found ways to remain civically and politically involved. In the following section, I describe several examples of youth civic engagement in Korea.

Examples of Youth Civic Engagement in Korea

Formal calls to support youth civic engagement in Korea have just begun, with several youth advocates and scholars seeking to expand opportunities and experiences to invite and support young people's active civic involvement. Although few formal opportunities have been supported and formal invitation and support remains low, young people have always found ways to participate in civic and political issues. This section presents three cases to describe how young people have met the challenges to their civic engagement and took action on political and civic issues that they found personally important.

THE YOUTH RIGHTS MOVEMENT

Influenced by the educational democratization movement in 1985, the youth rights movement has recently supported reducing oppressive practices in schools. The youth rights movement was ignited by a posting by a high school student Choi Woo Ju to an online forum on July 22, 1995, titled "A school that defiles the basic rights of students." He stated that the reality of school is that it violates student basic rights by forcing them into evening study and supplementary lessons. He wrote:

> As a citizen, I deserve to enjoy the dignity and value of humans. However, my 5 months of high school life have been filled with restrictions against my expectations. My own intentions were first ignored when the school required me to submit supplementary lessons and required evening self-study. I believed that learning should be pursued by my own initiative. I wished to study on my own after school. But a teacher told me to follow the requirements without grumbling. Otherwise, I could leave the school. My plea is that schools should not be operated by their head's arbitrary or tyrannical decisions any more. It means that schools must return time after school to students who deserve it. (Bae, 2012, p. 49)

The Department of Education investigated his civic complaint and ruled against him. This sparked other students to comment online about their experience of school and about how administrators and faculty ignored students' rights. Students across Korea responded by forming the student association Middle and High School Students Society for Welfare, which continues the work of protecting students' rights.

Several years later, in 1998, Im Yoo Bin, a student at Jeolla High School, posted a civil complaint on the website of Cheongwadae (the Korean presidential residence) titled "I accuse my school." He enumerated the main human rights issues of his school, including length of the school day (classes were scheduled until 10 p.m.), the regulation of hair length, and insufficient science laboratory equipment. He called for improved student services and increased free time for students.

As a result of Im's civil complaint, the school principal suspended him indefinitely from school because of false accusations against the school. In September, Im posted an apology at the bulletin board of Cheongwadae and was reinstated at school. This case was much criticized as typical of oppressing the freedom of expression.

The previous two cases had a huge impact on the spread of students' critical awareness of their schools and attempts to protect their human rights in the oppressive educational environment. A recent example of the youth activism is the Say No Society, a student association that opposes the standardized test, which was reintroduced after a ten-year hiatus. The organization believes that the test drives students to limitless competition. It took the lead in a signature-gathering campaign, a street campaign, and a class boycott.

Young people have continued to raise awareness about violations to their rights. Although initially they protested the general conditions of schooling in Korea, at the start of the new millennium, they began to advocate for their human rights. One well-publicized case in 2004 involved young people taking action to gain freedom of religion. At that time, students were enrolled in nearby public or private schools regardless of an individual's religion. The issue began when Kang Uiseok, a student at a private high school, demonstrated against being forced to attend Christian church services when he was not a Christian. Kang had not chosen to enter the Christian private high school he attended.

The school determined that his demonstration was "an activity to damage the ideology of the school," and he was expelled. Kang went on a hunger strike for forty-five days to protest his expulsion, and his health suffered as a result. As the news of his strike spread, many groups were formed, among them ROY (Right of Youth), which asserted that religious freedom should be given to all students, even those in private schools belonging to religious organizations. In the end, the school promised to give students the right to attend the church service of their choice. Subsequently, the courts ruled that Kang's expulsion from the school was improper. These examples describe actions young people took to improve their everyday life mainly in school. The following section describes several examples of how young people worked for larger political change.

YOUTH CIVIC ENGAGEMENT ON POLITICAL ISSUES

Young people have been working since the 1990s to reduce the voting age to eighteen. In 1960, the voting age was lowered to twenty years old. This differs from most countries, where voting rights are granted to much younger citizens (e.g., in approximately 130 countries, the minimum age required to vote is eighteen years; in some countries, including Great Britain, voting rights are guaranteed at the age of sixteen years). In Korea, when a person turns eighteen years old he or she is required to provide military service and to make tax payments. Youth argued that the voting age of twenty years old was not only unequal compared to other countries but also unfair considering their public duties. Young people have actively developed a movement for securing the voting age of eighteen, insisting that the unfair situation hinders their participation in social affairs.

In 2002, just before the presidential election, the Youth Association for Securing the Voting Age of Eighteen was founded. This network comprises fifteen organizations from all over Korea, including youth organizations, clubs, and student associations. In 2003, the network submitted a petition to the constitutional court arguing that depriving eighteen-year-olds of the right to vote was a violation of equal rights and that the election law ran counter to the spirit of the constitution. Their efforts were partially successful. In 2004, the voting age was lowered to nineteen. The movement to lower the age to eighteen continues to this day.

CANDLELIGHT MOVEMENTS

In the early 2000s, youth-led candlelight protests became models for peaceful resistant movements in Korea. Here I describe two examples. The first occurred in 2002, after two middle school girls walking on the shoulder of the road were struck and killed by a US army vehicle on a training exercise. Details of the event were not fully disclosed to the public, and compensation to the families of the two students was not properly made, given the unfair and unequal provisions of Status of Forces Agreement (SOFA), the military agreement between Korea and the US government. This led to a movement for the revision of SOFA.

Students of the Uijeongbu Women's High School visited the US military unit and delivered a written protest. This initial protest expanded into a candlelight protest that continued for more than a year. Young people founded a committee, proclaimed the Day for Action by Youth, developed an online signature-gathering campaign, and held a fundraiser. In undertaking these projects, they asserted their freedom of assembly against school and educational authorities and rules prohibiting participation in candlelight protests. Thus, they demonstrated their power through continued demands for the revision of SOFA and for an apology from the United States.

In May 2008, another candlelight protest was started by young people who opposed the importation of beef from the United States because of concerns about mad cow disease. This protest continued for several days, attracting a large number of people and raising awareness of issues of public health and national security. The group leading the initial assembly used mobile devices and the Internet to distribute information about the assembly. As a result, the protest attracted hundreds of thousands of people. It was reported that 60 percent of participants in the gatherings were young people. At the start of the movement, youth with the Internet ID name ANDANTE started an online signature-gathering campaign with the goal of impeaching the president for his decision to allow the import of beef from the United States. The campaign accumulated a surprising total of 1.39 million signatures. Subsequently, thirty-two candlelight cafés (another name for blogs) opened on the Internet. The number of cafés opened by middle and high school students was twice the number opened by university students. This is an instance of a large-scale citizen's movement in Korea led mainly by young middle and high school students. It is also an example of youth actively participating in social and political issues, and using virtual spaces to support their civic and political actions.

YOUTH CIVIC ENGAGEMENT IN VIRTUAL SPACE

According to research conducted by the Ministry of Information and Communication, 98 percent of Korean youth between the ages of six and nineteen have access to the Internet. The Internet is part of everyday life for the majority of youth in Korea. Having access to this virtual space has helped make it possible for youth to have a voice.

Online spaces, such as Cyber Youth, Tarea, and Idoo, have provided youth with places to have live discussions about their rights and social issues they care about. These spaces also supported young people in connecting with others who cared about similar issues, such as lowering the voting age, abolishing hairstyle restrictions in schools, and improving the youth labor environment. Idoo, especially, in its prime had thirty thousand to forty thousand youth who were actively involved. It was a hub for publicizing youth rights issues by reporting survey results on abolishing hairstyle restrictions, which gathered more than 160,000 signatures; lowering the voting age to eighteen; and repealing the National Education Information System of the Ministry of Education, which was vulnerable to identity theft (Bae, 2010).

From personal blogs to discussion forums, youth today in Korea have various options and much more freedom to communicate with one another. The openness and intimacy of the Internet has made it possible for more young people to participate and engage in political issues in a much shorter period of time. The means by which they engage in civic issues are also becoming more and more diverse, including simply replying to someone's posting, creating discussion forums, setting up personal web pages, making and posting UCC (Korea's version of YouTube) videos, joining volunteer groups, becoming active in cyber protests, and boycotting (Lee, 2009).

The introduction and rapid spread of social media networks has had a positive impact on youth civic engagement. Through Facebook and

Twitter, youth can acquire new information and express their own opinions. This provides an open and equal environment for all youth.

Conclusion: Developing Youth Civic Engagement in Korea

The growth of youth civic engagement in Korea is tied to the development of Korean society. Specifically, rapid economic advancement, political democratization, and the development of information technology have changed the image of youth in society and have improved youth participation in social, civic, and political issues.

Today young people in Korea, who are very well informed through the Internet and other means, have built a complex identity as both students and citizens. They are ready to jump from the fringe to the core of society. Young adults are expressing their desire to be independent, and they have a history of taking the lead in making changes in society.

Still, youth civic engagement is in its initial stages. The educational and sociocultural environment in which young people live has not changed much. Youth are still perceived as needing protection and supervision. This limits their opportunity for civic engagement.

According to the National Youth Policy Institute's (2008) research, the level of interest among young people in participating and being involved in civic work is high. Despite this interest, research has also shown that youth recognize a discrepancy between their expectations and reality. They do not experience themselves as having a political voice, and they do not think they receive enough information or education on how to participate.

In addition to this, there are some ongoing issues for youth civic engagement in Korea. First, in the rare cases when youth can participate in the governmental policy-making process, this usually involves young people giving their opinions and ideas. Little changes occur, though, on the basis of their input. Youth involvement is something required by policy but does not have much impact on the process of implementing or evaluating policy.

Second, there are limitations to the collecting of opinions from youth in certain situations. There is greater chance that the voices of marginalized youth (e.g., those who are working, are not in school, or who come from North Korea) are being neglected. By excluding these individuals, the group that participates in civic work becomes an elite group that no longer represents all youth.

Third, the biggest obstacle that youth civic engagement faces is adult attitudes. In general, adults' attitudes have not changed much. Adults still see young people as reckless, immature, and incomplete, and therefore not ready to be part of society. Korean society is still expecting its youth to stay out of the adult world and wait to become citizens later. This kind of outdated perspective results in the old-fashioned youth and education policies and practices that take away opportunities for young people to build skills and broaden the experiences that are necessary for everyday civic life. It continues to exclude young people from larger society. On the basis of these concerns, there are several things that we need to work on to vitalize youth civic engagement in Korea.

First, public understanding of youth civic engagement—what it means, why we encourage it, and how important it is—needs to be improved. We need to redefine concepts such as citizenship, youth citizenship, and civic engagement. It is important to make Korean society aware of the social status of youth and the importance of their role as citizens. Ultimately, we have to change the societal notion of youth as passive participants, subordinate and dependent on adults, to active participants who can contribute to the overall general good.

In addition, we must change education policy from the prep-school mind-set that focuses on citizens-to-be to one designed to provide a pathway for students to embrace the rights and responsibilities of living citizens.

Second, youth civic engagement must be more than just listening to students' ideas; it needs to be a process that invites and supports their opinions and their commitment to make a difference in Korea. We need to broaden the spectrum of participation beyond political engagement to various cultural domains. By introducing different cultural experiences through art or sports, young people can find more opportunities to connect to social issues.

Third, it is important that all opportunities be available to youth regardless of their academic performance or socioeconomic status. Youth participation is not just part of a checklist. It is crucial to make sure every voice is heard. By showing that their ideas matter, youth can become more empowered to make a contribution to our society.

Last, it is necessary to let youth take a closer look at where they live. Their own community is a great place to initiate civic work. As members of a community, youth can contribute their part to their own community just like adults do. By working in the community, they will build relationships with adult members and develop cooperative management models to allow them to work together. This experience will lay the groundwork for young people when they move on to the larger community.

For the development of society as a whole, it is essential for us to see young people not as citizens-to-be or as second-class citizens but as actual citizens who are competent at what they do and know their responsibilities and rights.

Reflection Questions

- How are a society and culture contexts for civic youth work ethos and practice?
- How might a student rights movement map onto a civic youth work model? Would civic youth work have worked in Korea before now? Why?
- What other job titles might fit for a civic youth worker engaged with students seeking educational and cultural reforms?
- How do the Korean sociocultural, economic, and political conceptions of youth influence the possibilities for youth engagement and for civic youth work practice?
- How does the UN Convention on the Rights of the Child work to promote civic youth work practice? Is an international instrument such as the convention by itself sufficient to change local understandings and practices on youth involvement? Why?
- What has been the role of new technologies in youth sociopolitical and cultural movements in Korea, Africa, and the Middle East from 2008 to today?
- How do you compare the youth engagement in this author's discussion of the student rights movement to youth engagement in the case study of the Mississippi gay, lesbian, bisexual, transgender, and queer youth rights movement?
- How is civic youth work practice implicitly and/or explicitly grounded in the civic rights and civic obligations and responsibilities of young people in a society? Absent these rights, is civic youth work feasible and safe for young people and for workers?
- What is symbolic youth engagement? How does it contrast with substantive youth engagement? With authentic, meaningful, and viable youth involvement?
- How generalizable is the author's assertion that in Korea adult opinion and, by extension, adult authority are crucial to whether small-scale youth engagement is viable and safe?
- How true is it in your opinion that a society's development depends on its perception of and response to young people as actual citizens who must be involved in viable and authentic ways on issues of concern to them and to the larger community?

CHAPTER TEN

Engaging Youth to Transform Conflict

A Study of Youth and the Reduction of War in Africa

Jennifer De Maio

On January 9, 2007, northern and southern Sudanese youth clashed once again. This time, however, they were not battling over religious and cultural differences or regional autonomy. Instead, they met in a basketball tournament held to mark the second anniversary of the signing of the Comprehensive Peace Agreement (CPA), which effectively ended twenty years of civil war in Sudan. The tournament was organized by the US Agency for International Development (USAID) and was intended to bring youth from the north and south together, to raise awareness of the peace agreement, and to foster the emergence of an active civil society.

Because peace is rarely permanent in contested spaces, developing strategies of conflict transformation and prevention is critical to human security. Protection of vulnerable young people in situations of armed conflict is an immediate concern. The past decade has witnessed an unprecedented increase in the involvement of young people, both as victims and as perpetrators, in armed conflict. The presence of a large number of young people in society is correlated with a higher incidence of civil war.[1] These so-called youth bulges are believed to affect states' political order and stability, and they have historically been associated

---

[1] *Youth* is defined here as an individual between the age of fifteen and twenty-four.

with periods of political crisis (Goldstone 1991, 2001, 2006). Urdal (2006) has established a link between youth bulges and armed conflict, terrorism, and riots. Youth are often targeted during conflict. The scarcity of opportunities in their societies can lead them to violence and acts of terrorism, and it makes them vulnerable to ideologies of war. Young men constitute the majority in most armed forces: it is estimated that there are three hundred thousand child and youth soldiers fighting in forty-nine countries.[2] As victims, witnesses, and perpetrators, youth are caught up in the cycles of violence and are often the unwilling heirs to legacies of grievances.

Given the central role they play in the perpetuation of violence, young people must be brought into the peace process and become active participants in conflict reduction and the development of early warning systems. To be sure, many have taken on active roles and created youth networks to try to build peace. The potential impact of youth is slowly being recognized as crucial in creating long-term stability, producing effective outcomes within communities, and offering protection from future conflicts. Through programs that emphasize bringing youth into civil society by including them in cultural, political, and social debates, young people are increasingly participating in the reconstruction of their countries. Despite these positive steps toward social and political participation, the international community and policy makers are still overlooking the capacity of youth to contribute to the reduction of conflict. Although young people are viewed as agents of violence, they are not necessarily identified as full actors in peace settings, and they are not recognized as having an active role as civil society actors, political constituents, or participants in measures to prevent violence. Young people are sometimes urged to be peacemakers, but they are seldom mentioned in responses to conflict through governance and political measures. If youth are given the chance to offer positive contributions to safety, there may be a greater opportunity both to improve security and to limit participation in violent action. Youth are central to postconflict reconstruction, but they are also key to the reduction of violence.

In the face of demographic realities, youth must be involved as partners in the process of reducing tensions in civil war. Engaging youth in conflict transformation and persuading them to organize and articulate their interests and needs is an essential step in building support at the community level for a political settlement of conflict. Youth are often the least visible in public forums. Their participation in decision-making processes, however, could significantly reduce the likelihood of

---

[2] This estimate has remained unchanged since 2001, as quoted by the Coalition to Stop the Use of Child Soldiers, and may not accurately reflect the number of youth currently involved in armed conflict. See http://www.child-soldiers.org.

the outbreak and/or escalation of violence. In this chapter, I posit that youth can play a constructive role in consolidating peace and averting conflict. The purpose of this analysis is threefold: first, to develop a theoretical understanding of the relationship between youth and conflict prevention; second, to explore case study evidence of efforts to achieve and sustain peace in Kenya, Rwanda, Liberia, Zambia, and Sierra Leone; and third, to consider the normative implications of viewing youth as critical partners in conflict reduction.

Youth in Civil War

According to the UN Population Fund (UNFPA) report "State of the World Population 2005," almost half of the world's population is younger than the age of twenty-five; 85 percent of all youth live in developing countries, which are currently facing the largest youth bulge in modern times; and in Africa and South Asia, children and youth together make up more than 60 percent of the total population. Recent research on countries with large young age structures—or youth bulges—suggests that these areas may be more prone to conflict (Urdal, 2007).[3] In most contested spaces, youth are viewed either as perpetrators of violence or as victims needing protection. And although the variables that cause civil conflict are many, the presence of large numbers of young people, particularly men, correlates with a higher likelihood of violence.

The relationship between youth bulges and a greater incidence of conflict depends primarily on several factors, including unemployment, lack of political openness, and expanded tertiary education (Braungart, 1984; Choucri, 1974; Cincotta, Engelman, & Anastasion, 2003; Goldstone, 1991, 2001; Huntington, 1996; Moller, 1968). When a surge in the number of young people coincides with a labor market that cannot provide enough jobs, the situation breeds frustration and disillusionment with the government, which can then motivate antigovernment actions. Large numbers of unemployed youth are cited as a source of recurring instability in the Middle East (Huntington, 1996; Zakaria, 2001). When economic insecurity is the norm, youth are more likely to seek order and safety in the form of armed groups, regardless of those groups' ideology or behavior (Punamaki, 1996). Militias, armed groups, and gangs are then able to mobilize youth for their own gains, evidenced by the estimated three hundred thousand young soldiers currently

---

[3] According to Urdal (2007), " 'In countries where youth make up 35 percent of the total adult population, the risk of conflict, with all other factors being equal, increased by 150 percent' compared to countries where youth make up only 17 percent of the adult population, as in most developed countries" (n.p.).

involved in armed conflict. Large youth cohorts lower the costs of war for rebel groups through the abundant supply of labor, thereby providing increased opportunities for factions to wage war against the government (Collier, 2000). The opportunity to engage in conflict at a lower cost combines with the motivation to use political violence as a rational means to redress economic, social, or political grievances (Gurr, 1970; Sambanis, 2002). Thus, when large youth cohorts find themselves excluded politically and/or economically, they may determine that the best—and perhaps the only—way of reacting is by joining a rebel group and engaging in antigovernment activities.

Evidence that the existence of a youth bulge can play a critical role in the emergence of armed violence in contested spaces presents a challenge for policy makers: how can the calculations of these youth cohorts be altered so as to make them perceive greater benefits from peace than from conflict? Youth bulges are a resource for rebels, but can they also be a resource for peace building? How can their energy be redirected so that they become agents for conflict aversion rather than violence? How can that be transformed so that they become agents for peace rather than rebellion? How can they be made to feel part of the process rather than viewed as threats? These questions are particularly relevant in societies in which youth feel marginalized.

Youth and Conflict Reduction Post–Civil War: Case Study Evidence

KENYA: VOTING FOR PEACE

After more than twenty years of debate and several attempts, on August 4, 2010, Kenya succeeded in passing a new constitution. The peaceful referendum process stands in stark contrast to the violence that erupted following the disputed 2007 presidential elections. The post-election violence claimed the lives of more than one thousand Kenyans and resulted in the internal displacement of many more. Since the country's independence in 1963, violent clashes among supporters of the various political parties have been a feature of Kenya's political activity. Resources, material benefits, and political and economic positions had traditionally been distributed along ethnic lines in Kenya, a practice that created intense competition among groups. As the date for the referendum approached, it seemed reasonable to expect that the violence that resulted after the 2007 elections would be repeated. Two months before the referendum, a bomb blast and stampede at a rally held by opponents of the constitution left six dead and dozens wounded. Reports of hate speech and threats were coming in from all over the country, particularly from the Rift Valley, which had been the

site of some of the most severe postelection fighting. When the constitution passed peacefully, scholars and policy makers were eager to
extract lessons from the Kenyan experience. Many cite as critical the
support of the political elite who, with a few exceptions, were in favor
of the adoption of the new constitutional framework. The international
community also put significant pressure on the parties in the disputed
presidential elections to reach a political settlement. In addition, the
parties were encouraged to employ legal mechanisms such as the Truth,
Justice, and Reconciliation Commission to address legacies of political
violence. Although the role played by political leaders during the referendum process was paramount, it alone does not fully account for why
67 percent of Kenyans voted in favor of the new constitution. What
seems particularly significant about the Kenya case are the efforts of
youth to engage in civic education efforts, to encourage debate on the
proposed constitution, and to develop effective early warning systems.

Youth groups contributed to building national cohesion and integration through their promotion of interethnic peace and reconciliation.
Youth in Kenya account for about 32 percent of the population and
form 60 percent of the total labor force (Kenyan Ministry of Youth
Affairs and Sports, n.d.). Kenyan youth comprise the country's largest
voting bloc. These youth have been raised in a society where opportunity has been eroded by widespread institutional collapse. Despite
these challenges, Kenyan youth are characterized by their optimism
and energy, which have translated into agitation for long-term systemic
changes. The nation's youth were among the first to campaign for the
referendum process. Working under the umbrella of the National Youth
Forum (NYF), groups like the Youth Agenda, the Kenya Muslim Youth
Alliance, and the Youth Peace Alliance distributed more than one million copies of the proposed constitution, held regional workshops with
youth leaders to collect the views of young people that were then presented to the Committee of Experts charged with drafting the document, and convened more than six hundred youth representing every
constituency in Kenya at a forum in November 2009 to discuss the proposed constitution. The NYF also hosted three town-hall meetings just
before the August 2010 referendum. The meetings, which were broadcast live on national television and streamed on the Internet through
YouTube, reached about four million viewers. In the months leading up
to the referendum, youth groups sent text messages (i.e., SMS, short
messages services) to a database of forty-five thousand cell phone
users. They tailored the messages to specific demographic sectors,
including women and other young people. The messages counted
down the days until the referendum and encouraged Kenyans to vote
and to vote peacefully (interview with H. Ole Naado, CEO of the Kenya
Muslim Youth Alliance, November 4, 2010). Groups in the country, such

as the umbrella organization Naivasha Network for Change, used theater and art to educate and engage their peers in the referendum process. Youth continue to be active advocates and actors in the implementation of the constitution. For example, NYF hosts youth town-hall meetings that are broadcast on local radio stations in each county. It still sends regular SMS messages, but now it focuses on promoting coexistence after the referendum. Youth throughout the country are being used as peace monitors. Extensive early warning networks have been established that enable people to send text messages to a publicly distributed number if they hear about or observe threats of violence. The new constitution is about a new vision for Kenya. That new vision for Kenya needs new and progressive leadership. There is a widespread sense among the youth that they are that new leadership and that their very livelihood and chances for success depend on the successful implementation of the constitution.

RWANDA: GENERATION GRAND LAC

A system of wars has developed in the Great Lakes region of Africa. From the genocide that devastated Rwanda to the conflict in Burundi to the continental war in the Democratic Republic of Congo (DRC), the region has suffered unprecedented violent conflict in recent decades that has ebbed and flowed across national borders. In an effort to promote stability and nurture an albeit fragile peace, USAID, in partnership with Search for Common Ground (SFCG), is using live youth radio to cross borders and counter the negative stereotypes and prejudices amongst youth in the region. Generation Grand Lac (GGL) was started in 2006 and, according to Chris Plutte, the country director for SFCG Rwanda, its primary goal is "to open up a conversation among youth, targeting university students, on regional issues that affect them all" (interview with C. Plutte, country director, Search for Common Ground Rwanda, January 12, 2009). Given the mistrust that exists among the DRC, Rwanda, and to some extent Burundi, the hope is that the program will open the lines of communication among young people to foster dialogue across ethnic lines. The radio programs are planned and hosted by young journalists from Rwanda, Burundi, and the DRC who meet once a quarter in a designated country and develop the shows for the following three months. Every Saturday for an hour, radio presenters from the three countries hold an open discussion on topics relevant to youth in the region: identity, rumor management, displaced and refugee youth, gender, and so on. The program is simulcast via web streaming and FM transmission, which allows audiences in the three countries to listen to and phone in to the same program at the same time. The experience illustrates to young listeners that the concerns and issues they face are shared across ethnic and national divides. It serves to bring them into a regional community that is working towards creating safe and stable environments. The program thus functions as a critical conflict prevention tool.

Another feature of the radio programs are the "listening clubs" they promote in different communities in the various countries. These listening clubs function in two ways: first, they create a space for the community to gather and listen to the show and call in with questions and/ or comments; second, the shows are followed by a debriefing and discussion of the topic of the program. Research conducted by the SFCG has shown that "regular GGL listeners are developing more constructive attitudes toward dealing with conflict, managing misinformation, and they are letting go of their prejudices in favor of a spirit of regional collaboration" (USAID, 2009, p. 2). In a survey in mid-2007, between 63 percent and 80 percent of university students listened to GGL in Kigali, Bujumbura, and Bukavu (USAID, 2009). These listeners were more open to the possibility of marriage with someone from another group, a key indicator of tolerance. "Generation Great Lakes continues to remind the youth of the region that by understanding each other, and based on what they have in common, they can build a stronger future together," commented Lena Slachmuijlder, country director of SFCG (USAID, 2009, p. 2).

In the past, radio served as a weapon of war in the region to ignite hatred and violence; it is now being used to encourage peace building and conflict prevention. Mass media such as radio and television play an important part in averting violence, promoting tolerance, and encouraging dialogue among young people. Such media can cross traditional societal divisions and invite audiences to participate in the creation of a new and better reality. Creative programs similar to those produced by Generation Grand Lac can be effective strategies for conveying positive messages and information. They can also raise awareness of community issues and grievances and suggest nonviolent means for addressing these. In addition, media can be used as a tool to promote public reward systems that promote conflict prevention and nonviolent practices (United Nations, 2003).

YOUTH CRIME WATCH: SIERRA LEONE, LIBERIA, AND ZAMBIA

Youth Crime Watch (YCW) started as a crime prevention and neighborhood safety program in the United States. It has since expanded to twelve other countries to demonstrate that young people can make a difference in improving the safety of their communities. The YCW's programs require that youth take on leadership roles in assessing problems and drafting courses of action as well as publicizing, promoting, and determining the sustainability of programs. The YCW promotes youth as central actors in crime prevention and safety at national and local levels and includes the following activities in their mission: anonymous crime reporting, radio-assisted youth patrols, mentoring, mediation, drug and crime prevention education, conflict resolution training, and peer and cross-age teaching (Social Program Evaluators and Consultants & Partners in Evaluation and Planning, 2003).

Since the end of the brutal war in Sierra Leone, crime, violence, and drug abuse among youth have been on the increase. In response, a group of young people came together to sensitize their fellow youth. Youth Crime Watch of Sierra Leone was established in October 2003 with the goal of young people taking an active role in reducing crime in institutions and communities with support from stakeholders such as civil society, local and international nongovernmental organizations, the government of Sierra Leone, the UN Mission in Sierra Leone (UNAMSIL), and the Civil Police Unit (CIVPOL). Their efforts made such an impact that a good number of youth changed their lifestyle to a better one. Today, Youth Crime Watch of Sierra Leone supports "watch out" activities, such as crime reporting, and "help out" activities, such as monitoring, mentoring, and mediation.

In Liberia, YCW youth participants work with the Liberian National Police and the UN Mission in Liberia (UNMIL) to develop and maintain an anonymous reporting system to exchange information. Schools are used for organizing programs and recruiting volunteers: these venues have proved effective because of the adult supervision and the large base for recruitment they provide. Through the use of anonymous tip boxes and preexisting emergency hotlines, participants provide information about mob violence, drug abuse, and theft. The YCW is planning to expand its efforts in Liberia to rural areas, where education infrastructure is minimal and where recruitment by armed groups and militias is less regulated. The YCW does not have a youth patrol unit in Liberia, fearing that the organizational structure of youth patrols too closely resembles that of armed groups and militias and could be detrimental to the peace process in a country facing a very recent history of civil war and the challenges of reintegrating and rehabilitating former child soldiers.

Youth Crime Watch Zambia (YCWZ) is actively involved in fostering dialogue among youth about the importance of crime prevention. The organization has planned youth leadership retreats at schools and trained participants about crime watching basics, including prevention and identification. The YCWZ has also held discussions on child abuse as part of its efforts to promote the prevention of crimes and protect the rights of children. In a radio program about child abuse, participants were asked to elaborate on the forms of abuse that are affecting children in schools and communities in Zambia. The most rampant forms of abuse that were identified included sexual abuse, verbal abuse, child labor, and child trafficking. Some of the possible solutions that were highlighted included the raising of awareness through campaigns and the work of various youth organizations, the establishing of anonymous crime-reporting systems for youth and children, and the making of regular follow-ups on cases of abuse. Radio programs are frequently used by the organization to provide general information about Zambia's Youth Crime Watch program, introducing the basic philosophy and tenets of the watch out, help out model. The aim of these programs is to develop civic responsibility in young people and to convey the central importance of youth involvement in stopping crime and violence.

Implications for Policy Makers

The cases discussed here suggest strategies for involving young people in conflict reduction and transformation. More important, they demonstrate that by empowering youth and making them feel that they can and do make a difference can have lasting impacts on how young people view their role as agents of change in society. The overwhelming presence of youth in contested spaces can be viewed as both a problem and an opportunity. Engaging youth in preventing conflict at an early stage of their development of ideas, opinions, and prejudices could have long-term benefits on the transformation and/or restoration of social order. Therefore, although it can be expected that youth bulges would be accompanied by increased unemployment and poverty, they can also be a unique opportunity to teach children less divisive views and to foster a generation versed in the language of peace and conflict management. The inclusion of youth in conflict transformation programs could over time bridge deep divisions in contested spaces. Intrastate stability and security could be strengthened with programs employing youth as active participants. The key to engaging youth in conflict reduction and peace building is to offer alternative means to addressing conflict. As we have seen with the cases presented here, if young people are offered possibilities for channeling their frustrations and differences in constructive ways, the likelihood of armed conflict decreases.

Success in transforming conflicts requires an understanding of the primary causes of war, local capacities and interests, and the willingness of the international community and other third parties to engage in conflict management efforts. Armed conflict has an undeniable impact on youth, and although young people are often invisible during international negotiations, they can play a critical role in conflict prevention. To successfully avert conflict, the international and local communities must empower young people and encourage them to take a lead in protecting their communities from violence. Youth need to be viewed as dynamic agents of peace who, rather than being the "problem," are critical to the solution (United Nations, 2005). In a research study conducted in Angola in July through October 2006 by Youth Ambassadors of Peace and Citizenship, a youth citizenship project implemented by Development Workshop, young people interviewed described how they are routinely marginalized and discriminated against by elders, as well as by the media, schools, churches, their local community, and civil society and political parties (Youth Ambassadors of Peace and Citizenship, 2007). They believe that they are viewed with suspicion and are seen as irresponsible, aggressive, and dangerous. Feelings of discrimination combined with their own lack of self-esteem and confidence can lead young people to exclude themselves from decision making. To transform young people into partners in the prevention of conflict, several obstacles must be overcome, including cultures of social exclusion, inflexible organizational cultures, problems of apathy, and unemployment (Youth Ambassadors of Peace and Citizenship, 2007). Each of these obstacles alienates young people and contributes to their absence from the decision-making process. If youth are brought into conflict prevention and peace-building procedures, their contribution could produce positive long-term results.

To gain more information about how to best involve young people in the conflict reduction process, the policy-operations gap must be addressed to determine which factors are likely to lead to violence. Such instruments could provide support for early warning and prevention mechanisms. Reliable early warnings provide the time necessary to prepare for short-term containment and relief strategies, and more important to design, build support for, and implement longer-term proactive strategies and development programs that can reduce the likelihood of future disasters. Young people can serve as an important resource in generating early warning signals. They could take part in several key activities, including planning and leading neighborhood watches, providing information about their perspectives and grievances to country experts, participating in public information campaigns to increase media involvement and ensure cohort support, and offering crime reduction education. By encouraging the participation of youth in early warning systems, the international and regional community would be creating a form of local buy-in in the process, thereby promoting the inclusion of civil society in the conflict transformation period.

Young people should be brought into the conflict prevention and transformation process as allies who have a significant capacity to influence their communities. More specifically, youth should actively contribute to the design, execution, and leadership of conflict reduction programs so that these incorporate the social, political, economic, and legal needs of such a major segment of the population. To be successful, it is essential that youth own the process of conflict transformation and are consulted and included in the discussion and addressing of grievances. Youth need to feel ownership over the process of reducing conflict and transforming their environments. Conflict reduction and the development of early warning systems should consist of broad participation and community buy-in; it is critical that youth take part in defining issues and devising solutions.

The likelihood of conflict decreases with the adoption of strategies and the establishment of institutions that address basic needs, including youth-oriented nongovernmental organizations, peace organizations, and regional initiatives. By the same token, the likelihood of conflict increases when destructive practices, such as the negative depiction of youth by the media, youth involvement in the shadow economy, and the exclusion of young people from peace processes and civil society forums, continue (Sommers, 1997). Young people have become increasingly involved in drawing attention to the indicators of the escalation of violence. It is crucial, however, that they develop the "skills and attitudes (appropriate within the local context) that enable them to handle conflict, which can be acquired through participation in decision-making processes and through education" (United Nations, 2003, p. 389). Although at the international level there is increasing recognition of the need to protect youth in contested spaces, warring parties are still not shielding children and youth. Experience from countries in conflict does not suggest that the "achievements on the international political, legal and normative level are being translated to actions on the ground" (United Nations, 2005, p. 141).

Central to the process of engaging youth in conflict transformation is the creation of community partnerships that mobilize and support youth. Local citizens have a more complete understanding of the priorities and demands for security and development, and they have a vested interest in ensuring that programs last. Programs are thus more likely to endure if there is community buy-in and if they are fully inclusive. In contested spaces, child soldiers and orphans often receive most of the attention, as programs are tailored specifically to them. This focus on specific populations can have an alienating effect on other youth in the community, can build resentment, and can undermine the potential efficacy of a program. To be successful, programs must be sustainable. As we have seen in the case studies discussed here, conflict reduction programs must be broadly youth driven and youth informed, and designed to foster dialogue along the contours of cultural pluralism.

The transformation of conflict has emerged to become an international priority. In implementing prevention strategies, efforts must be made to identify the frustrations and interests of youth who are caught in cycles of violence. To be sure, the reduction of conflict requires social inclusion. Enabling youth to make major positive contributions is one way to address factors that contribute to violence, increase global security, and prevent further armed conflict. It is therefore essential to accumulate and store knowledge on effective ways of engaging youth in transforming armed conflict.

Although we can develop guidelines, policy makers need to have a theoretical framework that they can adapt through informed analysis to various situations. For this to occur, the international community must take an active role in improving the necessary methods and intelligence with the knowledge that the tools that it uses must be adapted to each individual conflict situation. The continued development of a framework for conflict reduction and transformation through case study analysis should be the object of future research.

Reflection Questions

- How do these conceptions of youth in war fit or not with conceptions of youth in peace or as peacemakers and peacekeepers? With conceptions of why they should or should not be involved in civic engagement?
- What made it possible for young people to be involved in armed conflict? What made it possible for young people to be involved as peacemakers and peacekeepers?
- How does the involvement of young people as perpetrators in armed conflict in this African case study compare to their involvement in the Northern Ireland Troubles? What might this tell us about current practices of war making and conceptions of youth?
- In what ways might the demographic bulges in the number and percentage of youth in a society be related to perceptions of youth and to calls (by them and others) for their substantive involvement in civic life?
- In this chapter, mass youth groups have been active in national to local politics, as in Korea. Is this youth civic engagement, or is it something else and/or something more? Does small-scale, small-group civic youth work fit in this larger social movement? If so, how?

- What are the similarities and differences between the mobilization of youth and small-scale, small-group civic youth work?
- Is civic youth work as presented in this book culture bound in its ethos, knowledge, practice, and skills? If so, do the accounts from Africa and Korea suggest revisions?
- What is a nongovernmental organization, community-based organization, and international nongovernmental organization? How do these fit in typical US small-scale, small-group civic youth work?

CHAPTER ELEVEN

Croatian Youth Corner

Youth Participation and Civic Education from Practitioners' Eyes

Emina Bužinkić

Youth in Croatia

If you observe or research youth in Croatia, you would say that they are similar to other young people in many ways. Currently, young people make up 21 percent of the population in Croatia, at almost one million young people. In this way, Croatia mirrors much of Europe. One of the main differences is the context in which recent young generations in Croatia grew up, socialized, and developed. The past decades have brought radical changes to Croatian youth and those living in the western Balkans; the disintegration of Yugoslavia, followed by violent armed conflicts all around the region, specifically across and within the borders of Croatia, Bosnia and Herzegovina, Slovenia, Serbia, Montenegro, and Kosovo. More than a decade of violence in the region left many areas in ruins. Many young lives were lost, and lives have significantly changed. The process of Croatian democratic development is burdened with the history of one of the most ruinous wars in recent memory.

Croatian youth still live with the legacy of violence. The regional violence has had lasting impacts, including low political participation and voting, high unemployment, high levels of violence (according to official crime statistics), increasing violence among youth (according to current scientific research), high levels of xenophobia (according to recent research on discrimination), attacks on the rights of national minorities and returnees, high citizens' support of war criminals, and failing support to the accession to European Union. These consequences of the conflict continue to influence current institutional roles, citizens' rights, and social development on the economic and political levels. Croatians want social recovery, and young people advocate for a democratization process with openly designed spaces for citizen and youth participation. Young people want to address the legacy of violence and move beyond traditional patterns to create a new, safer, and inclusive environment.

Even though many youth have ideas of how to change their surroundings, most of them do not find the support they need. Governmental institutions have not made systematic steps toward enabling Croatian citizens to learn about democracy and the protection of human rights or toward supporting young people's political participation. Youth political participation is low, with only 5–7 percent of the youth population active in some form of civic activism (Ilisin, 2007); in reality, that number may be even lower because of the challenges of measuring civic activism in a postconflict society. Research has found that young people are not present in political institutions or the political system in general. Not surprisingly, researchers and youth workers both agree that young people are rather politically unmotivated and in many areas still very burdened by the legacy of violence.

Founding Croatian Youth Network

The end of armed conflict in Croatia brought some significant political changes; the country transformed from an authoritarian to a democratic way of governing. This dramatic political change opened up new processes for citizen participation, supported the establishment of nongovernmental organizations and other civil society organizations, supported basic rights such as freedom of speech, and supported a media boom. During this time period, young people were considered the strongest part of the population in every aspect: strength and ideas, length of life ahead, skills and knowledge, and motivation for change. With ideas of social change, many young people started organizing their local communities, creating youth groups, and working on political elections.

Among the most prominent examples of local youth organizing and political involvement is with the independent local election list. Since 2000, the Croatian political system has been parliamentary, and citizens vote for political parties or independent lists. One way to influence the political system is to create an independent list. In 2000, a group of young people created the Nezavisna Lista Mladih (Independent Youth List) in Kutina, a midsize town of some twenty-four thousand inhabitants (youth comprise 25 percent of the population), in a region that had been seriously affected by war and had a history of authoritarian political leadership. The platform of Nezavisna Lista Mladih was to work toward increasing youth participation in local matters and a focus on daily social problems affecting both young people and the general population. The youth group ran the campaign during the 2001 local elections and won several city council seats.

In 2002 the group founded the association Nezavisni Mladi Kutine (Independent Youth of Kutina), which advocated for creating and then adopting the first local youth action plan, a local strategy for improving overall quality of life for young people. This move supported more active youth political involvement. There were independent associations of youth for youth with an aim of changing the environment for youth development in the present and in the future. Those changes were often made under the slogan "a different world is possible." The Center for Peace Studies (http://www.cms.hr) and its program Youth MIRamiDA (*mir* means "peace," *ami* is French for "friend," and *da* means "yes"; there is also an analogy to a pyramid and building peace from the bottom up), a peace education program directed at informing, educating, and empowering youth activists for creating changes in their local communities, in Zagreb began to research youth political activism all around Croatia to show how youth efforts have created positive social change. The research was later published as *Youth Activism in Croatia*. This research further connected different youth groups from around the country and supported further cooperation in the youth sector.

These initiatives fit well with the general movement across Croatia to support greater democratization across civil and political arenas. There were efforts to increase citizen participation and to support the democratic development of governmental and societal institutions. All these efforts sought to stimulate policy changes. Young people were considered a social, potential community resource, as well as a creative engine for building up a healthy society, preventing wars, and creating a better way of life in the present and in the future. These metaphors were strong and lent support to young people's political activism at the time. This was a profound change from the previous image of young people.

Often neglected, manipulated, and ignored, youth became visible and active change advocates for sociopolitical reforms and more specifically for youth policy. They worked to create policies supporting better education, employment and mobility opportunities, cultural events, quality leisure time and health conditions, and inclusion in decision making. Those young people and youth groups who were advocating for local and state youth policies quickly realized that by cooperating, they stood a strong chance that policy would change in these areas.

This cooperative spirit also describes how the Croatian Youth Network (CYN) formed. Initially, young people throughout Croatia shared and discussed a wide range of ideas at youth events, such as cultural forums, festivals, concerts, youth association fairs, and peace-building workshops. This gradual sharing of ideas in nonformal settings supported later cooperative efforts and built support for the idea of joint action and representation. The CYN was established out of the need for cooperation and improved communication among a diverse group of youth organizations, regardless of their program identifications and organizational structure, and in full respect of their worldview and their political, racial, national, sexual, religious, and cultural identifications and those of young people whom they represented or advocated for, in order to advocate effectively and efficiently for the interests and needs of young people in Croatia.

In 2002 the first CYN general assembly was organized. The assembly comprised twenty-eight youth groups from all around the country. Groups included Independent Youth of Kutina, the Center for Peace Studies, and different social and political groups that work mainly on peace-building and cross-cultural efforts, as well as large national networks inherited from the earlier socialist government system (e.g., Jeunesse Musical of Croatia, Croatian Hostel Union, Scouts Alliance). Peace-building and multicultural work remained central to the overall work of CYN for many years.

From its beginnings, CYN has been based on democratic decision making and public work, in contrast to typical governmental practices at the time. It remains open to all interested youth organizations and initiatives, respectful of the integrity and independence of its members, and supportive of local youth organizations and initiatives. It began by working to build responsible partnerships with other interested organizations, institutions, and bodies of national and local governments, and it continues to do so. It has become a youth advocacy organization, bringing attention and focus to the interests and needs of youth. Also, given the history of Croatia, CYN actively promotes tolerance of difference and mutual respect between and among different ethnic groups, it works to protect human and minority rights, it promotes healthy lifestyles, and it supports young people's active and responsible participation in society and public decision making.

National Youth Action Plan and National Youth Council

In the same year that CYN was established, national authorities adopted a national strategic document on youth, the "National Youth

Action Plan." Monitoring its implementation became the responsibility of CYN, which functions both as the National Youth Council and the National Youth Umbrella Organization. The aims of the National Youth Council are to advocate for quality responses to youth problems in Croatia, to advise government officials on youth issues and youth strategies, and to monitor the implementation of national strategies.

Today more than sixty youth organizations participate in the network. Decisions are made using a very simple direct delegate system. With more than two hundred thousand beneficiaries of all the programs of member organizations, CYN works in several fields, including formal and nonformal youth education, independent culture and leisure time, youth mobility and tourism, sexual and reproductive health and rights, youth rights, employment and entrepreneurship, active youth engagement and political participation, and what the international community refers to as "dealing with the past" (work that is done in places with prolonged intergroup conflict to improve relationships among different social, ethnic, and religious groups). Work in these areas consists of advocacy and lobbying, analysis and research, education and training, and policy advising and monitoring. To do this work well, CYN continuously gathers ideas and input from youth activists, trainers, experts, researchers, and policy makers. Moreover, CYN has advocated for various national and local structural changes, has built strong partnerships in Croatia and abroad, and has supported several capacity-building programs for youth organizations and groups throughout Croatia.

Croatian Youth Network Achievements

Looking back on our work, Croatian Youth Network has achieved huge results, especially considering that the majority of work has been done on a voluntary basis with low financial and material support and little support from political structures. In the past nine years of our work, we have seen the following changes:

- Greater youth participation in decision-making bodies such as governmental advisory committees and local youth councils and advisory boards
- Structural changes in the legal system, such as the passage of the Act on Youth Advisory Boards, the Act on Volunteering, and the National Youth Action Plans, as well as national strategies on civil society development and strategic development of Croatia, local youth policy programs, and many other strategies related to youth

education, employment, culture, health, social care, civil society, and inclusion of citizens in shaping public policy

- The establishment of regional and local youth networks and councils (which has supported youth organizing and youth being able to solve problems in their communities)
- The education of hundreds of young people on democracy, human rights, civil society, political participation, volunteering in community, nonviolence, and peace building
- The education of numerous politicians, state and local officials, advisers, media representatives, and civil society organizations on youth participation and cooperation with youth groups
- The push for and leadership of many civic coalitions and initiatives
- Support for youth work and youth activities

Developing Youth Studies

The Croatian Youth Network continues to focus on developing systematic ways of introducing democracy into Croatia. Around the world, a primary way of doing this historically has been through formal education. Educational systems have been used successfully as a way to support social democratization. The CYN realized early on that changes in the Croatian educational system were necessary. Croatia has never had official education curricula on human rights, democracy, peace, active citizenship, or participation. These topics are not obligatory in elementary, secondary, or higher education curricula, although there have been nonformal programs supported by civil society organizations that youth could attend to develop their knowledge and skills in these areas. After years developing educational programs and conducting youth research, CYN and its partners saw a need to create an interdisciplinary educational program that supported more democratic ways of working with, understanding, and supporting young people.

More than a year ago, the Croatian Youth Network established the educational program Youth Studies in parallel with a lobbying and advocacy campaign to introduce civic education into schools at all levels (elementary to higher education). Both the advocacy and lobbying campaign and the Youth Studies program aim to support the development of knowledge, skills, and competences for young people's democratic citizenship. Given Croatia's history and recent violent conflict, both efforts focus on building young people's capacity in political literacy, political and democratic participation and decision-making processes, nonviolence, peace building and youth work in community, acceptance of interculturalism and diversity, sustainable development, and education for human rights. In addition, our approach combines experiential and cognitive learning theory and practice with action analysis and community-based research on youth issues. We pay additional attention to building a classroom that supports dialogic and collaborative learning among students, lecturers and trainers, mentors, and international experts.

The goals of our program are the following:

- To develop an understanding of individual responsibility in communities and participation in democratic actions and processes
- To build capacities in critical thinking, problem solving, research, and advocacy for sustainable solutions
- To deepen our understanding of youth policy development and social change by critically thinking about community (youth) work methods and techniques
- To deepen students' knowledge of their personal surroundings and communities

Currently, Youth Studies is a nonformal educational program focused on young people's everyday lives and ways to work with youth. The first cohort of twenty students participated in educational modules on civic or political education, youth participation and decision making, youth work and volunteering in community, and youth policy development. They attended lectures on youth and media, youth culture, subculture and counterculture, historical youth development, and opportunities for youth in the European Union. During the program, all students conducted research and policy analysis, and through support from Youth Studies staff and mentors, they created and implemented action plans either individually or in teams in local communities. Many of these projects have been published in our *Youth Studies Journal*, of which we have published three issues: "Youth and Society: Question of Identity," "Participation of Youth in Youth Policy Development," and "Education of Youth on Human Rights and Democratic Citizenship."

Currently, discussions about moving this educational program from nonformal to more formal settings are beginning. To keep the program available to young people currently working with nongovernmental organizations, we plan on maintaining the nonformal option. In addition, we are creating a formal program of study that will include greater emphasis on youth scholarship and youth work practice. Our hope is that several, if not all, Croatian universities will adopt this program as a regular offering during the academic year and as summer programs for students. What we do not want to lose as the program moves from nonformal to formal settings is the particular content of understanding young people's everyday lives and the collaborative learning methodology. Both currently face resistance in the Croatian academic system. We do not want to lose these because of the obvious benefits both have provided to the students in the Youth Studies nonformal program.

Youth studies students express their views:

- Lectures were useful, interesting, informative, and interactive. Lecturers were experts and they gave us more than expected.
- I have gained new focus and interests and that makes me extremely happy. I have found links with my old focus and reached another level of my knowledge.
- Individually oriented methods combining theoretical approaches and defining problems together with practical solutions and critical thinking. Excellent.
- Youth Studies was an excellent space for expression of ideas.
- Value of this group comes from diversity of people and fields they deal with. Our practical work reflects that diversity and shows their value of innovative youth dimension.
- Youth Studies was one of my biggest challenges. Mostly, I am fascinated with group participation.
- I am amazed by the group of different and engaged people. Topics were new to me; they were complex but interesting and motivating.
- The biggest pros of this program are its interdisciplinary approach and learning methodology.

As these comments suggest, students in the program support the content and methods. The program is unique in the Croatian context because it emphasizes issues that are not well integrated into formal education programs. It stimulates conversations around diversity. It builds capacity in information sharing, cooperation, and networking. It stimulates creativity. It also builds strong group cohesion, which we have found to be important for those who want to work on social change. For these reasons, we will continue to develop the Youth Studies program as a civic education program led by youth, for youth, and with youth.

Conclusions

The Croatian Youth Network emerged during the end of a prolonged and devastating war in Croatia. It succeeded through building strong collaborations and partnership and providing a space for young people, who had been marginalized, to participate in the country's democratic, economic, social, and educational development. Through its efforts,

Croatian youth policy has been created with young people from around the country rather than simply for them. The CYN continues to advocate for youth participation and seeks to improve the everyday lives of young people in Croatia by creating more opportunities for young people to thrive and, more recently, to have the opportunity to learn how they, too, can contribute to the ongoing development of their local and national communities.

Reflection Questions

- In your opinion, what are some long-term consequences of civic conflict and war on young people's willingness, ability, and opportunity to take on viable roles as community citizens?
- Is there a civic and citizen psychology?
- How does a nation's political culture work to invite, deflect, disenfranchise, and otherwise influence the possibilities of civic youth work?
- Is it more reasonable to restrict youth civic engagement to youth issues or to include any issues important to the young people who participate?
- Is it conceivable to you that a small-scale, small-group youth civic engagement project involving eight to ten teenagers can become a national mass movement? How might this happen?
- What must civic youth workers know about and know how to do before they begin work with a youth group? What is the worker's expertise: Youth work? Small-group work? Public policy making? Relevant youth issues? The politics of social change?
- How does the Croatian case help you answer the previous questions?
- Is it reasonable to expect that democratic civic practices in Croatia, Kenya, Northern Ireland, Israel, and Korea differ in details, if not in spirit and, thus, that civic youth work practice in each country is both somewhat similar to and different from practice in other countries? Is there only one legitimate model of civic youth work practice?

PART 4

Developing Civic Youth Work

Teaching and Training Civic Youth Workers

Creating Spaces for Reciprocal Civic and Youth Development

R. W. Hildreth
and Ross VeLure Roholt

How do you teach a youth worker to cocreate democratic space with young people? This seems counterintuitive—individuals are not spaces. We typically think of youth workers in terms of their social and professional role. Teaching youth workers is considered a process of helping them develop knowledge and skills of working with youth. Yet the very process of working with young people, doing things, in a physical and social space has the potential to transform these interactions into engaging spaces. We have all seen this—the classroom, youth program, or informal spaces that are alive, that are crackling with energy. Often, these engaging spaces are in deteriorating physical places—it is the work and youth workers that make them engaging! In this volume we have seen numerous examples of cases in which the "engaging" spaces are not merely physical ones. Katie Johnston-Goodstar and Joanne Krebs tell the story of how ordinary images in the media can be used to create spaces of questioning, critique, and critical thinking that support young people in telling their own stories and in beginning the process of taking on public issues and making a difference in ways that young people feel are important and necessary. Katie Richards-Schuster and colleagues also describe a space that is not simply physical but that emerges within a group of young people and supporting adults to change the culture with respect to attitudes toward sexual orientation.

However, we wish to push the metaphor a bit farther. We know that youth workers can help create engaging spaces, but we think that highly skilled practitioners actually embody an engaging space in their very being. The way they talk, walk, and carry themselves transforms the space for those around them regardless of any particular activity. We believe that this is a way of being-in-the-world that can be developed through study and practice. In this chapter we share our experiences with how this can be done.

We draw on our collective experiences over the past fifteen years working with individuals to become better youth workers. We do not offer a step-by-step recipe but rather a broader discussion of how we frame the development of civic youth workers, as well as a discussion of some essential ways we work with them. We have found that youth work is not something that can be taught directly. You cannot give a lecture on how to "become" a youth worker (at least an effective one). Yet we can all learn to be more effective in our work with young people. Because youth work is an embodied, contextual way of being with young people, teaching civic youth workers is more of an experiential process. It requires joining theory to practice to person (Higgs & Titchen, 2001). It requires the creation of spaces in which student youth workers can do youth work, reflect on how it went and what their efforts created, consider what they might do differently, and then bring this knowledge with them into practice. Thus, teaching is a matter not merely of preparation (although preparation is important) but also of supporting and creating space for ongoing reflective practice. The old aphorism "plan tight and implement loosely" captures how the process unfolds in training and teaching civic youth workers.

We begin here by discussing three elements that should be developed simultaneously—the what, how, and who of youth work—to build the curriculum of civic youth work. Then, we discuss some of the ways we have found to be useful in helping individuals become better civic youth workers. In the concluding section, we discuss civic youth work as a distinct orientation and field.

Three Elements to Develop Simultaneously

Educating for practice has unique characteristics. Higgs and Titchen (2001) describe education for practice as requiring a simultaneous focus on three forms of knowledge, what they call propositional, professional craft, and personal. Most often, higher education focuses on propositional knowledge forms, and examples of these can be found in any introductory textbook in every major in a university. This knowledge is the knowledge of theory, research, and scholarship broadly conceived.

Propositional knowledge that has been used in teaching civic youth workers includes informal and experiential education theory (Boud & Miller, 1996; Conrad & Hedin, 1982; Jeffs & Smith, 2005), participatory action research (Cammarota & Fine, 2008), youth civic engagement scholarship (Sherrod, Torney-Purta, & Flanagan, 2010), youth participatory practice (Checkoway & Gutierrez, 2006), youth studies theory (James, Jenks, & Prout, 1998), and youth development theory (Delgado, 2002; Hamilton & Hamilton, 2004). Our model of training civic youth workers includes propositional knowledge, but it does not focus on this alone.

In agreement with Higgs and Titchen (2001), we too have found that propositional knowledge, or the knowledge of "what," alone cannot support good practice. Although we did not create our educational programs on the basis of the scholarship of Higgs and Titchen (2001), we too have learned the value of bringing together learning about theory with learning about practice with learning about self. In college classes and community-based trainings, as instructors, we seek to combine knowledge "about," knowledge of how to do, knowledge of self (i.e., the youth worker). These three are simultaneously focused on in the youth work training and education we describe. Because of this, we lean more toward experiential and critical approaches to training civic youth workers. The aim is for participants to be able to do work with young people democratically and to understand how they can use who they are to facilitate this work, as well as to know about democratic theory and develop a beginning mastery of democratic skills.

Many youth work and youth development training programs focus simply on developing propositional knowledge (Huebner, Walker, & McFarland, 2003) or offer an array of activities to do with young people. Higgs and Titchen (2001) take issue with these forms of practice education because they often miss the critical element of practice—knowing how to do. Good and skillful practice in caring professions, which for us is one home of civic youth work, requires an ability to do good things in the right way. It joins together the technically correct with the morally good (Benner, 1984). This often requires knowing what to do in a specific situation or a particular context, with specific, actual young people. Generalized and theoretical knowledge can provide insights, but the knowledge we are after is learned by doing the work. When we train, we model civic youth work practice, and when we teach well, we cocreate supportive environments in which participants can rehearse their work and reflect on their practice, so that they too can develop a beginning to more advanced professional-craft knowledge of civic youth work.

Finally, good caring practice also requires a solid understanding of the personal knowledge we carry with us into our practice (Higgs &

Titchen, 2001). No matter how hard we try, we can never be objective practitioners. In our experience, when practitioners strive to be objective, they often end up being, at best, ineffective and, at worst, causing damage and harm to those in their groups.

From the beginning to the end of the education of civic youth workers, we invite participants to master a better understanding of their own biographies. We want to challenge the misconception that young people are more similar than unique. One way to introduce this is a better understanding of how we all come to the training with unique stories and experiences. These inform our decisions about what should be done and how. By not understanding their own biographies and experiences, participants often assume that what they think should be done comes from a universal understanding rather than from a personal and unique understanding. We have also found that once participants better understand their own biographies and experiences, they become more skillful at learning this about the youth they are working with—that is, who is in their group and what the particular group of young people might be interested in addressing.

In training we facilitate, and we constantly reflect on how well we are keeping these three ways of knowing in harmony. We look to the group to better understand which of the three we should focus on at a particular moment and which we can bring in later on. For each group, this varies, and therefore the training does too. What remains core to the trainings are the ways we approach the work and the overall process we implement.

Educating Youth Workers: Reorienting, Reframing, and Reflective Practice

Over the past fifteen years we have worked together and individually in a variety of settings to help individuals become better in their work with young people. We have worked in a number of different venues and settings—in informal conversations, in one-shot ninety-minute workshops, in college courses, with cohorts in a youth work major, and with professional development cohorts. Although these vary in duration and intensity, the same principles hold for all. In the following sections we discuss three approaches we use to teach youth workers.

REORIENTING

In trainings, workshops, and college classrooms, we often confront novices who want step-by-step guides to get started. And this makes sense; working with young people can be scary! This is especially true when you emphasize, as we do, working with rather than working on, and working democratically rather than working autocratically. When you are just beginning to learn this way of working with young people (as with most new learning), even for some experienced youth workers, many ask for straightforward and step-by-step instructions on what to do and when. Beginning students always ask for tools, techniques, and activities! Then there are those with more experience (e.g., coaches, recreation center workers, baby sitters), who generally are more relaxed and have a good feel for working with young people. For those who are comfortable and those who are uncomfortable with young people, we begin with a process of reorientation. But what does this mean? What is an orientation toward youth? And why might we have to do it?

In the most basic sense, an orientation is how we see young people. Crucially, our orientations always include taken-for-granted ways of looking at, being in, and responding to (youth in) the world. We often begin by asking students, "When you see a group of young people hanging out in the street late at night, what thoughts run through your head? What parts of your biography does this experience activate? Would it matter if these young people were in a small town or in the big city?"

How do we help youth workers reorient? We often start by disrupting relations of expertise. In any educational situation, there are expectations about how things are done. In general, there is an expert authority (e.g., instructor, facilitator, trainer) who is there to teach, to deliver a curriculum, or to implement a program for students and/or trainees. The trainees are there to receive wisdom, tips, activities, and insights and to put these into their practice. We resist this model, and good youth work should resist it as well.

We never walk in and say, "This is how you should work with youth, this is how you create an engaging space, and this is how to develop as a youth worker." Instead, we typically begin with a question: "We have ninety minutes here together. What do you want to do?" In doing so, we model youth work training as a cocreative process that builds participants' experiences and expertise. Of course, many people find this frustrating—some say, "Why don't you just tell us what to do?!" Our response to this is, "Well, what do you want to do?" Civic youth work education and training models practice how civic youth work could be done with young people. As facilitators, we model what civic youth workers sound like, look like, think like, see like, hear like, and so on, so that participants not only learn about the practice but also can experience what it might be like for young people to meet someone who responds to them in this way. This can often be scary or create confusion with participants. It is at these moments that the training really begins. We continue to invite participants into a democratic process in which shared understanding is built and shared decision making becomes normalized and routine. This means not giving up our authority but reimagining it in cocreative ways.

In this cocreative model for education and training, we help people explore their own experiences and taken-for-granted ways of being. In a real sense, participants' experiences represent our collective textbook. They provide the material for trainings to happen. Thus, we invite youth workers to explore, discuss, and analyze their own experiences, professional development, and biography. In other words, we cannot reorient without some sense of our basic orientations toward youth in the world.

REFRAMING

However, our basic orientations toward what we do and why we do it are not necessarily self-evident or straightforward. Not only is every description contextual and intensely personal; there are many different ways to describe every experience. This leads to our second essential way of working—reframing. To reframe is to open up different ways to make sense of one's experiences. Reframing involves, first and foremost, the process of listening to the frames that people use to talk about their experiences. These frames may be explicit or implicit—they represent one's basic orientation. The work or reframing involves repeating the original frame back to the participant. This often begins by the facilitator asking for permission to summarize what the participant just said. In our work, the first few days (and much of the training) are filled with "Let me see if I have this right—what I think you are saying is . . ."

Reframing helps enlarge experience by allowing us to see its broader and deeper dimensions. There are three basic ways to reframe experience. The first way is to draw on multiple perspectives. When youth workers describe their experience, we invite them to reconsider that experience from a different perspective. This could be as simple as asking, "How do you think kids in your youth group would describe this same experience? If you were your supervisor, how you would read this experience? What if you were the parent of a teenager?"

Another way to reframe draws on different domains and levels of experience, which can include educational, political, social, psychological, moral, and the like. Reframing can take the form of asking straightforward questions about a particular experience: "What do you think young people were learning?" (educational), "Who had power, who made decisions, and did this change over the course of the group?" (political), "What did this experience teach you about yourself, and what do you now know about yourself that you didn't necessarily know when you started the training?" (psychological), "How has the group changed since the training began?" (social), and "What was the right thing to do, what should we do, and what should you do?" (moral). However, we have found that direct questions are not always the best way to reframe. Rather, we try to repeat back what we heard in the descriptions and then turn it toward a different interpretive framing to enrich and extend our understanding of the experience.

An example of this is the epigraph to the introduction to this book, a quote from a South African youth worker in one of our trainings. During one of the conversations, this youth worker told a powerful story about how a group of young people joined together to address increasing levels of violence in their township. Another participant asked, "How did you know that they could do this?" The youth worker responded, "They could do it, so we let them." This sentence opened up a new framing when the facilitator offered an alternative framing: "We let them, so they could do it." Here the facilitator illuminated the way that figured worlds (Holland, Skinner, Lanchicotte, & Cain, 1998) are formed and can be transformed, simply by introducing a new way of understanding young people and how they become capable of doing something. Is it that they have developed the skill so they can now do it, or is it that people have supported their doing it so that now they can do it?

A final way to reframe involves more intensive explorations of the theories of youth, youth work, sociology, education, and politics. Theories are more explicit and systematic treatments of these dimensions of experience. Although we can talk about theories in any training setting, the integration of theory and civic youth work practice is better suited to longer-term efforts such as college courses, intensive workshops, professional development cohorts, and so on. To learn theory generally involves reading, which takes time to do and to discuss. This is not to say that one must learn theory first and then put it into practice; rather, it is better to put theory and practice in conversation with each other. By doing so, youth workers develop a grounded understanding of their work with youth.

A theoretical grounding gives youth workers a better understanding of the lives of young people and their social worlds. It allows them to tap into the deeper relations that structure their lived experiences. Sociological theories help youth workers develop a deeper understanding of the lives of young people—their social worlds, subcultures, location in larger discourses of power, and the social forces that perform opportunities and choice. Educational theory gives us better understandings of the multiple ways in which people learn and different approaches to teaching and learning, as well as to youth development. Social psychology helps us become more aware of how young people develop and how identities influence behavior. Political science and political sociology give us better understandings of youth policy, broader structures of power, and how young people might bring about social and policy change. Postmodern, poststructural, and critical theories examine the construction of the category of youth and how social discourse incites moral panic about youth.

Crucially, when youth workers have better theoretical understanding, they can test and challenge existing theories. They can also build grounded theory of youth work practice (Charmaz, 2006). In many settings, youth work teachers have become enamored of a particular theory. We believe that multiple theories should be put into conversation with one another so that youth workers can use all those theories to make sense of particular facts and situations.

REFLECTIVE PRACTICE

All this talk, all this reorienting and reframing, must be done in conjunction with actual, in-the-community youth work practice. Regardless of participants' skill level, we begin by talking together about our lived experiences with youth. These talks become part of our textbook. Our focus is to connect what we have learned together with theory about young people and with actual examples from our own practice. These are the case examples we use to reimagine what might be possible if a youth worker had made different choices. By constantly moving from the everyday realities of doing civic youth work to thinking about what we do, how we do it, and what happened, we make connections between theory and practice, and at times, we enlarge and deepen both. The hope is that youth workers develop complex repertoires of action, that they can make sense of any experience in multiple ways and have multiple ways of responding. No longer do they have to apply theory to practice. This becomes part of their very being, making them who they are. It is common to hear, "She is a natural youth worker; she makes it look easy." Indeed, some people have a great deal of natural ability. However, we also believe that most individuals, through careful and reflective practice, can develop mastery. What some people call natural we call expertise (Dreyfus & Dreyfus, 1991).

Conclusions

In this chapter, we have provided an introduction and overview to how we facilitate, train, and educate beginning to advanced civic youth workers and what we have learned about how to support and expand this practice. We challenge many of the typical ways youth workers are trained currently, with a focus on propositional knowledge, and instead broaden what they should know to include both professional craft knowledge, how to do the work, and personal knowledge of who is doing the work.

Reflection Questions

- What is the expertise of civic youth work?
- Why argue that experiential learning is the best learning strategy? Does this hold for all professional education, training, and development?
- What are the phenomenological and existential goals of the authors' pedagogy? What do they want the trained and/or expert youth worker to be able to do, and how do they want the trained worker to do this? Do the authors begin with clear outcomes for their students and trainees, or do they begin in other places?
- What do you suspect that the authors are not telling you when you read their philosophy, strategy, and practice for training beginning workers?
- Are there contradictions or tensions between being a student and a trainee in one setting and being a civic youth worker in other settings? In the United States and in other national contexts? What does one role (student) teach about the other (civic youth worker) and vice versa?
- Why does the civic youth worker have to know about youth?
- Are the essentials of civic youth work practice in the worker's knowledge, knowledge of civic youth work method, elsewhere, or all the above? What is the minimum one should know to be a (true) civic youth worker?
- Why do you suspect that the authors have been effective teachers and trainers of civic youth workers?

CHAPTER THIRTEEN

Understanding Civic Youth Work

Touchstones for Practice

Ross VeLure Roholt,
Michael Baizerman,
and R. W. Hildreth

In this chapter, we aim to contextualize the civic youth work stories with short practice stories on youth work and on the history of two movements directed at understanding, responding to, and changing young people, primarily in the United States, since the 1980s: healthy and/or positive youth development and youth civic development. Especially important in the latter, we believe, is our deepening and enriching conceptions of youth as citizens, in both narrow (role) and broad (civic engagement) terms, and our joining these in a view of youth as living citizen(ship). We offer also a brief introduction to civic youth work practice and to logic models that explicate basic elements of civic youth work programming. Along the way, we present our take on the practice stories as six themes that we find common across all of the examples.

Readers will note the limited discussion on youth, whether in developmental or in constructionist frames, the latter our preference, and the absence of the words adolescent and adolescence in our writing. To us, these refer to the scientific young person, whereas *youth* refers to the young person in everyday life. The former belongs to developmental science and is in its language game of applied science. Our ontological and existential frames are different and are grounded in interpretive science, with its task of understanding, not explaining scientifically.

What Is Youth?

Because this text is about young people and a particular way of understanding and working with them, we begin with a brief note about our understanding. We distinguish youth the individual from youth the age-graded (analytic) population group, from a youth age cohort of actual young people, from youth the metaphor, from youth the symbol, from youth as institutionalized sociocultural and sociolegal and sociopolitical social role(s). These frames of understanding are rarely explicit when scholarship, news, popular media, and the community talk about young people.

We understand youth as an age-graded social role, one also graded by sex, social class, and other social and cultural factors. This social view says that specific young people can be understood as doing and being "youth" because they are taking on and living a localized, time-bonded way of doing youth. Youth the social role is lived on the ground of everyday life in each young person's everyday life worlds (for more, see VeLure Roholt, Hildreth, & Baizerman, 2009). To understand a particular young person is to get at his or her living-self, that is, how that person experiences his or her body, time, space, and relationships (Van Manen, 1990): "This is what it is like to be her." One gets at this through narratives and anecdotes, stories, memories: this is who the young person is. Descriptions, not analysis, provide the data, the substance of him- or herself and his or her self.

Youth policy drives youth programming, and this drives youth programs and services that drive and are the contexts for youth work practice. All these are about changing young persons; these can also be directed at changing (the constituents of) the social role "youth." And they can also be about how individuals, groups, and populations take on and perform, that is, how they do youth. The current major frame for understanding young people and the life period of adolescence is the developmental science–based view and practice called healthy and/ or positive youth development.

What Is Positive Youth Development?

During the 1960s, youth were active as social disruptors and social reformers, disclosing through their activism what they considered the corruption, disingenuousness, fraud, and objectifications of the capitalist state of the United States. There were two main youth-led sociopolitical movements—anti–Vietnam War and the so-called counterculture (Baizerman, 1974). Then, adult commentators led a confused public in wondering how youth came to be so "rebellious," and they looked to answers in child rearing, parenting styles, and various other social institutions and social practices. Most, then and now, forgot that youth were venerated in the 1940s during World War II as soldiers and "patriots," whereas soon after, there was a moral panic (in the United States) about juvenile delinquency and youth gangs, followed by the period of counterculture activism and cultural innovation.

The 1980s and 1990s in the United States was a time of seeming youth political apathy, the opposite of sociopolitical activism. This was a return, it seemed, to the 1950s, when individualism and individual non-involvement in sociopolitical structures and processes was attributed to effects of World War II and the Korean War. This time, as in all other times, the adult public and researchers made a moral assessment of young people. "Something is wrong with our kids," they said. "They don't want to get involved," they claimed. "What did we or what are we doing wrong, as parents and as society? What should be done? What can be done? What must we do now?" American social science was joined to American pragmatism in a youth development industry. The term used to frame this was *positive and/or healthy youth development.*

Positive youth development presents itself as scientific and hence the most truthful frame for understanding young people and their needs. It can be read as a scientific social movement (Eaton, 1962). It views all young people metaphorically as having strengths (e.g., Silbereisen & Lerner, 2007). This sets it apart from earlier adolescent and youth development theory and change theories, which typically viewed adolescence as a problematic time and adolescents as deficient (Lerner, Wertlieb, & Jacobs, 2003).

In a positive youth development frame, young people are redefined from problems to resources to be developed (Hamilton & Hamilton, 2004). This redefinition of young people became clear in the goals of youth development programming. Typical youth program goals seek to reduce problematic behavior and outcomes for young people, such as drug use, sexual activity, and violent behavior. In the positive youth development framework, program goals describe what they want young people to be and become rather than what they want to prevent (Eccles & Appleton Gootman, 2002). Eccles and Templeton (2000) proposed what they called the 4 Cs of youth development: confidence, caring, competence, and connectedness. Lerner (2007) expanded on these, adding character and contribution for 6 Cs. Other frameworks also exist, including Connell, Gambone, and Smith's (2000) three goals for youth development programs: supporting young people in learning how to connect, be productive, and navigate through systems and life changes.

Recently, these two approaches—problem focused and positive youth development—were critiqued as inadequate (Ginwright, Cammarota, & Noguera, 2005). These authors disagree with the assumptions of both that something natural or essential exists in young people; young people are neither essentially problems nor resources (Cammarota, 2011). And neither theory adequately accounts for "the complex social, economic, and political forces that bear on the lives of urban youth" (Ginwright & Cammarota, 2002, p. 82). Both deficient and healthy youth development theories tend to make moral claims and call them scientific. Research on and with urban youth has raised important questions for youth development as an enterprise, and it shifts our focus from changing them to supporting them in understanding self, their community, and the larger world, as well as how they can change social conditions that negatively affect them. Supporting healthy development for urban youth requires helping young people develop and sustain positive identities, inviting and supporting their participation in improving their communities, and recognizing how others may also suffer from oppression (Cammarota & Romero, 2011). Civic and political development can be a space of youth development.

What Is Civic Development?

Positive youth development is a scientific, professional ideology and frame for understanding young people, their development, and best practices for enhancing healthy development. Civic life is one domain of everyday life wherein healthy development can be developed and expressed. It is focus and space for youth engagement, for doing civic work. For example, many of the stories have discussed how by being involved in advocating for policy change in Mississippi (chapter 4) or educating peers about safe driving (chapter 8), young people have supported their own development and created improved community conditions for themselves and others.

Civic development is a focus of youth civic engagement scholarship, yet it remains theoretically underdeveloped (Wilkenfeld, Lauckhardt, & Torney-Purta, 2010)—so too were (and are) interventions to enhance youth civic engagement. For example, interventions were designed to teach young people civic knowledge, skills, and attitudes, with an overall aim to reduce apathy toward normative political activity (e.g., voting, political campaigning). Research raised important questions about youth political apathy and interventions seeking to change youth apathy. First, scholarship indicated that young people may not engage in normative political behaviors as much as they used to, whereas most do participate in both community service and by volunteering. These findings challenged earlier conceptions that apathy was the problem, and they complicated the idea of youth civic development. Youth civic engagement came to be understood as more than just participating in normative political activity. Here was an opening to a richer theoretical understanding and to new policy and programmatic interventions.

Civic development refers to the practices and processes that invite and support young people to engage in the work of democracy (VeLure Roholt et al., 2009). This can include voting and political campaigning, as well as activities associated with building social capital (e.g., volunteering, service learning) and working to address community issues or problems (e.g., public work; Kari & Boyte, 1996). It is about understanding how people come to be "informed and committed participants in the affairs to the community" (Flanagan & Van Horn, 2003, p. 273). This expanded understanding of civic development raised questions about why young people gave so much time to volunteering and other service activities and so little time to formal political activity. Yates and Youniss (1999) suggest that young people participate in these activities because they are supported in doing so and because there are multiple pathways for their involvement, from church and community groups to school requirements. This differs significantly from political activity, for which few pathways exist for young people to meaningfully participate.

Civic development picks up on the development science themes of interdependence and bidirectionality (Lerner, 2006). Civic development is the result of interactions between the person and the context. Although there are individual dispositions and assets that support civic development, there are also social, cultural, and other contextual factors that enhance or inhibit young people's and the young person's civic development. This view led to a shift from teaching civic knowledge, skills, and attitudes to what and how these invitations and structures are supported in different contexts, and to what interventions are necessary to enhance these under different environmental configurations (Hart & Kirshner, 2009). To support civic development, it has been argued, the focus must be on both the individual and the context. Policy and community practice both are important for the civic development of young people (Youniss & Levine, 2009).

Two steps have been taken to get at the richness of the ideas and practice of civic youth work. Positive youth development and civic development were introduced and the relations between these were suggested. The next step is to bring these together with concepts of youth and of civic youth development.

What Is Civic Youth Development?

Much of the recent scholarship on civic development has focused on how to build young people's civic knowledge, skills, and attitudes. It has sought to explore what developmental opportunities are required for young people to identify with the common good and become informed and committed participants in their community (Flanagan & Van Horn, 2003). The practice stories in this volume are joined to ten years of research and evaluation work to describe how this can be done. This approach challenges the assumption that young people are not interested in, do not care about, and do not want to contribute to their communities. In this view, it is more likely that they have never been meaningfully invited to express their concerns or supported to do something about these. Here the focus shifts from individual outcomes such as knowledge, skills, and attitudes to considering how practice creates enabling environments that support young people's civic and political participation in their communities.

Civic youth development is also bidirectional in conception and practice (Lerner, 2006). Not only do young people shape their context; the context also shapes them. How does context shape civic youth development? Examples include the negative relationship between levels of poverty and high child saturation (e.g., the proportion of children to adults in any given area) and youth civic engagement (Hart & Kirshner, 2009). A lack of attention to youth issues also leads young people to not engage in formal politics (Gimpel & Pearson-Merkowitz, 2009). Furthermore, the general images of young people as risky, violent, egotistical, and immature (Males, 1999; Youniss & Levine, 2009) pose additional challenges to youth who want to be involved in their communities. They are viewed as scary, different, and unqualified. It is not surprising that young people we have talked with in our studies tell us that they do not have many opportunities to be meaningfully involved in their communities. Typically, they are viewed as spectators, victims, or criminals. Civic youth development begins by offering young people an invitation to participate as citizens. All the practice stories begin by assuming young people have something to offer and (but not only) something to learn. They directly challenge the negative images of young people and show how the young people figured out ways to overcome other barriers and deflections from participating in civic and political work present in their context.

Youth civic engagement does not take place in neutral environments. This challenges the more romantic images of youth civic engagement as radical or as undisciplined or as too controlled by adults, and it places the work closer to other, adult political efforts and activity. By engaging in civic and political activity, young people come into contact with both allies and opponents. When young people begin to make strong arguments for their political positions and causes, what they assume to be their basic rights, including their right to express their opinion, are taken away by adults. To support civic youth development, young people need opportunity, time, and support to reclaim their basic rights and to work toward social change.

To support young people's active involvement in civic and political activity and to prevent further nonengagement or disengagement, civic youth development is typically a small-group activity. Civic youth development begins by building relationships and trust among group members. The group provides a safe(r) space in which young people can participate in civic and political work (VeLure Roholt, Hildreth, & Baizerman, 2003). It is a rehearsal space in which they can improve their public voice prior to making a public statement and doing other public work (Boyte & Skelton, 1997).

Building trust, relationships, and a group is recognized as important to sustaining most civic and political work. Lederach (2005) calls relationships "the center of social change" (p. 75). In civic youth work, the group provides a space for extended discussions about what its members want to do and how they want to do it. Most solutions to pressing issues emerge "from relational resources, connections, and obligations" (Lederach, 2005, p. 77). The group provides a stable environment in which to address and work, often in a fluid and hostile political context. Within the group, solutions can be worked out and actions taken, and when successful, celebrated. When actions fail, the group can provide support and encouragement to try again. The group can be a microdemocracy. It is in the group that members can learn and be supported in continuing to engage in the larger work of democracy in the larger community.

Civic youth development requires action. It is not enough to talk about issues; young people must also be provided with the invitation and support to act on the issues that they find personally meaningful. Civic youth development is strengthened when young people engage in the cyclical processes of discussion, analysis, reflection, and action (Freire, 1970). In contrast to much that has been written about it, youth civic development occurs by focusing on supporting young people in engaging civic and political issues, in taking action on those issues, and then in reflecting on the action they took. Conrad and Hedin (1982) proposed this idea long ago on the basis of their evaluation of experiential education programs. They found that "change[s] in behavior often precede rather than follow changes in attitude" (p. 66). They go on to critique the traditional form of citizenship education, which "proposes that instruction in proper attitudes about personal and social obligations will lead to responsible behavior" (p. 66). Responsible civic action by individuals and small groups seems to be best learned and practiced in small groups, with adult guidance. Civic youth worker is one type of adult presence. It is to that topic that we move next.

If civic youth development, that is, lived citizenship, is a goal and if youth policy and derivative programs and services are directed toward that goal, then civic youth work is the praxis and the practice that can best make this happen. We get to a discussion of that work by beginning with two general introductions about work with youth and youth work.

What Is Work with Youth?

The phrase "work with youth" is in the vocabulary of human services. It is more than and different from being a friend of a young person. It implies a contractual relationship, explicitly or implicitly, to intentionally be with a youth by "doing" something with this young person. The phrase can refer to volunteer and paid work both, typically within an organization. In this phrasing, usage gets closer to the exclusive auspices of agencies and/or organizations with respect to "work" and on whose behalf that work is undertaken. At this time, society is hypervigilant about adults having unsupervised contact with teens (and children). This moral panic pushes the phrase "work with youth" into the realm of human services, and often into the realm of youth work.

What Is Youth Work?

Youth work is a job, youth work is a field of practice, and youth work is a semiprofession in the human services, an occupation that does not have all the criterion of a profession but also is not fully nonprofessional—all similar yet have important differences. Here the focus is not on work with young people but on the field of practice and the semiprofession—there are a variety of terms for this that vary by country (e.g., child-care worker, youth pedagogue, teen recreation worker, high school teacher) and by setting (e.g., child-care agency, hospitals, juvenile court, sports, ministry).

The field of practice and the semiprofession of youth work are in overlapping families of resemblance (Manser, 1967) in that in the United States there is no single, consensual, legitimate definition, philosophy, methods, employing organization, and the like. Both are more like relatively open spaces than closed formal occupations or exact sets of activities. In their current forms and meanings in the United States, each includes a broad range of occupations in a wide range of settings, including an array of semi- to full professions, groups, and organizations with different goals, philosophies, methods, funding, and so on.

In the youth work field of practice and in youth-serving agencies, youth work clearly means human service practice, a practice that can range from being similar to social work to being similar to counseling and recreation, and having roles similar to that of a probation officer. It all depends on setting: the particular employing organization and its funding sources, its purpose and/or mission, its goals, and its methods.

In the US youth work field of practice and in youth-serving agencies, youth work is a more or less intentional practice of working with young people to meet a vast array of purposes and goals, using a range of methods, and it is carried out by adults (typically) who have some to no academic training in the area but perhaps some in-service training from the employer, such as on how to do the work that the employer, employing agency, and/or funder requires.

In other countries, including Canada, Norway, the Netherlands, and Northern Ireland, this (seeming) confusion does not exist to the same degree, because youth work is an occupation with legitimized academic and professional training, and with employment by a smaller range of legitimized and funded groups and organizations. There are also professional groups, professional courses, and legal frames for practice.

Currently, policy changes and organizations in many countries are converging, with the result that, at best, youth work (as a profession) in after-school recreational and related work is marginalized and schools have after-school supervision of children and adolescents under plans such as daylong learning and the extended school day. This shows that although both school and recreation are youth work fields of practice, there are great differences between agencies and fields of practice in their goals, philosophies, and methods of what is done, to whom, when, where, how, and why. In practice and in everyday talk within and outside the field and the profession, school is not youth work! Youth work takes on a tighter meaning and practice in the context of citizenship. With this scaffolding in place, we introduce civic youth work and the civic youth worker.

What Is Civic Youth Work?

Civic youth work is the intentional practice of inviting, supporting, preparing, and evaluating young persons to be active citizens now and to continue to be lifelong citizens. It is an emergent field of practice and emergent type of semiprofessional youth work, defined first by VeLure Roholt et al. (2009; see also VeLure Roholt & Cutler, 2012).

Civic youth work is part pedagogy, part social action, and all praxis—it joins the knowing and doing of an individual young person or group of young people on a topic of interest and concern, a topic that calls or addresses their interests and compels them to act.

Civic youth work is like general youth work in that the youth worker works with young people, partly inviting, coaching, and teaching about normative approaches to understanding social troubles and social problems in the youths' near or faraway environments (see chapters 2–4), and partly inviting, coaching, and teaching about nonviolent (see chapters 3, 4, 10, and 11) and socially just ways to respond to the issue, topic, or problem that the youth or youth group took on or engaged (see chapters 6 and 8).

Civic youth work is unlike classical and typical US youth work practice because it is based less on perspectives, goals, values, methods, and skills basic to human service work and more on those basic to social and political action work. However, civic youth work is grounded in a belief that the civic development of a young person is a worthy personal and social good, and as such, it is an element of the youth's overall sociomoral development. In reflecting on civic youth work as a pedagogy, it can be considered a type of experiential learning (Conrad & Hedin, 1982), or what used to be called action learning (Revans, 1983), and it is similar to the best practice of service learning (Waterman, 1997). Its practice contrasts clearly and sharply with most school-based civics education teaching styles and substance in the United States, and it is more similar to civic education outside of the United States, such as in Scotland and Ireland. When performed as we advocate, the actual work feels more youth work–like than school teacher–like.

Understood by its philosophy, purpose, value nexus, method, and skills, civic youth work clearly falls in the family of youth work practice, although it is also different enough from most other practices to be recognized as its own type of practice, as we recognize here. Table 13.1 summarizes the two ideal youth work practices.

Civic Youth Work, Vocation, and Citizenship

An element of the civic youth work ethos is vocation—calling, address, and response. Vocation is a venerable concept for understanding the citizen's role and how individuals come to be compelled to become— that is, to do and to be—living citizens.

Vocation in both religious and secular uses is a call from God or an address from one's everyday life world or the larger world. Both religious and secular vocations compel one to discern the truth of the call and address and, having done that, to act to fulfill the invitation, call, and address: the individual takes on a social station, or a social role, and becomes that role, thinking, feeling, and acting in everyday life from within that role. In this way, we are deeply and profoundly social and cultural beings. Vocation joins the person to social role and to everyday life. In this way, people with vocation craft themselves in their response to the compelling call.

In a vocational frame, citizen becomes grounded to everyday life as a compelling call to do and be citizen in age-(in)appropriate ways.

Table 13.1. Comparing Classical and Civic Youth Work

	Classical and/or typical youth work	*Civic youth work*
Philosophy	Youth centered and youth involved	Young people are citizens now!
Purpose	Supports personal and social development	Invite and support young people's civic and political development, and community and social change
Value nexus	Accepting and valuing young people	Cocreating, community change, social justice
Method	Informal and nonformal learning, experiential education, conversation, relationship building	Experiential and community-based learning, democratic group work, youth participatory action research and evaluation, critical education
Skills	Animating, facilitating	Cocreating, cosustaining, reflecting on the effectiveness of social action, reading the external sociopolitical environment

When youth are living citizens, they are following the narratives of their self; they are "doing" citizenship as teenagers or young people in their everyday life worlds and beyond. A civic youth worker advising a small group of youth can facilitate the call and address to make a difference in the world. The youth worker cocreates with the group democratic and engaging spaces.

Engaging Spaces: Civic Youth Work Practice

Se hace camino al andar.
(You make the road by walking it.)
—*Antonio Machado*

Just as you make the road by walking it, you make the space by making it! As metaphor, engaging spaces are spaces that are personally meaningful; they capture our attention and interests. In these spaces we are engaged! Engaging spaces are also cocreative, processual, and fluid; they develop through engagement with others.

Space is typically conceived as place. It is bounded, contained, located; it is here or there, in or out. We present an alternative view of space here.[1] In civic youth work, youth workers and young people together bring spaces into existence; that is, they cocreate the spaces. Even though there may be a place or venue in which youth work occurs, that place does not constitute a space before the cocreative act. Youth workers have a special responsibility to keep the space open and available and to facilitate the ongoing cocreation of necessary space. We believe that this is a process that anyone can learn.

Cocreating engaging spaces begins with young people's lives, their experiences, problems, wants, and needs. This something-we-want may come from a desire to make something happen or to change something, such as how to reduce fatal accidents among young drivers (chapter 8). Civic youth work is a group practice. If the civic youth worker and the youth group want to work on teen driving safety, then the group will imagine where in the material world of cars, roads, drivers, police, and so on, there might be a space to work on that project. Or we might imagine this something-we-want as something we want to do in a particular place, such as a museum (chapter 3). Something-*we*-want means that the thing that is wanted results from a group process between youth worker and young people, who work to define what compels them, what they want to do, what change in the material world and its people they want to try to bring about, what real world need or want they want to meet and fulfill.

So, how do civic youth workers bring about new spaces for engagement? As in the epigraph to this section, "we make the road by walking." That is, we bring into existence the space we want and/or need for our work by doing the work, by responding to the ordinary needs and/or wants that propelled or maybe compelled us to act to bring about that which we want to do or that which we want to change.

Practice Themes of Civic Youth Work

These general introductions to civic youth work as a process of co-creating and co-sustaining with young people spaces for group work on issues of compelling concern and interest to them do not tell much about how this work is done. The chapters do tell some of this, but they

---

[1] Sources for this section include Evans and Boyte's (1986) classic work *Free Spaces*. The scholarly literature on space, place, site, and venue in geography and the social sciences is immense.

lack the detailed and concrete stories of who, when, where, how, and for what reasons, and to what effects; they lack the concrete, particular everyday realities of the work.

However, in this chapter, we do provide a link between the general introduction on how to do this work and the concrete and specific. To do this, we describe six overarching themes of civic youth work practice that we have drawn from an analysis of the case studies. We then bring the themes and stages of civic youth work practice together with programmatic logic models in a brief introduction to the ethos, craft orientation, and practices of civic youth work.

However, there are some problems that arise in presenting the themes here. For example, there may be a danger in the limited variety and location of the policy, programs, projects, and training efforts. Obviously, the cases in this book are a sample, from an unknown universe of civic youth work practices worldwide. In this sense, the six themes can be considered hypotheses on the characteristics of civic youth work worldwide and across domains of work with youth. A second problem is related to sampling: civic youth work is a normative, moral practice, as is all youth work, which can be effective locally, especially when the practice fits with local social, cultural, and political life, when it is socially and culturally appropriate. It may be that our dialogue with the authors brought out these six themes, thus distorting the authors' actual ways of working because they named their actual work in our terms and located it in our categories. A third problem has to do with distortion. Is civic youth work "civic youth work" if it meets the test of our six themes? That is, is our notion cultural bound? Related, is a fourth concern: Are we proposing that there is an essence to civic youth work and that to be called civic youth work a particular effort must have that essence? Or are we proposing that there are essentials that a civic youth work effort must meet to be able to claim that it is civic youth work? Our position is that civic youth work, as youth work in general, is best understood as a family of resemblances (Manser, 1967) in which some civic youth work efforts share certain elements but not others with some or all other civic youth work programs, policies, and practices. Although these issues may be of interest primarily to academic scholars of youth work and civic youth work, the substance of the issues is real and immediate for practitioners too. All of this gets at the questions of what youth work is and what good youth work (practice) is. And it gets at questions of cross-national and cross-cultural practice, including the question of what we can learn from and offer to others working in other countries and with a variety of populations. These are perennial issues that we treat as concerns here, and hence we have responded to them, if only briefly and incompletely.

The practice of cocreating youth spaces can be found almost anywhere where there are youth workers and young people. As the chapters in this book reveal, doing this work does not require a particular physical location or a particular youth work approach (e.g., civic engagement, leadership development, arts enrichment). This work is done in schools, community centers, and museums. Nor must the work be specific to a particular activity. Examples in the book show ways to support youth participation in research, program evaluation, the arts, policy making, peace building, social change, and community building. Although spaces such as these can occur just about anywhere, they do not occur naturally—skilled youth workers doing intentional work construct them. A particular program type (e.g., arts based, service learning, youth organizing) in itself does not bring about such spaces. Instead, the spaces are created in and through particular youth work practice. As the stories in this book teach us, without such intentional work, there are no engaging spaces. What is this practice? Is it teachable? What do the stories here teach us about how engaging spaces can be cocreated and cosustained?

Engaging youth spaces are brought into existence by how a youth worker practices. First, in agreement with good general youth work practice, creating engaging spaces begins by demonstrating care for young people and building trusting relationships with them (e.g., Maier, 1990; Mayerhoff, 1971). If these things are missing, engaging spaces can be neither created nor sustained. But demonstrating care is the simple first step. The chapters herein suggest six other youth worker choices and practices that create and sustain engaging youth spaces. These include the choices to cocreate with young people, to focus on inquiry, to take action, to encourage risk taking, to listen for vocation, and to support public performance. These six practices are found within and across all the chapters herein. We now examine each of the six practices.

COCREATING WITH YOUNG PEOPLE: DOING THE WORK TOGETHER

Involving young people to participate in decisions that affect them has become common among programmers and funders. It has been codified in the UN Convention on the Rights of the Child and has been used as a basis for policy making and policy and program evaluation in several countries. But as a practice choice, this involvement is less understood. The chapters in this book describe how youth workers can make youth involvement real in programs. This is an alternative: in most youth programs, adults develop program plans before working with groups of actual young people. Although many of the chapters discuss work in formal settings, civic youth work can work in most settings. As seen, workers engage young people—they work *with* them—rather than providing a service to young people. A youth participant from Manchester Craftsmen's Guild (chapter 7) expressed this well: "We have the same opportunity to create something [as adults do]."

A common practice in the chapters here is working with young people to figure out what they want to do together. This process is variously called creative work, critical practice, collaborative work, and public work. In this work, young people have many opportunities to shape the direction and focus of their individual and collective work as a group. They contribute to creating the group ethos, and they take over when willing and capable. Rather than occupying static roles, youth take on roles based on the group's wants and needs. For example, at one moment, they may be a student and then moments later a teacher. Several of the chapters provide examples of this role shifting. A good example comes from Northern Ireland (chapter 3), where young people were at one moment museum visitor and soon after museum exhibit curator. In the United States, in Mississippi, young people shifted from student to policy maker to social change activist on gay, lesbian, bisexual, and transgender issues (chapter 4). Also, in the United States, in Minnesota, young people shifted from students to critical researchers to policy advocates (chapter 2).

This role shifting occurs when youth workers pay attention to what is known as incidental learning (Turner, 2006). Incidental learning occurs without planning and emerges often from and in discussion, reflection, and planning work with youth. In cocreating with youth, workers notice what emerges in conversations, and this becomes a priority. Adults do not teach the group; they facilitate the group's reflection on what they are learning—as individuals and as a group—and what they, individually and collectively, want to do given what they have learned together. Although many of the programs that the chapters describe have predetermined foci, typically driven by funders (e.g., students had to focus on heritage in the project described in chapter 3 on Northern Ireland), the programs typically did not have a predetermined outcome required of the group. The group, as a group, could decide how it would meet these external expectations in the context of what they wanted to do as a group. The youth worker often facilitated this joining of what was expected with what was wanted. For example, in Israel, groups of young people were asked to focus on road safety, but they were allowed to create their own response to the problem (chapter 8), and in Minnesota, students at the New City School were asked to help develop policies for the school (chapter 6). Cocreation can easily be grounded in group inquiry.

ONGOING INQUIRY: OBSERVATION, ANALYSIS, ACTION, REFLECTION, AND QUESTIONING

Youth workers can choose to focus on asking questions rather than on giving directions or answers, as the stories in this book show. Questions were the way the work started with evaluation (chapter 5), action research (chapter 2), policy work (chapter 4), and museum work (chapter 3). Questions keep the space open, democratic, analytic, and reflective. In a deep sense, workers come to the young people as an embodied question or interrogatory, not as an answer. Their presence asks young people to choose and to act (in existential terms).

Questions open up time and space for young people to reflect on their work, to critique what they have planned, and to design and redesign when necessary. Questions create a group process that is iterative and incremental rather than totalizing. Youth work together, building in the moment; the results are not predetermined. The shape, texture, and speed of the work is jointly decided and acted on, always with an ear and eye to learning through attention, analysis, and reflection, led at first by youth worker and then by group members.

Through the use of questions, reflection comes to be ordinary and ongoing. The value of reflecting on one's work is well known and basic to experiential learning and participatory action research and evaluation. In these chapters, youth workers did not want reflection to be only part of their work; instead, they chose to have reflection be the central theoretical and practical focus of their work. They aimed at praxis, the joining of action with reflection (Freire, 1970). To create praxis, youth workers had to avoid what Freire (1970) calls verbalism, or remaining stuck in talking about what you are going to do, and activism, or acting without thought or consideration of alternatives. By choosing to create praxis, youth workers focus on reflecting on what the group is going to do, is doing, and has done, and on supporting the group as it takes action.

TAKING ACTION: DOING THE WORK

In all the chapters here, young people took action, whether challenging unjust policies and unsafe environments for gay, lesbian, bisexual, and transgender youth in Mississippi or creating a museum exhibit. Young people were not only learning about something or receiving training; they were actually doing the work. In learning theory, these chapters are about experiential learning. All programs described here accept and live out the basic idea that action precedes attitude change (Conrad & Hedin, 1982). To support young people's active learning through engagement, youth workers chose to support group actions rather than to focus on longer periods of training or passive, school-like education.

It is in and through action that learning can happen for young people, the larger group, and youth workers. In taking action, young people begin to learn how they can transcend what is typically expected of them individually and as a group; as a group, they begin to learn how to support group members and the group's overall work; and youth workers learn how to best support the group and the talents of each member. Youth workers stop and reflect with the group, when the action succeeds and when it fails. Both are opportunities for the group members to learn about what they can do to enhance their work and, often, to move beyond what they believed possible before they began the work.

Taking action also challenges both young people and the community's idea of what youth is and what can be expected of and from them. Both youth and adults too often believe that youthhood is a time of waiting, of being not ready for prime time (Konopka, 1973). This assumption is challenged directly when youth workers support and encourage young people to take action, even when the group is not certain whether it will achieve its goals. The purpose here is to have action experiences, experiences of acting as a group and as individuals, and of doing something more than talking about issues, as Freire (1970) warned against. A result of group action, whether or not the action is successful in meeting the group's goals, is to challenge how adults and young people contest dominant and inaccurate images of youth as lazy and apathetic people (Males, 1999) who do not experience or share a compelling interest in making a better world and, given their age, who do not have the experience or skills to do so.

SUPPORT RISK TAKING: GOING BEYOND THE SAFE AND BORING

The stories described in the chapters can be read as young people taking risks. Group participation typically required that youth challenged societal expectations of age and competence, which was risky for both youth workers and young people. The stories are not about age or age-appropriate youth roles or activities, both of which are popular in work with youth and in developmental theories. Instead, these young participants took on challenges new to them and unusual for young people in their local area.

Young people in these chapters were invited to work outside of their comfort zones in responsible ways. Among the acts and actions that they likely viewed as risks were giving their opinions on issues that mattered to them and putting themselves at the center of the social issue they were working on. For many youth, it is risky to begin to tell others what they deeply care about, and for many others it is even more of a risk to work publically and visibly to address what they view as a compelling social issue. The young people in Mississippi took risks by naming themselves to the larger world as gay, lesbian, bisexual, transgender, or allies and then they continued to take risks by working to change the larger social climate for such youth. Other young people took risks that may not appear to us or other adults as profound. In one evaluation project, young people were responsible for collecting data necessary for their project (chapter 5). Some young people might experience this as risky: if they did not collect the data or if they lost the data, the entire project could be in jeopardy. In the Manchester Craftsmen's Guild (chapter 7), youth took risks in presenting their art for public critique. In Northern Ireland (chapter 3), the risks young people took could have led to violence. All the programs described herein occur in a context in which young people both were doing things, acting, in ways beyond what is typical for them and in ways which may be scary for them, and were taking on new roles, many of which had not been previously available to them or their peers. Thus, they did not know how to perform these roles, and learning to do so, is a risk in itself: it takes courage to take on a new role.

The youth workers invited and supported this risk taking. They and the group together figured out what each new role required of them— what and how to think, feel, and act. They learned to work safely in what could be dangerous territory. In this way, they learned to accomplish new tasks, and they thereby learned new skills. Workers assumed that young people could do this social and psychological work and understood the value for them, for other young people, and for the larger community. Taking on new roles is also a strategy for inviting one to a vocation.

LISTENING TO THE VOCATION

The first requirement of youth workers is that they listen to what young people say and what young people mean. They do not silence the voices of young people but choose instead to work with young people to build a specialized vocabulary and interpretive frames and orientations that fit the larger ideas that the group is talking about and wanting to learn more about. Youth workers also pay full attention to young people's questions, and they treat those questions as relevant and substantive. The youth workers honored and witnessed young people by hearing, being addressed by, and responding to their queries. This is the core of any youth work practice. Here, this practice is also crucial because questions may lead to higher risk to youth workers themselves and their work, but they also may build the group's action agenda.

PERFORMING PUBLICALLY

One focus of engaging spaces is youth development; a second is making a contribution to the near or greater community. To us and to the chapter authors, these things are reciprocal. In every story, young people made a valuable contribution to their community. For example, the Manchester Craftsmen's Guild continues to create high-quality art exhibits in and for the community; young people working in the Northern Ireland museum created heritage exhibits for the whole community at a time of lessening intercommunity violence. Other young people worked to address the social problems of road accidents or to improve the living conditions of gay, lesbian, bisexual, and transgender youth through policy advocacy and social activism. These practices support youth development and social development both and at once in reciprocity (Pittman, 1991).

Public performance has the added benefit of reducing the age separation that is so common throughout the everyday lives of youth and adults. Public acts work to reconnect young people to larger adult social worlds. As young people work on their projects, they enter into social spaces that are too often reserved for adults.

FROM CIVIC YOUTH WORK PRACTICE THEMES TO MODELS FOR PRACTICE

In these six themes we find the ethos, craft orientation, and practices of civic youth work as Weberian ideal (see Gerth & Mills, 1958). In a sense, we are in an analogous model of practice to that of the applied philosophy school of therapy (Caruso, 1964; Frankl, 1969) and some aspects of existential therapy (Cooper, 2003) in that the concrete, particular, and practical are tightly hitched to the abstract, general, and theoretical. In civic youth work the abstract and theoretical are part sociobehavioral and developmental science and part philosophical anthropology and notions from ontology and epistemology, both existential and phenomenological; however, the particular and practical are connected to social and political group work, community organizing, and practice skills in democratic, social, and community development.

The six themes must be treated as a whole, an integrated, interpenetrating reticulum in which there are multiple synergistic interactions. Simply, each theme needs and plays off the others for the whole to work and for any one theme to be effective in practice.

The final sections of this chapter contain the promised civic youth work logic models and an overview of civic youth work ethos, craft orientation, and practice.

Civic Youth Work Programming Logic Model

It is increasingly common in human services and youth services to require that programs and projects explicate and provide a program logic model for funding and evaluation (Knowlton & Phillips, 2009). The now-classic program logic model moves in time and action from inputs to activity to outputs to outcomes, with the latter typically divided into short, medium, and long term. Least obvious are outcomes that are measurable. Usually, youth agencies and workers focus on outputs, such as attendance and frequency of participation and meetings, rather than outcomes, such as changes in understanding and gaining mastery of skills, when advocating for funds, and they focus on activity rather than outcomes when describing their work. Funders no longer accept these diversions. Note that in any program logic model, items can be moved across categories, when warranted; for example, "changes in the young person" can be a measurable output or an outcome.

The program logic model in table 13.2 summarizes the stories contained in the chapters of this book and our conception of civic youth work programming. Caveat emptor! This model is schematic and intended to stimulate thinking about civic youth work.

Civic Youth Work: Ethos, Craft Orientation, and Practice

Any human services practice can be understood by examining its ethos, craft orientation, and practices. Here we sketch these for civic youth work.

ETHOS

The ethos of a practice is its philosophical understanding of its purpose, its core values and beliefs, and its assumptions about the larger world and its particular world. In science, this includes notions of the human being, of psychology, of how individuals change, and the like. For civic youth work, the core ethos includes notions about youth as individual, as population, as metaphor, and as symbol, as well as notions about age and development.

The civic youth work ethos is a conception of youth as a socially constructed, age-specific social role that individual young people take on and live in everyday life in socially normative ways, thus giving cultural meaning to the role for themselves and for adults. It is a conception of the young person and youth as interested, available, and able to take responsibility for responding to everyday and larger public issues

Table 13.2. Civic Youth Work Programming Logic Model

Inputs	Activity	Outputs	Outcomes (by different levels of analysis)
Youth worker Young people Program context and policy Philosophy of civic youth work practice Practice approaches and methods	Group work Team building Critical questioning Joint decision making Building shared understanding	Changes in youth worker skills Changes in young person Changes in program Changes in youth work philosophy Changes in practice methods and approaches	Individuals (e.g., young people taking on citizen role, lived citizenship) Group (e.g., improved ability to work as a team, handle conflicts, implement social action) Theory (e.g., ongoing refinement of civic youth development theory) Program (e.g., increase support for democratic and critical youth work) Strategy for organization development (e.g., increased commitment to democratic ways of working with young people) Youth worker (e.g., increase skill in co-creating, co-sustaining social action, strengthening belief in civic youth work) Civic youth work practice (e.g., increased clarity of why to do this work, what the work entails, and how to do it)

that compel them to act. Young people are there, ready to be called and addressed by their world and the larger world.

CRAFT ORIENTATION

The craft orientation (Bensman & Lilienfeld, 1973) of a practice is how the practice (e.g., profession, field) defines its work and its stance toward that work and toward the larger world. The ethos and craft orientation of a practice overlap. In the human services, each semiprofession or full profession defines for itself its craft orientation. This has resulted in multiple frames of craft orientation within and across many professions. The same is true in general youth work (VeLure Roholt & Baizerman, 2012). We propose that the ethos and craft orientation of civic youth work overlap and in turn are the substance of its practices. That is, the six themes constitute ethos and craft orientation, and how they are put into the world with young people is the core of civic youth work practice (table 13.3).

PRACTICE

Each of the six themes is operationalized as a civic youth work way of working with young people. That is, each theme is activated as a practical way of working, as a skill, as expertise, as an ideal practice (Gerth & Mills, 1958). Ideal strategy abstracts and distorts elements of the actual so as to emphasize other elements; ideal does not mean "best."

Civic youth work practice makes concrete, specific, and particular—that is, real—the theme of seeing young people as capable and responsible and able to make a difference on issues that call or address them when they in a group cocreate and cosustain space for working out and acting out their considered response (VeLure Roholt et al., 2009). In the

Table 13.3. Ideal Youth Work Practices

Ethos	This is what we believe	Youth is a socially constructed, age-specific social role
Craft orientation	Six themes	Cocreating, risk taking, public performance, listening to vocation, taking action, ongoing inquiry
Practice	Putting all of this into practice	Seven stages of civic youth work

following sections we provide a seven-stage process that we take as basic to civic youth work practice.

Developing Group Wants and Needs

Civic youth work begins by talking with young people not only about issues they want to address but also about how they might want to address them. Johnston-Goodstar and Krebs (chapter 2) describe how this took place in a critical media literacy project. They openly discussed with young people what engagement meant to them and discovered that some typical practices often supported by youth workers and youth scholars may not be the best fit for young people or their specific contexts. Strategies such as public protest created the possibility of harm for them and others involved, given their gender, race, and class, as well as the relationships among young people in a particular neighborhood and local police and school officials. Instead, the group cocreated an action that considered these risks and supported the change young people wanted to make.

Imagining Spaces for Group Action

Finding spaces that support youth action is challenging and fraught with difficulties. Too many people do not image young people as political and social actors, and they become nervous when they are doing something out of the ordinary, even when what they are doing is for the benefit of the community. Germanic (chapter 8) found ways to navigate this difficult terrain by engaging local leaders and partnering with organizations throughout Israel. By doing so, young people had strong support in taking meaningful action on an issue that was compelling to them—road traffic safety.

Making Space by Doing the Work

As we have already discussed, civic youth work is about doing real work. Space is created when young people do work that matters to them and to others. Shumer (chapter 5) demonstrates how he made space with young people in the two evaluation projects he facilitated. Together, they made evaluation space by constantly asking questions, and then they made civic and political space as they began to talk about the reactions of teachers and the changes they wanted to see in their neighborhoods. In working on the project, young people learned about evaluation practice and began to imagine where they could work to improve their own communities. By doing the work, they also came to understand that they could make changes: they were able.

Sustaining the Space by Ongoing Work

Spaces do not continue when the work stops; they are sustained only through ongoing work. The Mississippi Safe Schools Coalition (chapter 4) shows how safer spaces for gay, lesbian, bisexual, and transgender youth were sustained because young people continued to work on this issue. By working first to build a coalition and then to create mechanisms to monitor local situations for young people and to advocate for policy change, and finally to develop processes that allowed for increasing numbers of young people and allies to support the work, they sustained an active, civic, political, and democratic space. This is easy to imagine, and young people have far too much experience with what happens when ongoing work ends.

Linking the Space to Larger Worlds

All these stories told in the chapters of this book are powerful because they did not occur in isolation or silence. Each project chose to make the issues it was concerned about visible and vocal to larger audiences and worlds. What often started out as a small project, as in a museum (chapter 3), could literally become as big as a rock concert. When young people became visible, both supporters and opponents began to view them as skillful; talented; and in some cases, dangerous, as when young people were not content with making changes only in their local area. They also cocreated larger spaces for and involved more young people in civic and political work. Although these projects all began as a small group of young people joining with caring adults to do something, they became much larger, as did the spaces they co-created and co-sustained.

Evaluating the Work

Almost every story told in this book describes how evaluation became an ongoing process in the work the group was doing. Some of the evaluation related to how the youth participants experienced the group and what they learned (chapter 11), whereas others would ask the group to evaluate the group's progress and how well the group was progressing on its project. Rea (chapter 3) used evaluation to co-assess with the silk mural group whether group members had the skill to create the mural as a group or whether they needed help; they asked for help. Evaluation, both formal and informal, was a practical, everyday, ordinary activity in all the chapters.

Modifying the Practice

A practice can work for a while and then not be effective, or external and internal demands can require new practices. Rea (chapter 3) had several conditions to be addressed for the work in the museum to be successful. This meant that she had to modify the practice, not only from how it had proved successful in other museums but also from how it had been done in her own organization. Much of this modification was cocreated with young people. By asking the group to come up with ways to address concerns and issues that others raised—whether funders, museum curators and staff, or Rea's supervisor—the group figured out together what they needed to do to satisfy many stakeholders and to create a project that they believed in and valued.

A Final Note

In this chapter, we have shown the substance of civic youth work, without explicating the many ways it is actually practiced. On the level of abstraction that we have maintained, we have shown that civic youth work falls into the family of normative youth work practices, and although its particulars are contextual, there are common themes across contexts in the United States and internationally.

We write about cocreating spaces as integral to civic youth work, aware that there are many types of spaces, from imaginary to material, and that there are large bodies of scholarly (Casey, 1993), practice (Schutz, 1997), and popular literatures that address the notion of space. Some of the terms we have used include *civic space*, *public space*, and *lived citizenship*. Our civic youth work takes place in the move from imagined to actual space, wherein young people work as a group on an issue of compelling interest to them. Along the way, they work in aporetic space, the space of wonder, imagination, questioning, and emergence (e.g., Ankr, 2006; Burbules, 1997).

For the development of this practice, we must still engage in empirical studies of practice and its effectiveness, and explicate in concrete detail how civic youth work can be and is practiced.

We invite young people, practitioners, and scholars to respond to this call, especially after the youth-led Arab Spring of social reform and the emerging youth-led challenge to Wall Street in the United States.

Reflection Questions

- What is missing for you from this chapter?
- What is a touchstone? Why is it used as a metaphor here, in contrast to the more typical frame of competency or competencies?

- Do the authors succeed in making the case for civic youth work as authentic practice, distinguishable from the more general youth work? In what ways do they succeed and/or fail in their attempt?
- Is a model and theory of positive youth development necessary (and/or sufficient) for this model of civic youth work?
- How might this chapter read if it had been written by our colleagues in Israel, Korea, Northern Ireland, Croatia, or Kenya? What might they have written instead?
- For you, what are the essentials that define civic youth work?
- For you, what is the unique expertise of civic youth work?
- For you, what are the major themes about civic youth work across the chapters?
- Does the authors' seven-stage process fit with your own experience, thoughts, and practice? How should their model be modified?

References

Allen, J., & Brown, B. (2008). Adolescents, peers, and motor vehicles: A perfect storm? *American Journal of Preventative Medicine, 35*(3), S289–S293.

Ankr, M. (2006). *Aporetic openings: An ethics of uncertainty*. (Unpublished PhD dissertation). European Graduate School, Sass-Fee, Switzerland.

Arnett, J., Offer, D., & Fine, M. (1997). Reckless driving in adolescence: "State" and "trait" factors. *Accident Analysis and Prevention, 29*(1), 57–63.

Bae, K. N. (2010). *Youth right movement and challenges in Korea. Korean Association of Civic Youth Studies Fall Seminar Manual on Civic Youth in Korea*. Seoul: Korean Association of Civic Youth Studies.

Baizerman, M. (1974). Towards analysis of the relations among youth counterculture, telephone hotlines, and anonymity. *Journal of Youth and Adolescence, 3*(4), 293–306.

Baizerman, M. L. (1994, June). *A proposal: The call of vocation, work and healthy youth development*. (Unpublished manuscript.) University of Minnesota.

Barber, B. (1992). *An aristocracy of everyone*. New York: Ballantine.

Bartolome, L. (2008). Beyond the methods fetish: Toward a humanizing pedagogy. In M. Villegas, S. Neugebauer, & K. Venegas (Eds.), *Indigenous knowledge and education: Sites of struggle, strength, and survivance* (pp. 125–147). Cambridge, MA: Harvard Educational Review.

Batsleer, J. (2008). *Informal learning in youth work*. London: Sage.

Battistoni, R. (2000). Service learning and civic education. In S. Mann & J. Patrick (Eds.), *Education for civic engagement in democracy: Service learning and other promising practices* (pp. 29–44). Bloomington, IN: ERIC Clearinghouse for Social Studies and Social Science Education.

Benner, P. (1984). *From novice to expert: Excellence and power in clinical nursing practice*. Menlo Park, CA: Addison-Wesley.

Bennett, S. (2000). Political apathy and avoidance of news media among generation X and Y: America's continuing problem. In S. Mann & J. Patrick (Eds.), *Education for civic engagement in democracy: Service learning and other promising practices* (pp. 9–28). Bloomington, IN: ERIC Clearinghouse for Social Studies and Social Science Education.

Bensman, J., & Lilienfeld, R. (1973). *Craft and consciousness: Occupational technique and the development of world images*. New York: Wiley.

Biesta, G. J. J., Lawy, R. S., & Kelly, N. (2009). Understanding young people's citizenship learning in everyday life: The role of contexts, relationships, and dispositions. *Education, Citizenship and Social Justice, 4*(1), 5–24.

Boud, D., & Miller, N. (1996). *Working with experience: Animating learning.* New York: Routledge.

Boyte, H. (2003, Summer). Putting politics back into civic engagement. *Campus Compact Reader,* 5–8.

Boyte, H., & Skelton, N. (1997). The legacy of public work: Educating for citizenship. *Educational Leadership, 54*(5), 12–17.

Braungart, R. (1984). Historical and generational patterns of youth movements: A global perspective. *Comparative Social Research, 7*(1), 3–62.

Bryk, A. S., & Schneider, B. (2002). *Trust in schools: A core resource for improvement.* New York: Russell Sage Foundation.

Buber, M. (1957). *Pointing the way: Collected essays.* New York: Harper and Bros.

Burbules, N. C. (1997). Aporia: Webs, passages, getting lost and learning to go on. *Philosophy of Education Yearbook,* 33–43.

Cammarota, J. (2011). From hopelessness to hope: Social justice pedagogy in urban education and youth development. *Urban Education, 46*(4), 828–844.

Cammarota, J., & Fine, M. (2008). *Revolutionizing education: Youth participatory action research in motion.* New York: Routledge.

Cammarota, J., & Romero, A. (2011). Participatory action research with high school students: Transforming policy, practice, and personnel with social justice education. *Education Policy, 25*(3), 488–506.

Canella, C. (2008). Faith in process, faith in people: Confronting policies of social disinvestment with PAR as a pedagogy for expansion. In J. Cammarota & M. Fine (Eds.), *Revolutionizing education: Youth participatory action research in motion* (pp. 189–212). New York: Routledge.

Caruso, I. (1964). *Existential psychology: From analysis to synthesis.* New York: Herder and Herder.

Casey, E. (1993). *Getting back into place: Towards a renewed understanding of the place world.* Bloomington: Indiana University Press.

Charmaz, K. (2006). *Constructing grounded theory: A practical guide through qualitative analysis.* Thousand Oaks, CA: Sage.

Checkoway, B., Dobbie, E., & Schuster-Richards, K. (2003). The Wingspread symposium: Involving young people in community evaluation research. *CYD Journal, 4*(1), 7–11.

Checkoway, B., & Gutierrez, L. (2006). Youth participation and community change: An introduction. *Journal of Community Practice, 14,* 1–9.

Checkoway, B., & Richards-Schuster, K. (2003). Youth participation in community evaluation research. *American Journal of Evaluation, 22*(1), 21–33.

Checkoway, B., Richards-Schuster, K., Abdullah, S., Aragon, M., Facio, E., Figueroa, L., et al. (2003). Young people as competent citizens. *Community Development Journal: An International Forum, 38,* 298–309.

Choucri, N. (1974). *Population dynamics and international violence: Propositions, insights and evidence.* Lexington, MA: Lexington.

Cincotta, R. P., Engelman, R., & Anastasion, D. (2003). *The security demographic: Population and civil conflict after the Cold War.* Washington, DC: Population Action International.

Civic Mission of Schools. (2003). *Civic Mission of Schools*. New York: Carnegie Corporation of New York and Center for Information and Research on Civic Learning and Engagement.

Cohen, P. (1997). *Rethinking the youth question: Education, labour and cultural studies*. Hampshire, UK: Macmillan.

Coles, R. (1989). *The call of stories*. Boston: Houghton Mifflin.

Collier, P. (2000). Doing well out of war: An economic perspective. In M. Berdal & D. Malone (Eds.), *Greed and grievance: Economic agendas in civil wars*. Boulder, CO: Rienner.

Comer, J. (1980). *School power: Implications of an intervention project*. New York: Free Press.

Connell, J. P., Gambone, M. A., & Smith, T. J. (2000). Youth development in community settings: Challenges to our field and our approach. In G. Walker (Ed.), *Youth development: Issues, challenges, and directions* (pp. 281–300). Philadelphia: Private/Public Ventures.

Conrad, D., & Hedin, D. (Eds.) (1982). Youth participation and experiential education. *Child and Youth Services, 4*(3–4), 1–154.

Cooper, M. (2003). *Existential therapies*. Thousand Oaks, CA: Sage.

Cousins, B., & Earl, L. (Eds.) (1995). *Participatory evaluation in education*. Bristol, PA: Falmer Press, Taylor and Francis.

Cousins, J., & Whitmore, E. (1998). Framing participatory evaluation. *New Directions for Evaluation, 80*, 5–23.

Craft, A. (2005). *Creativity in schools: Tensions and dilemmas*. London: Routledge.

Davis, J., Soep, L., Remba, N., Maira, S., & Putnoi, D. (1993). *Safe Havens: Portraits of educational effectiveness in community art centers that focus on education in economically disadvantaged communities*. Cambridge, MA: President and Fellows of Harvard College.

Delgado, M. (2002). *New frontiers for youth development: Revitalizing and broadening youth development*. New York: Columbia University Press.

Delgado, M., & Staples, L. (2008). *Youth-led community organizing: Theory and action*. Oxford: Oxford University Press.

Delli Carpini, M., & Keeter, S. (1996). *What Americans know about politics and why it matters*. New Haven, CT: Yale University Press.

de Tocqueville, A. (2006). *Democracy in America*. New York: Random House. (Originally published 1835).

Dewey, J. (1909). *Moral principles in education*. Boston: Houghton Mifflin.

Dewey, J. (1916). *Democracy and education: An introduction to the philosophy of education*. Retrieved from http://www.twinsphere.org/library/philosophy/nonanalytic/modern/American/Dewey,%20J.%20-%20Democracy%20and%20Education.pdf.

Doyle, E., & Smith, M. (1999). *Born and bred: Leadership, heart and informal education*. London: YMCA George Williams College for the Rank Foundation.

Dreyfus, H., & Dreyfus, S. (1991). Towards a phenomenology of ethical expertise. *Human Studies, 14*, 229–250.

Duncan-Andrade, J., & Morrell, E. (2008). *The art of critical pedagogy: Possibilities for moving from theory to practice in urban schools*. New York: Peter Lang.

Earthman, G. I. (2002). *School facility conditions and student academic achievement*. Los Angeles: Institute for Democracy, Education, and Access, University of California, Los Angeles.

Eaton, J. W. (1962). *Stone walls do not a prison make.* Springfield, IL: Thomas.

Eccles, J., & Appleton Gootman, J. (Eds.) (2002). *Community programs to promote youth development.* Washington, DC: National Academy Press.

Eccles, J. S., & Templeton, J. (2000). *Community-based programs for youth: Lessons learned from general developmental research and from experimental and quasiexperimental evaluations.* Cambridge, MA: Harvard University Press.

Evans, S., & Boyte, H. (1986). *Free spaces: The sources of democratic change in America.* Chicago: University of Chicago Press.

Fetterman, D., Kaftarian, D., & Wandersman, A. (Eds.) (1996). *Empowerment evaluation: Knowledge and tools for self-assessment and accountability.* Thousand Oaks, CA: Sage.

Fielding, M., Bragg, S., Craig, D., Cunningham, I., Eraut, M., Gillinson, S., et al. (2005). *Factors influencing the transfer of good practice* (Department for Education and Skills Research Report No. RR615). Nottingham, UK: DFES Publications.

Finn, J., & Checkoway, B. (1998). Young people as competent community builders: A challenge to social work. *Social Work, 43,* 335–345.

Flanagan, C., & Van Horn, B. (2003). Youth civic development: A logical next step in community youth development. In F. Villarruel, D. Perkins, L. Borden, & J. Keith (Eds.), *Community youth development: Programs, policies, and practices* (pp. 273–296). Thousand Oaks, CA: Sage.

Frankl, V. (1969). *The will to meaning: Foundations and applications of logotherapy.* New York: World.

Freire, P. (1970). *Pedagogy of the oppressed.* New York: Continuum International.

Fullilove, M. T. (2004). *Root shock: How tearing up city neighborhoods hurt America and what we can do about it.* New York: Ballantine Books.

Gallagher, T. (2004). *Education in divided societies.* Hampshire, UK: Palgrave Macmillan.

Gay, G. (2000). *Culturally responsive teaching: Theory, research, and practice.* New York: Teacher College Press.

Gay Lesbian Straight Education Network. (2004). *State of the states.* New York: Author.

Gerth, H. H., & Mills, C. W. (1958). *From Max Weber: Essays in sociology.* New York: Oxford University Press.

Gibson, C. (2001). *From inspiration to participation: A review of perspectives on youth civic engagement.* New York: Carnegie Corporation of New York.

Gimpel, J., & Pearson-Merkowitz, S. (2009). Policies for civic engagement beyond the schoolyard. In J. Youniss & P. Levine (Eds.), *Engaging young people in civic life* (pp. 81–101). Nashville, TN: Vanderbilt University Press.

Ginwright, S. (2003). Youth organizing: Expanding possibilities for youth development. *Funders Collaborative on Youth Organizing, 3,* 1–18.

Ginwright, S. (2008). Collective radical imagination: Youth participatory action research and the art of emancipatory knowledge. In J. Cammarota & M. Fine (Eds.), *Revolutionizing education: Youth participatory action research in motion* (pp. 13–22). New York: Routledge.

Ginwright, S., & Cammarota, J. (2002). New terrain in youth development: The promise of a social justice approach. *Social Justice, 29*(4), 82–95.

Ginwright, S., Cammarota, J., & Noguera, P. (2005). Youth, social justice, communities: Towards a theory of urban youth policy. *Social Justice, 32*(3), 24–40.

Ginwright, S., Noguera, P., & Cammarota, J. (2006). *Beyond resistance: Youth activism and community change.* New York: Taylor and Francis.

Goldstone, J. A. (1991). *Revolution and rebellion in the early modern world.* Berkeley: University of California Press.

Goldstone, J. A. (2001). Toward a fourth generation of revolutionary theory. *Annual Review of Political Science, 4*, 139–187.

Goldstone, J. A. (2006). A clash of generations? Youth bulges and political violence. *International Studies Quarterly, 50*(13), 607–629.

Goodman, S. (2003). *Teaching youth media: A critical guide to literacy, video production and social change.* New York: Teachers College Press.

Gurr, T. R. (1970). *Why men rebel.* Princeton, NJ: Princeton University Press.

Hamilton, S., & Hamilton, M. A. (Eds.) (2004). *The youth development handbook: Coming of age in American communities.* Thousand Oaks, CA: Sage.

Hanna, P. (1936). *Youth serves the community.* New York: D. Appleton-Century.

Hart, D., & Kirshner, B. (2009). Civic participation and development among urban adolescents. In J. Youniss & P. Levine (Eds.), *Engaging young people in civic life* (pp. 102–120). Nashville, TN: Vanderbilt University Press.

Higgs, J., & Titchen, A. (2001). *Practice knowledge and expertise in the health professions.* Oxford, UK: Butterworth Heinemann.

Holland, D., Skinner, D., Lanchicotte, W., Jr., & Cain, C. (1998). *Identity and agency in cultural worlds.* Cambridge, MA: Harvard University Press.

Huebner, A., Walker, J., & McFarland, M. (2003). Staff development for the youth development professional: A critical framework for understanding the work. *Youth and Society, 35*(2), 204–225.

Huntington, S. (1996). *The clash of civilizations and the remaking of world order.* New York: Simon and Schuster.

Ilisin, V. (2007). Political values, attitudes and participation of youth: Continuity and change. In V. Ilisin (Ed.), *Croatian youth and European integration* (pp. 69–148). Zagreb: Institute for Social Research.

James, A., Jenks, C., & Prout, A. (1998). *Theorizing childhood.* Oxford, UK: Polity Press.

Jeffs, T., & Smith, M. (2005). *Informal education: Conversation, democracy, and learning.* Nottingham, UK: Educational Heretics Press.

Johnston-Goodstar, K. (2009). *Critical indigenous pedagogy of place: Locating and engaging justice with indigenous youth.* (Unpublished PhD dissertation.) University of Washington, Seattle.

Johnston-Goodstar, K., & Nagda, R. (2010, January–February). Becoming protagonists for integration: Youth voices from segregated educational spaces. *InterActions: UCLA Journal of Education and Information Studies, 6*(1), 1–16.

Kari, N., & Boyte, H. (1996). *Building America: The democratic promise of public work.* Philadelphia: Temple University Press.

Kellner, D., & Share, J. (2005). Toward critical media literacy: Core concepts, debates, organizations, and policy. *Discourse: Studies in the Cultural Politics of Education, 26*(3), 369–386.

Kellner, D., & Share, J. (2007). Critical media literacy, democracy, and the reconstruction of education. In D. Macedo & S. R. Steinberg (Eds.), *Media literacy: A reader* (pp. 3–23). New York: Peter Lang.

Kenyan Ministry of Youth Affairs and Sports. (N.d.). *Welcome from the Ministry of Youth and Sports.* Retrieved from http://www.youthaffairs.go.ke.

Kirlin, M. (2003). *The role of civic skills in fostering civic engagement.* (Working Paper No. 06). College Park, MD: Center for Information and Research on Civic Learning and Engagement.

Knishkowy, B., & Gofin, R. (2002). Seat belt use among teenagers in two Israeli family practices. *International Journal of Adolescent Medical Health, 14*(1), 51–54.

Knowlton, L., & Phillips, C. (2009). *The logic model guidebook: Better strategies for great results.* Thousand Oaks, CA: Sage.

Konopka, G. (1973). Requirements for healthy development of adolescent youth. *Adolescence, 8*(31), 1–26.

Kumar, R., O'Malley, P. M., & Johnston, L. D. (2008). Association between physical environment of secondary schools and student problem behavior: A national study, 2000–2003. *Environment and Behavior, 40*(4), 455–486.

Lederach, J. P. (2005). *The moral imagination: The art and soul of building peace.* Oxford: Oxford University Press.

Lee, J. E. (2009). *The effects of social participation activity by internet on the political efficacy in the high school.* (Unpublished MA thesis) Ewha Womans University (Seoul).

Lerner, R. (2006). Developmental science, developmental systems, and contemporary theories of human development. In W. Damon & R. Lerner (Eds.), *The handbook of child psychology* (Vol. 1, pp. 1–19). Hoboken, NJ: Wiley.

Lerner, R. (2007). *The good teen: Rescuing adolescence from the myths of the storm and stress years.* New York: Crown.

Lerner, R., Wertlieb, D., & Jacobs, F. (2003). Historical and theoretical bases of applied developmental science. In R. Learner, F. Jacobs, & D. Wertlieb (Eds.), *Handbook of applied developmental science* (Vol. 1, pp. 1–28). Thousand Oaks, CA: Sage.

Lippman, P. (2010). *Can the physical environment have an impact on the learning environment?* Centre for Effective Learning Environments, 2010/13, OECD Publishing. doi: 10.1787/5km4g21wpwr1-en.

Llewellyn, K., & Westheimer, J. (2009). Beyond facts and acts: The implications of "ordinary politics" for youth political engagement. *Citizenship Teaching and Learning, 5*(2), 50–61.

London, J. (2000). *Youth-led research, evaluation, and planning: The experience of youth in focus.* Las Vegas, NV: Focal Point.

London, J. (2002, June 7–9). *Youth involvement in community research and evaluation: Mapping the field.* Paper submitted to the Wingspread Symposium on Youth Involvement in Community Research and Evaluation, Racine, WI.

Lopez, M. H., Levine, P., Both, D., Kiesa, A., Kirby, E., & Marcelo, K. (2006). *The 2006 civic and political health of the nation: A detailed look at how youth participate in politics and communities.* College Park, MD: Center for Information and Research on Civic Learning and Engagement.

Madison, S. (2005). *Critical ethnography: Methods, ethics and performance.* Thousand Oaks, CA: Sage.

Magnuson, D., & Baizerman, M. (2007). *Work with youth in divided and contested societies.* Rotterdam, the Netherlands: Sense.

Maier, H. W. (1990). A developmental perspective for child and youth care work. In J. Anglin, C. Denholm, R. Ferguson, & A. Pence (Eds.), *Perspectives in professional child and youth care* (pp. 7–24). New York: Haworth Press.

Malamud, R. (1998). *Reading zoos: Representations of animals and captivity.* New York: New York University Press.

Males, M. (1999). *Framing youth: 10 myths about the next generation.* Monroe, ME: Common Courage Press.

Mandle, J. (2009). *Paths to the park.* Retrieved from http://juliamandle.com/proj ects/paths-to-park#.

Mann, S., & Patrick, J. (2000). *Education for civic engagement in democracy: Service learning and other promising practices.* Bloomington, IN: Educational Resources Information Center.

Manser, A. (1967). Games and family resemblances. *Philosophy, 42*(161), 210–225.

Maxwell, L. E. (2007). Competency in child care settings: The role of the physical environment. *Environment and Behavior, 39*(2) 229–245.

Mayerhoff, M. (1971). *On caring.* New York: HarperCollins.

Mezirow, J., & Associates (1990). *Fostering critical reflection in adulthood.* San Francisco: Jossey-Bass.

Moller, H. (1968). Youth as a force in the modern world. *Comparative Studies in Society and History, 10,* 238–260.

Morrell, E. (2004). *Becoming critical researchers: Literacy and empowerment for urban youth.* New York: Peter Lang.

Morrell, E. (2006). Youth-initiated research as a tool for advocacy and change in urban schools. In S. Ginwright, P. Noguera, & J. Cammarota (Eds.), *Beyond resistance! Youth activism and community change: New democratic possibilities for practice and policy for America's youth* (pp. 111–128). New York: Routledge.

Murphy, J. (2004). Against civic schooling. *Social Philosophy and Policy, 21*(1), 221–265.

National Association of Secretaries of State. (1999). *American youth attitudes on politics, citizenship, government, and voting.* Lexington, KY: Author.

National Commission on Civic Renewal. (1998). *A nation of spectators: Final report of the national commission on civic renewal.* College Park, MD: Institute for Philosophy and Public Policy.

National Youth Policy Institute. (2008). *A study on the level of Korean youth rights in comparison with international standards III.* Seoul: Author.

Noddings, N. (1984). *Caring: A feminist approach to ethics and moral education.* Berkeley: University of California Press.

Patton, M. Q. (2008). *Utilization focused valuation* (4th ed.). Thousand Oaks, CA: Sage.

Pittman, K. (1991). *Promoting youth development: Strengthening the role of youth serving and community organizations.* Washington, DC: Academy for Educational Development.

Polkinghorne, D. (1988). *Narrative knowing and the human sciences.* Albany: State University of New York Press.

Proweller, A. (2000). Re-writing/-righting lives: Voices of pregnant and parenting teenagers in an alternative school. In L. Weis & M. Fine (Eds.), *Construction sites: Excavating race, class and gender among urban youth.* New York: Teachers College Press.

Punamaki, R. L. (1996). Can ideological commitment protect children's psychological well-being in situations of political violence? *Child Development, 67,* 55–69.

Putnam, R. D. (2000). *Bowling alone: The collapse and revival of American community.* New York: Simon and Schuster.

Revans, R. (1983). *ABC of action learning.* Kent, UK: Chartwell-Bratt.

Rogoff, B. (1990). *Apprenticeship in thinking: Cognitive development in social context.* Oxford: Oxford University Press.

Ross, M. (1955). *Community organization: Theory, principles, and practices.* New York: Harper and Row.

Sabo, K. (Ed.) (2003). *Youth participatory evaluation: A field in the making* (New Directions in Evaluation, Vol. 98). San Francisco: Jossey-Bass.

Sabo Flores, K. (2008). *Youth participatory evaluation.* San Francisco: Jossey-Bass.

Sambanis, N. (2002). A review of recent advances and future directions in the quantitative literature on civil wars. *Defence and Peace Economics, 13*(3), 215–243.

Schutz, A. (1997). The metaphor of space in educational theory: Henry Giroux through the eyes of Hannah Arendt and Michael Foucault. *Philosophy of Education Yearbook,* 352–360.

Sherrod, L., Torney-Purta, J., & Flanagan, C. (2010). *Handbook of research on civic engagement in youth.* Hoboken, NJ: Wiley.

Shumer, R. (2003, October). *City Scan report, 2002–2003.* Hartford: Connecticut Policy and Economic Council.

Shumer, R. (2004). *City Scan report, 2003–2004.* Hartford: Connecticut Policy and Economic Council.

Shumer, R. (2006, August). *Final report: Youth engaged in service and community based organization study.* Jackson: Mississippi Commission on Volunteer Service.

Shumer, R. (2007). *Youth-led evaluation.* Clemson, SC: National Dropout Prevention Center, Clemson University.

Silbereisen, R., & Lerner, R. (2007). *Approaches to positive youth development.* Thousand Oaks, CA: Sage.

Smith, A., & Robinson, A. (1996). *Education for mutual understanding: The initial statutory years.* Belfast: University of Ulster, Centre for the Study of Conflict.

Smyth, P. (2007). The stumbling progress of community relations youthwork in Northern Ireland: 1968–2005. In D. Magnuson & M. Baizerman (Eds.), *Work with youth in divided and contested societies* (pp. 46–60). Rotterdam, the Netherlands: Sense.

Social Program Evaluators and Consultants & Partners in Evaluation and Planning. (2003). *Youth crime watch of America: 2001–2002 national outcome study.* Detroit: Author.

Sommers, M. (1997, March–April). *The children's war: Towards peace in Sierra Leone.* New York: Women's Commission for Refugee Women and Children.

Strickland, W. (2007). *Make the impossible possible: One man's crusade to inspire others to dream bigger and achieve the extraordinary.* New York: Currency/ Doubleday.

Taubman-Ben-Ari, O., & Mikulincer, M. (2007). Traffic psychology and behavior. *Transportation Research, 10*(2), 123–138.

Terry, S. (1998, August). Genius at work. *Fast Company.* Retrieved from http://www.fastcompany.com/magazine/17/genius.html.

Thompson, K. (1998). *Moral panics.* New York: Routledge.

Turner, C. (2006). Subject leaders in secondary schools and informal learning: Towards a conceptual framework. *School Leadership and Management, 26*(5), 419–435.

United Nations. (2003). *World youth report 2003* (Chapter 14: Youth & Conflict). Retrieved from http://www.un.org/esa/socdev/unyin/wpayconflict.htm#WYR2005.

United Nations. (2005). *World youth report 2005.* Retrieved from http://www.un.org/esa/socdev/unyin/wpayconflict.htm#WYR2005.

UN Population Fund. (2005). *State of world population 2005: The promise of equality.* New York: Author.

Urdal, H. (2006). A clash of generations? Youth bulges and political violence. *International Studies Quarterly, 50*(3), 607–629.

Urdal, H. (2007, March 5). *Demography and conflict: How population pressure and youth bulges affect the risk of civil war.* Retrieved from http://www.wilsoncenter.org/event/demography-and-conflict-how-population-pressure-and-youth-bulges-affect-the-risk-civil-war#field_speakers.

US Agency for International Development. (2009). *Success story: Great Lakes Radio unites youth.* Retrieved from http://www.sfcg.org/articles/usaid_drc_2008.pdf.

Van Manen, M. (1990). *Researching lived experience: Human science for an action sensitive pedagogy.* Albany: State University of New York Press.

VeLure Roholt, R., & Baizerman, M. (2012). Preparing the next generation of professoriate in youth studies: Mapping the contested spaces. In D. Fusco (Ed.), *Advancing youth work: Current trends, critical questions* (pp. 127–140). New York: Routledge.

VeLure Roholt, R., Baizerman, M., & Steiner, M. (2002). Museum development, youth development: Examples from a flourishing site. *Museum Ireland, 12,* 48–56.

VeLure Roholt, R., & Cutler, J. (2012). Youth work as engagement. In D. Fusco (Ed.), *Advancing youth work: Current trends, critical questions* (pp. 173–181). New York: Routledge.

Velure Roholt, R., Hildreth, R. W., & Baizerman, M. (2003). *Year four evaluation of Public Achievement: Examining young people's experiences of Public Achievement.* Retrieved from http://www.publicachievement.org/pdf/evaluations/report2002-03.pdf.

VeLure Roholt, R., Hildreth, R. W., & Baizerman, M. (2009). *Becoming citizens: Deepening the craft of youth civic engagement.* New York: Routledge.

Vygotsky, L. S. (1986). *Thought and language.* Cambridge, MA: MIT Press. (Originally published 1934.)

Walker, T. (2002). Service as a pathway to political participation: What research tells us. *Applied Developmental Science, 6*(2), 183–188.

Waterman, A. (1997). *Service-learning: Applications from the research.* Mahwah, NJ: Erlbaum.

Watts, R. J., & Flanagan, C. A. (2007). Pushing the envelope on youth civic engagement: A developmental and liberation psychology perspective. *Journal of
Community Psychology, 35*(6), 779–792.

Weis, L., & Fine, M. (2000). *Construction sites: Excavating race, class and gender
among urban youth.* New York: Teachers College Press.

Westheimer, J., & Kahne, J. (2004). Educating the "good" citizen: Political choices
and pedagogical goals. *PS: Political Science and Politics, 37,* 241–247.

Whitmore, E. (Ed.) (1998, Winter). *Understanding and practicing participatory
evaluation from new directions for evaluation.* San Francisco: Jossey-Bass.

Wilkenfeld, B., Lauckhardt, J., & Torney-Purta, J. (2010). The relation between
development theory and measures of civic engagement research on adolescents. In L. Sherrod, J. Torney-Purta, & C. Flanagan (Eds.), *Handbook of
research on civic engagement in youth* (pp. 193–220). Hoboken, NJ: Wiley.

Wortham, S. (2001). *Narratives in action: A strategy for research and analysis.* New
York: Teachers College Press.

Wuthnow, R. (1995). *Learning to care: Elementary kindness in an age of indifference.*
Oxford: Oxford University Press.

Yates, M., & Youniss, J. (1999). *Roots of civic identity: International perspectives on
community service and activism in youth.* Cambridge: Cambridge University
Press.

Young, E., Green, H. A., Roehrich-Patrick, L., Joseph, L., & Gibson, T. (2003). *Do
K-12 school facilities affect education outcomes?* Nashville: Tennessee Advisory Commission on Intergovernmental Relations.

Youniss, J., & Levine, P. (2009). *Engaging young people in civic life.* Nashville, TN:
Vanderbilt University Press.

Youniss, J., & Yates, M. (1997). *Community service and social responsibility in youth.*
Chicago: University of Chicago Press.

Youth Ambassadors of Peace and Citizenship. (2007, June). *Youth participation in
decision-making* (Angola Research Paper). Luanda, Angola: Developmental
Workshop.

Youth Council Northern Ireland. (n.d.). *Placing the values of equity, diversity, and
interdependence at the core of the policy and operations of youth organizations.* Belfast: Author.

Zakaria, F. (2001). The roots of rage. *Newsweek, 138*(16), 14–33.

Zinn, H. (2009). *The Zinn reader: Writings on disobedience and democracy.* New
York: Seven Stories Press.

Contributors

Michael Baizerman is professor in and director of youth studies, School of Social Work, University of Minnesota, where he has taught since 1972. He is an active researcher with students on behalf of municipal agencies and their youth services. He is active internationally, with long-term work in Northern Ireland and Laos, and with shorter-term work in Korea and the Middle East. He writes regularly with colleagues on youth work, youth studies, and program evaluation.

Emina Bužinkić is a twenty-seven-year-old activist living in Croatia. She has been leader of the Croatian Youth Network as its vice president, president, and secretary-general from 2004 to 2011, advocating for youth needs and youth policies. Since 2002 she has been working with the Centre for Peace Studies as a Youth MIRamiDA coordinator, peace-building youth trainer, and advocate of peace education. For many years she has worked on the issues of migration and postcolonialism as a researcher, monitor, and trainer. Currently, she is program coordinator at Documenta—Centre for Dealing with the Past, and she has been director of the Youth Studies Program in Croatia. She is engaged as a policy analyst, publicist, and trainer.

Yun Jin Choi is a professor in the Department of Adolescent Science, Chung-ang University, Seoul, Korea. In recent years, her scholarship has focused on youth rights and youth policy. She has worked as researcher for the Korean Institute for Youth Development and founded the organization YES21, which focuses on youth educational strategies in Korea. She is an active scholar and educator and continues to advocate for young people's inclusion in civic and political decision making in Korea and worldwide.

Jennifer L. De Maio is an associate professor of political science at California State University, Northridge. She has a PhD from the University of California, Los Angeles, an MSc from the London School of Economics, and a BA from Georgetown University. Her first book, *Confronting Ethnic Conflict: The Role of Third Parties in Managing Africa's Civil Wars* was published in 2009. De Maio has also published and presented papers on civil wars and conflict management in Africa, including a recent article on the problem of exclusivity in peace processes, which appeared in the journal *Civil Wars*, and a piece on preventive diplomacy published in *World Affairs*.

Anna C. Davis is a current R. Scott Hirt intern with the Southern Poverty Law Center and a recent graduate of Southern Mississippi University. She was a founding member of the Mississippi Safe Schools Coalition and is a current member of the MSSC's Queer Youth Advisory Board.

Tracy Galvin is currently a PhD scholar at the University of Limerick. She holds a BS in physical education and mathematics and a specialist diploma in teaching, learning, and scholarship at third level. Galvin teaches at the Department of Education and Professional Studies at both undergraduate and postgraduate levels.

Ofir Germanic is a student in the master program Youth Development Leadership at the University of Minnesota. Until 2011, he headed up the Youth Department of Or Yarok, Green Light, in Israel.

Joshua Green earned a master of fine arts degree from Cranbrook Academy of Art. Formerly vice president of operations for youth and arts at Manchester Craftsmen's Guild, he is presently executive director of the National Council on Education for the Ceramic Arts.

R. W. Hildreth is an assistant professor of political science at Southern Illinois University–Carbondale. His research interests include democratic theory, the pragmatist philosophy of John Dewey, youth civic engagement, and transnational activism. He is currently finishing a book manuscript titled *Living Citizenship: John Dewey, Civic Engagement, and the Renewal of Democratic Life*.

Katie Johnston-Goodstar, PhD, MSW, is an assistant professor in the Youth Studies Department at the University of Minnesota's School of Social Work. Her research broadly focuses on participatory action research with urban and Indigenous youth, urban and Indigenous youth development, critical media literacy, and histories of social work and youth work in Indigenous communities.

Joanne Krebs, MEd, is a youth worker whose practice joins community and critical education, participatory action research, and critical media literacy. She has worked in schools and communities for more than a decade and currently collaborates with young people on community-based action research projects examining districtwide school policies, and she uses social and other media forms to explore diverse youth identities and to pursue social justice agendas.

Terrance Kwame Ross is executive director of Origins, a company that aims to promote an equitable and humane multicultural society through quality education for all. He also cofounded New City School and currently teaches regularly at the University of Minnesota in both the undergraduate Youth Studies Program as a community faculty and in the Youth Development Leadership Masters Program as a lecturer. Both programs are located in the School of Social Work, College of Education and Human Development.

Izzy Pellegrine is a student at Mississippi State University and founding member of the Mississippi Safe Schools Coalition. She has participated in social justice efforts at the local and national level and is a current member of the MSSC's Queer Youth Advisory Board.

Lisa Rea has an MA in cultural heritage and museum studies. From 2004 until 2007 she worked for Public Achievement Northern Ireland as the museums and communities youth worker, where she cocreated several museum-based projects with groups of young people throughout Northern Ireland and Ireland. She continued to work for Public Achievement as a freelance consultant until 2010. From 2009–2010, she managed a project between the Lisburn YMCA and the Lisburn Museum. Since the beginning of 2011, she has been spending time at home enjoying time with her baby son, Linus.

Katie Richards-Schuster is an assistant research scientist with the Michigan Youth and Community Program at the University of Michigan's School of Social Work. Her work focuses on youth participation and community engagement. As part of her work, she has partnered with the Mississippi Safe Schools Coalition in its youth engagement and participatory research efforts.

Rob Shumer has been involved in education for more than forty years. He has taught from middle school through graduate school. Shumer is the former director of field studies at University of California–Los Angeles and the founding director of the National Service-Learning Clearinghouse and the Center for Experiential Education and Service

Learning at the University of Minnesota. He is also the past president of the Minnesota Evaluation Association, former board member of the National Society for Experiential Education, and current board member of the International Association for Research on Service-Learning and Community Engagement. He currently teaches courses on civic engagement, participatory evaluation, and constructivist curriculum, and he has conducted more than twenty-five research and evaluation studies on national service, service learning, civic engagement, and participatory evaluation. He also serves as the internal evaluator for the National Research Center for Career and Technical Education and recently conducted two national studies on career and technical education programs.

Mary Ann Steiner holds a master's degree in education in youth development leadership from the University of Minnesota and is currently a PhD candidate in learning science and policy at the University of Pittsburgh. Steiner is the director of the Center for Lifelong Science Learning at the Carnegie Museum of Natural History, in Pittsburgh.

Ross VeLure Roholt is assistant professor of youth studies, School of Social Work, University of Minnesota, where he teaches courses on civic youth work. He is an active community-based participatory researcher and has completed several studies on youth work, civic youth work, and youth involvement in democratic and social development. He is active internationally, with long-term work in Northern Ireland, Laos, and Japan, and with shorter-term work in Morocco, Korea, the Netherlands, Jordan, Israel, Palestine, and Ireland. He has written widely on civic youth work, completing a special edition for *Child and Youth Services* (2008), a philosophical training curriculum for Public Achievement Northern Ireland (funded by the Peace Institute), a handbook for civic youth workers, and a training for trainers with the Institute for Rights and Democracy in Canada. He continues to work with young people to respond to compelling issues both locally and globally.

Sarah Young is a doctoral student in social work at the University of Alabama, where she is a Point Scholar. She also serves as one of the founding members and core adult ally for the Mississippi Safe Schools Coalition.

Index

Note: Page numbers followed by "f" or "t" refer to figures or tables respectively.

action, taking, 175–176
activist spaces, creating, 62–63
American Civil Liberties Union (ACLU) of Mississippi, 46
arduous and mindful practice, 21–22
automobile accidents, in Israel
Or Yarok (Green Light), 104–106
young people and, 103–104

banners, use of, at Manchester Craftsmen's Guild (MCG), 87–90
Birnbaun, Ezra, 7

candlelight movements, in Korea, 121–122
Choi Woo Ju, 119
circles of influence, reckless driving and, 105–106, 105f
City Scan program, 57–59
civic development, defined, 163–164
civic organizations, decline of, 4–5
civic youth development, defined, 164–167
civic youth work. See also youth work
vs. classical youth work, 170t
craft orientation of, 181
defined, 168–169
ethos of, 179–181
practice themes of, 171–173

programming logic model of, 179
vocation and, 169–170
civic youth work practices. See also practice
craft orientation, 181
eight-stage process for basic, 182–184
engaging spaces and, 170–171
ethos of, 179–181
history and context of New City School (NCS) and, 68–70
ideal, 181, 181t
New City School (NCS) program model for, 70–74
schools as site for, 67–68
themes, 171–173
from themes to models for, 178
civic youth workers, 2–3. See also youth workers
creating engaging spaces and, 151–152
educating, 152–154
reflective practice and, 158
reframing, 156–158
reorienting, 154–156
stories of, 3–4
civil war, youth in, 126–129
implications for policy makers, 134–137

civil war, youth in (*continued*)
  Kenya case study, 129–131
  Rwanda case study, 131–132
  Youth Crime Watch programs,
    132–134
classical youth work, vs. civic youth
    work, 170t
co-creating spaces, 173–174
collaborative work, 174
comfort zones, getting young people
    outside, 38
community civic groups, decline of,
    4–5
community mobilization, 45
conflicts. *See* civil war, youth in
Craft, Anna, 86
craft knowledge, professional, 152
craft orientation, of practice, 181
creating spaces, concept of, 52–53
creative work, 174
Critical Media Literacy in Action
    project
  about, 22–24
  as engaged space, 24
  research and production process of,
    26–28
critical pedagogy, 24, 25
critical practice, 174
Croatia, youth in
  achievements of Croatian Youth
    Network and, 143–144
  founding of Croatian Youth
    Network, 140–142
  "National Youth Action Plan" and,
    142–143
  violence and, 139–140
  Youth Studies program, 144–146
Croatian Youth Network (CYN)
  achievements of, 143–144
  founding of, 140–142
  Youth Studies program of, 144–146
curatorial voice, 38–39

democracy building, 32
Dewey, John, 67
dialogue, in engaging youth work
    practice, 39–40

Dodson, Dan, 7
domains, of youth work, 4

engaged spaces. *See also* spaces
  civic youth workers and, 151–152
  Critical Media Literacy in Action
    project as, 24
  future prospects for, in public
    schools, 29–30
  transformative possibilities of,
    28–29
engagement, 6, 7
  vs. engaging, 6–10, 8t
engaging spaces. *See also* spaces
  civic youth work practices and,
    170–171
  civic youth workers and, 151–152
  creating, 173
  future prospects for, in public
    schools, 29–30
engaging youth work practice, in
    Northern Ireland, 38–40
ethos, of practice, 179–181
evaluations. *See* youth participatory
    evaluations

Freire, Paulo, 39

Gay Lesbian and Straight Education
    Network (GLSEN), 49, 52
gay-straight alliances (GSAs), 45, 52
Generation Grand Lac (GGL), 131
Green Light (Or Yarok). *See* Or Yarok
    (Green Light) Association for
    Safer Driving in Israel

Hackshaw, Jim, 7
Harlem Youth Opportunities
    Unlimited (New York City), 7
heritage, created by young people,
    33–34
Heritage Lottery Fund (Northern
    Ireland), 34

Im Yoo Bin, 119
Independent Youth List (Nezavisna
    Lista Mladih) (Croatia), 140–141

Independent Youth of Kutina (Neza-
    visni Mladi Kutine) (Croatia), 141,
    142
innovations, in schools, 80
Israel
    Leading the Way project, 105–111
    Or Yarok (Green Light), 104–106
    young people and automobile acci-
    dents, 103–104

Kang Uiseok, 120
Kenya, case study of youth and
    conflict reduction in post-civil
    war, 129–131
knowledge, forms of, 152–153
Korea, youth civic engagement in,
    115–116
    candlelight movements, 121–122
    developing, 123–125
    economic, social, and political
    contexts of, 116–118
    political issues and, 120–121
    virtual space and, 122–123
    youth rights movement as example,
    119–120
Kronenfeld, Danny, 7

Leading the Way project, 105–106. *See
    also* Or Yarok (Green Light) Asso-
    ciation for Safer Driving in Israel
    cultural adjustments and, 107–108
    defined, 108
    effectiveness of, 110
    goals of, 106–107
    replication model, 110–111
    structure of, 108
    youth participation, 108–109
lesbian, gay, bisexual, transgendered,
    and queer-identified (LBGTQ)
    youth, 43
    in Mississippi, 43–44
Liberia, Youth Crime Watch in, 133
listening clubs, 132

Machado, Antonio, 170
Manchester Craftsmen's Guild
    (MCG), 81–82, 178

after-school youth program of,
    82–83
banners at, use of, 87–90
philosophy and culture of, 86–89
physical environment of, 83–85
studio and workshop vignettes,
    89–90
teaching artists' story, 95–97
transformations of youth and
    teaching artists at, 98–101
youth experiences at, 90–91
youth stories of exposure to mate-
    rials, art culture, and thinking at,
    92–95
Mandle, Julia, 89
marginalized youth, 44
McMillan, Constance, 50
mindful and arduous practice, 21–22
Mississippi, LGBTQ youth in, 43–44
Mississippi Commission on Volunteer
    Service (MCVS), 59
Mississippi Safe Schools Coalition
    (MSSC), 44–45
    in action, 48
    annual queer and allies conference,
    48–49
    creating spaces and, 52–53
    formalizing role of young people in,
    46–47
    future work of, 53
    impacts of, on young people and
    policy, 51–52
    lessons learned from work of, 53
    local and state legislative activities
    of, 49–50
    origins of, 45–46
    Prom Watch, 50–51
    Queer Youth Advisory Board
    (QYAB), 44, 47–48
    Second-Chance Prom, 44, 51
    Stories Project, 49
Mobilization for Youth (New York
    City), 7
museums, youth group work in, 35–37

networking, 45
New City School (NCS) (Minneapolis)
    civic youth work program model of,
    70–74

New City School (*continued*)
history and context of, 68–70
outcomes and general goals of
informal youth work of, 78t
support for youth development
education and, 76t
youth development and, 74–75
youth work and, 75–79
Nezavisna Lista Mladih (Independent
Youth List) (Croatia), 140–141
Nezavisni Mladi Kutine (Independent
Youth of Kutina) (Croatia), 141
Northern Ireland
approach to engaging youth in,
34–38
creation of silk mural, 37–38
engaging youth work practice in,
38–40
Heritage Lottery Fund in, 34
Public Achievement, 34
the Troubles and, 32
working with youth in, 32–33
young people creating heritage in,
33–34

Okuda, Hiromu, 92–95
Okuda, Mieko, 92–95
Or Yarok (Green Light) Association for
Safer Driving in Israel, 104–106.
See also Leading the Way project
national conferences, 110

peacekeeping, 32
pedagogy, critical, 24, 25
personal knowledge, 152, 153–154
positive youth development, defined,
161–163
practice. *See also* civic youth work
practices
critical, 174
educating for, 152–154
mindful and arduous, 21–22
reflective, youth workers and, 158
practice themes, of civic work
practice, 171–173
professional craft knowledge, 152
programming logic model, of civic
youth work, 179, 180t

Prom Watch, 50–51
propositional knowledge, 152–153
Public Achievement (Northern
Ireland), 34
public performance, 178
public work, 174

Queer Youth Advisory Board (QYAB),
44. *See also* Mississippi Safe
Schools Coalition (MSSC)
retreats of, 47–48
structure of, 47
train-the-trainer model of, 47–48
questions, using, youth workers and,
175

reckless driving. *See also* Leading the
Way project
circles of influence and, 105–106,
105f
reasons young people engage in,
106–107
reflective practice, youth workers and,
158
reframing, youth workers and, 156–158
reorientation, youth workers and,
154–156
response classroom approach, 13, 70.
See also New City School (NCS)
(Minneapolis)
Right of Youth (ROY) (Korea), 120
risk taking, supporting, 176–177
Ross, Frank, 81
Rwanda, Generation Grand Lac (GGL)
in, 131–132

safe spaces, creating, 52–53
Say No Society (Korea), 120
schools
future prospects for engaging
spaces in, 29–30
innovations in, 80
as site for civic youth work practices, 67–68
Schwartz, Mike, 6–7
Search for Common Ground (SFCG),
131
Second-Chance Prom, 44, 51

Sierra Leone, Youth Crime Watch in, 133
silk mural project, in Northern Ireland, 37–38
Slavin, Sy, 7
spaces. *See also* engaged spaces; engaging spaces
  creating, of legitimate engagement, 21–22
  creating activist, 62–63
  creating safe, 52–53
stories
  of civic youth workers, 3–4
  organization of, 11–14
  reasons for, 10–11
Stories Project, of MSSC, 49
Strickland, Bill, 81–86
Sturgis, Ceara, 50
Sudan, 126

taking action, 175–176
train-the-trainer model of organizing, 47–48
Troubles (in Northern Ireland), 32

vocation
  civic youth work and, 169–170
  listening to, 177
voting, young people and, 4–5

Wilcox, Preston, 7
work with youth, defined, 167

young people
  co-creating with, 173–174
  study of, 1–2
  voting and, 4–5
youth. *See also* civil war, youth in; Croatia, youth in
  approach to engaging, 34–38
  defined, 151
  marginalized, 44

Youth Association for Securing the Voting Age of Eighteen (Korea), 121
youth civic engagement. *See also* Korea
  change in theme and tone of, 5–6
  ideal-type orientations to, 8t
Youth Crime Watch (YCW), 132–133
  in Liberia, 133
  in Sierra Leone, 133
  in Zambia, 133–134
youth development
  as focus of engaging spaces, 178
  positive, defined, 161–163
youth disengagement, 4–5
Youth Engaged in Service (YES) program, 59–63
youth participatory action research (YPAR), 24–25
youth participatory evaluations, 55
  City Scan program and, 57–59
  defined, 55–56
  potential outcomes of, 56
  Youth Engaged in Service (YES) program, 59–63
Youth Studies program (Croatia), 144–146
youth work. *See also* civic youth work
  classical vs. civic, 170t
  defined, 167–168
  domains of, 4
youth workers. *See also* civic youth workers
  listening to vocation and, 177
  supporting risk taking, 176–177
  taking action and, 175–176
  use of questions and, 175

Zambia, Youth Crime Watch in, 133–134
Zinn, Howard, 29